HOLLYWOOD
ON TRIAL

HOLLYWOOD
ON TRIAL

McCarthyism's War
against The Movies

MICHAEL FREEDLAND

with Barbra Paskin

ROBSON
BOOKS

First published in the United Kingdom in 2007 by
Robson Books
10 Southcombe Street
London
W14 0RA

An imprint of Anova Books Company Ltd

ISBN 10: 1 86105 947 7
ISBN 13: 9781861059475

A CIP catalogue record for this book is available from the British Library.

10 9 8 7 6 5 4 3 2 1

Typeset by SX Composing DTP, Rayleigh, Essex
Reproduction by Spectrum Colour Ltd. England
Printed and bound by Creative Print & Design, Ebbw Vale, Wales

This book can be ordered direct from the publisher.
Contact the marketing department, but try your bookshop first.

www.anovabooks.com

For my Sarala
Who has given me everything

CONTENTS

ACKNOWLEDGEMENTS

Acknowledgements for this book begin, end and carry through almost every page with the name Barbra Paskin, a journalist and writer of great talent and for whom the term 'with' is hardly sufficient.

We have worked together many times, on previous books and on radio programmes for BBC Radio Two, including the genesis of this volume, which was also called *Hollywood On Trial*. When this book became a reality, Barbra undertook hours of discussions, phone calls and emails about how the project should proceed. She suggested interviewees – most of whom had never spoken before – mainly victims and their family members from the vicious era we have come to call McCarthyism. Barbra not only suggested names, she also interviewed dozens on my behalf, complementing the interviews I did myself, showing a skill, persistence and, most importantly, a sense of dedication and perfectionism that is little short of wondrous. At times, I accused her of bullying me. I am grateful for it today. As indeed I am for the interviewees who willingly gave up their time to be spoken to by Barbra and myself.

I am also very grateful to Jeremy Robson, who first offered the project his blessing, and for the immense encouragement from Barbara Phelan and my copy-editor Clive Hebard. I am also extraordinarily grateful to Merle Kessler for her help in the early days of this undertaking.

Those interviewed were: Ed Asner, Dan Bessie, Sonya Dahl Biberman, Paul Buhle, Walter Bernstein, Jean Rouverol Butler, Larry Ceplair, Hope Corey, Michael Cole, Kirk Douglas, Jean Porter Dmytryk, Jonathan Foreman, Ellen Geer, Bernard Gordon, Julie Garfield, Betty Garrett, Sondra Gorney, Roderick Gorney, Madeline Lee Gilford, Lee Grant, Marsha Hunt, Sylvia Jarrico, Bill Jarrico, Tony Kahn, Hal Kanter, Jeff Lawson, Gabriela Maltz Larkin, Kate Lardner, Patrick McGilligan, Hilda Ornitz, Eileen Penn, Ronald Radosh, Joanna Rapf, Alex Raksin, Ann Strick, Mary Davenport Salt, Peter Spelman, Bella Stander, Eric Sherman, Francesca Robinson Sanchez, Joan Scott, Nikola Trumbo, Christopher Trumbo and Rosanna Wilson-Farrow.

Thanks too to the late Larry Adler, Norma Barzman, Theodore Bikel, Betsy Blair, Norman Corwin, Joanne Crawford, Oliver Crawford, the late Glenn Ford, Larry Gelbart, Arthur Marx, the late Zero Mostel, the late Gregory Peck, David Raksin, Jill Robinson Shaw, Evelyn Keyes, Carol Eve Rossen, Stanley Rubin, the late Artie Shaw, the late Sidney Sheldon, the late Erle Jolson Krasner, Dennis Sykes and Gloria Stuart.

To them all my sincerest thanks.

Michael Freedland

Chapter One
The Shame of It All

Who do you think they're really after? Who's next? Is it your minister, who will be told what he can say in his pulpit? Is it your schoolteacher, who will be told what he can say in the classroom? Is it your children themselves? Is it YOU who will have to look around nervously before you can say what is on your mind?

Actor Fredric March, on the radio programme, *Hollywood Fights Back*, 1947

She was nine months' pregnant and had been groomed as one of the darlings of the most glamorous studio in Hollywood. Her husband was – certainly in most people's eyes – on the verge of becoming a superstar. The term hadn't yet come into common usage (or perhaps any kind of usage) but after two sensationally successful movies, who could doubt that he was up at the top of the list?

Yet as Betty Garrett kissed Larry Parks goodbye that morning in March 1951, both knew that it was all about to come crashing to the ground. Once her baby had been born, she now so firmly understood, MGM weren't going to get back on the phone with an offer of another role like the one she had had with Frank Sinatra and Gene Kelly in the 1949 film *On the Town*. Much more significantly, for her husband there would be no new follow-up to *The Jolson Story* of 1946 and *Jolson Sings Again* three years later, the second sequel that the 'trades' had been predicting for months.

Parks made his way to Washington, where he would be told to give the details that would as surely wreck his career as it threatened to emotionally destroy him and his family. He was to be at the beginning of a re-gathering storm, a Hollywood storm that was no trick of light and sound, for this storm was all too real and reverberated through the entire country. It struck the rest of America like an explosion. A thud of something that couldn't be immediately identified, followed by rumblings – the sound of people who thought they had safe jobs in the

1

film capital crumbling under an unforeseen weight. That weight was called McCarthyism – named after a drunken, bullying demagogue called Joseph McCarthy, a man who had given a new word to the English language and threatened to take America back to the dark ages.

Lillian Hellman, who made as big an impression on the era as any of her famous colleagues, once remarked: 'The McCarthy group – a loose term for all the boys, lobbyists, congressmen, State Department bureaucrats, CIA operators – chose the anti-Red scare with perhaps more cynicism than Hitler picked anti-Semitism.'

McCarthy was the man who could have been convicted of bad arithmetic as quickly as for distorting the American Constitution. 'I have a list' was his favourite phrase – a list of the number of Communists who worked in the State Department or perhaps the Army. One day he would say he had 205 Communists on his list; the next day, one hundred – and so it went on. Anyone who picked up that list might have found either McCarthy's laundry details or, more likely, the most recent bill from his friendly neighbourhood liquor store.

Such was the man who saw every Communist as a Soviet agent, which itself was far from the truth. McCarthy, who won his Senate seat in Wisconsin in no small way thanks to the support of Harold Christoffel, a Communist leader of the United Auto Workers union, set himself up as the white knight of the anti-Red crusade. His so-called 'investigations' bore as much resemblance to democracy as an elephant to a mouse. The incredible thing was that the elephant was this ugly, slurring junior senator from Wisconsin and the mouse was the President of the United States, leading other mice scurrying through his State Department into the offices of big business, the laboratories of the nation's scientists, the classrooms of its teachers and back to where much of it had started, the studios of those gentlemen in Tinseltown, known collectively as the moguls.

Ironically, McCarthy himself had nothing to do with the Hollywood investigations. Long before he came on the scene, chairing the Senate Internal Security Committee, the House Un-American Activities Committee (which gave another new word to the language, the acronym HUAC) was searching for Reds under the beds. Being labelled a Communist was the most dangerous epithet to be thrust on a person. Almost as bad was the term 'fellow traveller', which described someone who appeared to share the Marxist philosophy without actually owning a party card. And there was yet another word being added to the lexicon: blacklist. Being named or summoned to appear before HUAC was a ticket to oblivion, an entry on a sheet of paper locked away in movie producers' drawers that would spell the end to even the most high-flying career. It was a list that conveniently salved the consciences of those people who were looking for a means of getting at those whom they considered to be too left wing by far.

Author, academic and civil-rights expert Paul Buhle noted that, 'the hearings had been turned into a grand opportunity for anti-Communists, liberal anti-Communists, to join with conservative anti-Communists and absolutely drop the future of blacklistees under the margins of American cultural life.'

The American writer and former Soviet spy Whittaker Chambers wrote in his autobiography *Witness*: 'It is not the Communists but the ex-Communists who have co-operated with the government who have chiefly suffered.' This was only partly to be the case with the Hollywood set, many of whom – notably including at the very start of the anti-Hollywood campaign, Larry Parks – were damned if they did co-operate and equally damned if they did not.

The Tinseltown trials were part of a wider battle that the committee and its supporters decided was essential in an age when in American Establishment eyes, Communists had replaced Nazis as the number-one enemy. Actors, directors, producers and their colleagues were considered dangerous because, unlike most German spies, these were not foreigners who spoke with strange accents. If nothing else, what HUAC longed for was that vital part of the Hollywood system – publicity. It figured, and rightly, that having stars listed in their own cast of characters was as important for getting their message across as it was for any motion picture or studio. The fight, so HUAC maintained, was against Communist infiltration and its attempts to get American atomic secrets. By attacking Hollywood they were finding a way of warning the great American public of the threat at large in the same way as studio publicity hacks praised a star's home life or sporting activities to indirectly publicise their pictures.

The climate of the times gave the all-embracing term McCarthyism to the germ that McCarthy himself would soon be spreading like manure. He may have had nothing to do with the first anti-Hollywood hearings back in 1947, but his influence was stamped all over those that came four years later. In the meantime, as other investigations were taking place, it was Hollywood that grabbed the headlines and the national and international attention and made famous the name of its chairman J Parnell Thomas and his committee. It has to be said that in 1947 it seemed to Thomas and his self-satisfied men sitting high on the dais in California and Washington DC that their work was exclusively for the good. In fact, it was the seeding of an infection which made people sick and sometimes killed them. It killed careers, too, and, as these pages make clear in some cases for the first time, had a cataclysmic effect on families, many of whom were forced into exile.

As the writer-director Hal Kanter now puts it: 'I don't think I can think of a more contemptible, more despicable irony than was the House Un-American Activities Committee. There was no interlude in American history that was more anti-American than the Un-American Activities Committee. I was awfully uncomfortable in that whole period.' The eminent veteran broadcaster Norman Corwin – often described well into his 90s as America's poet laureate of radio – put it to me: 'There was hysteria. I was aware that this was a period of sordid lunacy. This was a period of insanity and cowardly sordid insanity. It had no saving grace. The country was in a seizure.' The courts, the press and the broadcast media all participated in a grotesque pageant. 'It infected the courts, infected the press. A garage mechanic could be fired if he were accused of reading subversive literature.'

Was it just hysteria? Was America in a state of collective paranoia? The question has to be asked because events unfolded at a strange time for the United States. The Cold War was certainly at its most frozen. Winston Churchill had proclaimed the existence of 'an Iron Curtain' when he made his famous speech at Fulton, Missouri in 1946. Before long, the Berlin airlift would seal, seemingly for ever, the existence of that curtain between East and West. But, as Paul Buhle made clear in conversation with Barbra Paskin, it was a time when 'the Soviet Union was completely exhausted economically, socially and every other way, and there was no conceivable threat to the United States – except in the minds of Harry Truman and others who really sought to finalise US power across the entire world.'

Perhaps the psychologists advising HUAC – if there were such people – decided that theirs was a way of maintaining a fiction which would give them a perverse sense of power. But the President? After all, wasn't Truman soft on Communism? Not if you studied international politics or noted his virtual declaration of the Cold War, he wasn't. But according to HUAC, there was a good chance that the American public would think he was – especially since there was a presidential election campaign about to get under way, with the incumbent, who had taken office on the death of Franklin D Roosevelt, facing New York Governor

Thomas E Dewey. It was intimated that opposing Communist values was a way of supporting Dewey, a Republican. Once – regrettably to the committee – Truman won that election, HUAC focused on other targets. It was then able to say how pleased it was that it was Truman who instituted 'loyalty boards' in all government offices.

Why both the Democrat Harry Truman and the Republican Dwight D Eisenhower both seemed to give HUAC their blessing is, according to Norman Corwin, 'a haunting question. Both administrations were themselves trapped. So much so that there were the famous McCarthy hearings, when McCarthy accused the Army of having a nest of Communists.' As for Hollywood, no one seemed to point out that out of 30,000 workers in the film industry in 1947, no more than 300 could be shown to have had associations with the Communist Party, either then or before. And that did not mean actual membership. Nevertheless, the deceptively simple sentence, 'Are you now or have you ever been a Communist?' was enough to send shivers down the spines of people who had never seen a red flag and for whom a hammer and sickle were mere symbols of the working man. The defendants' protests were frequently shouted down by the chairman of the committee, the man with a different kind of hammer, a man who before long would be sent to the same jail as some of his victims. They were asked to name names (a phrase which in itself haunted people who had never had reason to tell anything but the truth) or confirm names of people who the committee had decided were Communists. If they refused, the accused found themselves on a blacklist – a fact later revealed in more than 8,000 government documents that covered the hearings – with often disastrous repercussions.

A lot of the controversy centred around two factors: the aid and assistance given to the committee by rival Hollywood unions, and by plain and simple anti-Semitism which, as we shall see later on, was a near-permanent feature of the investigations.

The names of the Screen Writers Guild (SWG) and the Screen Actors Guild (SAG) will crop up constantly in this story. Their histories are not proud ones. Both guilds co-operated with the studios in making the blacklist work. They could have argued that their job was to keep their members working – including those who might be incriminated by association with Communists. They could have done, but they didn't. They merely wanted to keep the studio bosses happy and to preserve what they considered to be a 'gentlemen's club' or at least a gathering of artists, rather than to entertain the notion of anything as nasty as trades unions, a concept taboo in conservative post-war times.

When the moguls backed the establishment of the pompously named Motion Picture Alliance for the Preservation of American Ideals (MPAPAI), the Guilds rejoiced. They were on the side of the angels. After all, this was the group which, a year before it all blew open, was given carte blanche by the SAG. As it declared: 'The Screen Actors Guild has in the past, does now and will in the future rigorously oppose by every power which is within its legal rights any Fascist or Communist influence in the motion picture industry.'

The reputedly right-wing International Alliance of Stage Employees (IASE) had existed since the early 1930s, as had the Conference of Studio Unions (CSU), which was declared by HUAC's supporters to be a Communist front body. The moguls regarded the International Alliance as 'their' union. All it needed for open warfare was a strike. When Herbert Sorrell, head of the Conference, called one, there were riots. Picket lines were exposed to teargas by the studios' own police forces. Some demonstrators were actually clubbed. This turned into the catalyst that HUAC welcomed with the open arms of a grim reaper. The moguls, HUAC knew, had to accept the idea of rooting out Communists or risk massive box-office losses. And since some of the studios were turning out on average a new film every week, this was an important consideration. What the studio bosses had to decide was whether to go along with the new ethos or to continue to employ people who may have held party cards, but who were helping them to turn in a profit. If the moguls had been brave, they would have taken the second course. But they were not and the saddest period in American domestic politics since the Civil War dawned.

It was a time that was deadly both in its intent and in its results. There were suicides, while others died early deaths from heart attacks and strokes. These were caused not just by the anxiety of knowing – or, even worse, *not* knowing – that their name was on some list or other, but from the struggles, as Paul Buhle points out, 'to make a living and make house payments and afford to send the children to school, and so on.'

J Parnell Thomas put his cards on the table from the beginning: 'This committee under its mandate from the House of Representatives has the responsibility [of] expressing and spotlighting subversive [elements] wherever they may exist. It is only to be expected that Communists would strive desperately to gain entry to the motion picture industry simply because the industry offers such a tremendous weapon for education and propaganda.'

Why so many writers, actors, artists and assorted intellectuals became, if not members of the party, sympathetic to many of its values, is perhaps the most fascinating aspect of this sad, terrible story. Many of them were super rich, living in Beverly Hills' mansions, driving Cadillacs and the occasional imported Rolls-Royce. They held meetings around their swimming pools, protesting at the conditions of Mexican farmers, supporting striking longshoremen and worrying about the Spanish Civil War. As the writer Norma Barzman commented about the late 1930s: 'First of all, you have to remember the times, the whole history of the Depression, fascism. The Soviet Union was the only country helping the democratic government of Spain.' This extended to a general feeling that Russia was the only bastion of anti-fascism – an illusion smashed with the signing of the Hitler-Stalin pact. And then came World War Two and Hitler's invasion of the Soviet Union.

Exiled musician Larry Adler would put this into perspective: 'Our enemy became our ally – and then our enemy again. But I became involved when our enemy suddenly became a friend. However, that didn't help me because to the Un-American Activities Committee one of the things held against me was that I did shows for the Russians. I talked to them – and so did Eleanor Roosevelt. I belonged to an organisation of which she and Dwight Eisenhower were members. But I was the one who was blamed. I got into trouble for it. That's why I came to England. I was more or less immune from propaganda of any kind.' Adler was just one of a whole slew of Hollywood personalities who chose exile rather than appear before the committee. It took time for a lot of them to change their political allegiances.

Interview after interview confirms just how serious it was to be called before HUAC and how unreasonable it all seemed at the time. Sylvia Jarrico, widow of Paul Jarrico, the writer who became one of the iconic figures of the blacklist period, told Barbra Paskin: 'Fascism had appeared in the world and it was felt by serious political thinkers, people who felt that fascism had to be fought every day and in every possible way, to prevent the destruction of liberties. And they felt that the strongest fighters against fascism were the Communists. I believe that's what did it. It happened all over the world, intellectuals all over the world felt that the Communist party was an organising centre for the resistance to fascism.'

The fact that Paul had been named was of no surprise to him. He once said: 'I was pretty well known as left of centre, considerably left of centre. There was no secret about my political orientation and I in fact produced a film called *Hollywood Ten* in the summer of 1950 on the eve of their going to prison.'

'He was not a man to hide his politics,' his wife now says. What might have surprised him was that among the people who named him was Richard Collins, who had been his writing partner and was one of the original Hollywood Nineteen – the first people to be called to Washington by HUAC, later whittled down to the famous Hollywood Ten. 'He felt disgusted' about that, Sylvia says. Eventually, the Jarricos would talk about the *real* Russia, the country of the gulags, the purges and the wholesale disregard for human life. Sylvia Jarrico says: 'Many people felt very ignorant and felt sorry that they hadn't been more knowledgeable to be able to be more realistic and more effective in the fight against fascism. And to have accepted, to have taken certain things for granted. One of the classic conceptions attributed to Marx was that it's not only important to understand the world, you must also change it. And I remember saying to Paul at that time that with these revelations, one can say it is not only important to change the world, one must also understand it.'

What Paul didn't expect was the speed with which the blacklist hit him. On the day that he was served with the pink slip summoning him to appear before HUAC, he was barred from entering the RKO parking lot and the studio complex. 'That's how quick it was,' he recalled, years afterwards.

There is an argument that Communism in America was an even more intellectual movement than it was in Britain, where Cambridge University was the seeding ground for the spies Burgess, Maclean, Philby, Cairncross and Blunt, and the BBC had its own communist cell. HUAC's members believed Communism was an intellectual conspiracy, even though it had an essentially working class following. There was in particular another more subtle purpose of a committee that, when it was established in 1937, had claimed to be after fascists as much as it was Communists. Its first official target was Franklin D Roosevelt's New Deal, which it said enabled the Works Progress Administration (WPA) and the Federal Theatre Art and Writers organisation to be infiltrated by Communists. The fact is, HUAC was also dedicated to pursuing Jews. Most of its victims were writers and most of those writers were Jews. This was obvious from the statements of members of both Houses of Congress, like Representative John Rankin of Mississippi, who, in a tirade from the floor of the House, proceeded to loudly reel off the original names of Jewish Hollywood stars. Gerald K Smith, America's principal anti-Semitic rabble rouser, praised the service the committee was giving to the nation. A convicted Nazi spy paid tribute to HUAC and the leader of the German-American Bund (a fascist movement) did the same. Every time a witness refused to name names of fellow travellers or suspected Communists, Rankin, Smith and their cohorts rejoiced. Refusing to name names was publicised by the committee as proof of disloyalty to the Stars and Stripes.

The message was easily delivered and taken. As the then young left-wing actor Ed Asner said for this book: 'I learned very early on to keep my mouth shut.'

There was good reason for that. Plainly, the act of naming names was not always a protection from further harassment at the hands of HUAC. Larry Parks all but went on his knees before the committee as he begged not to be asked to 'crawl in the mud' to give names. Eventually, in sheer desperation, he confirmed names which the committee had presented to him. Shortly afterwards, the star of *The Jolson Story* and *Jolson Sings Again*, who had seemed destined to become one of the biggest names in Hollywood, was told his contract with Columbia was cancelled. He made only one more film – in a supporting role eleven years later.

HUAC chose Hollywood as its principal victim, as much because of the glamour it represented as for the chance to publicise its own beliefs, for the individuals summoned to testify were often big names who attracted journalists, photographers, TV channels and the general buzz of celebrity. The committee believed that the then current vogue for *film noir* was an indication of liberal influence. Apparently, the feeling was that dark movies, as distinct from the colourful get-up-and-sing pictures which ironically starred HUAC enemies like Gene Kelly and Judy Garland, were anti-American in concept. HUAC was helped by the fact that a number of the men behind the *films noirs,* including the recent assault on anti-Semitism, *Crossfire* (1947), from soon-to-be-blacklisted director Edward Dmytryk, actually were on their hit list.

Eight movie writers, one producer-writer, Adrian Scott, and one director Dmytryk, would be jailed for, in effect, falling into HUAC's carefully laid trap – by the way they tried to avoid answering questions, they gave the committee precisely what it wanted – a chance to convict them of contempt of Congress.

In a storm of controversy, these Hollywood Ten became the totems of what was undoubtedly a witch-hunt. Twenty-six stars chartered a plane to go to Washington to complain. HUAC loved the publicity this afforded their cause. It loved even more the fact that a whole tranche of these stars eventually reneged on their support for the Ten. The storm became a hurricane, a hurricane in which a principal part was played by men in grey suits wearing fedora hats – a uniform not normally seen in California, even in the 1940s. The FBI was responsible for issuing the subpoenas (yet another word that became part of everyday language in Hollywood) which brought the accused into the hearings. Not just that. It has been alleged – although never actually proved – that they weren't satisfied with *real* evidence. Detective agencies were said to be employed specifically to draw up phony files on people.

Eric Sherman, son of director Vincent Sherman, told Barbra Paskin that MGM studio head Dore Schary confronted his father with an 18-page dossier that had been compiled against him. 'It had a list of donations my father had made to the Communist party. Item after item. And Communist cell meetings my father had attended. My father told Dore it was a total fabrication.'

Paul Buhle says about that: 'The amount of false information generated was enormous – because, as in the case of the committee, it was said that a very large sum of money could change the status of an actor or writer or director overnight.' If that were so, it says a great deal for the integrity of the wealthy actors, writers and directors who did go through the torments inflicted by HUAC – and initially by the FBI men themselves.

They were seen everywhere. There was the story of a New York restaurateur whose business was floundering and, in desperation, inserted an advertisement in the *Daily Worker* (itself never banned even in the height of the McCarthy troubles). It said Joe's Tavern was the place 'where radicals congregate.' After the ad appeared, the establishment was crawling with what the FBI director J Edgar Hoover called 'G-men', taking note of everyone who chose to eat there. The amazing thought is that Communist influences quite legally existed in America at the time – and not just care of the *Daily Worker*. The Stanley Theater, just off New York's Times Square, used to show Soviet films. Every time a picture of Stalin came on the screen, people stood up and cheered.

Being put on the blacklist was to become a badge of honour – but one that its holders could well have avoided. Avoiding the blacklist was too often a sign of cowardice. Those who did name names or who rushed to show how much they loved America and its flag seemed to do so without care for the pain of those they incriminated. The hounding of witnesses was all part of the shame wrought by the whole process. It took bravery to stand up for oneself. Some did it with panache – notably

Lillian Hellman, who famously declared, 'I cannot and will not cut my conscience to fit this year's fashions.'

To protest in Hollywood was not fashionable at all. Yet there was a sense of collaboration about those who played the HUAC game, treachery which resembled the actions of the Fifth Columnists of World War Two and those supporting Francisco Franco against the Republicans in the Spanish Civil War (the side which many of the blacklistees had gone out of their way to support). That treachery was demonstrated in no small way by the manner in which professional bodies in the film capital rushed to show their love for their country and its institutions.

In 1946, the Screen Actors Guild was growing deeply concerned about reports branding it a deadly shade of crimson as a union under Communist influence. In June of that year, SAG president Robert Montgomery issued a statement rigorously opposing any Fascist or Communist influence. When he handed over the SAG presidency in March the following year to Ronald Reagan, the SAG mandate became even stronger. As we shall see, Reagan, along with Gary Cooper and Walt Disney, became one of HUAC's key 'friendly' witnesses in the first wave of Hollywood hearings that year.

In November 1947 SAG officers had to swear an anti-Communist loyalty pledge. In September 1950 SAG instituted what they described as their own 'voluntary' loyalty oath where members could come forward of their own volition to repudiate Communism and swear allegiance to America. In July 1953, amid massive national anti-Communist fervour, the loyalty oath became mandatory. It would remain in force for the next 21 years (although in 1967 it became an optional oath). The screen directors followed suit. In case anyone had any doubt where right-wing film people stood, they formed the Motion Picture Alliance (MPA) – with John Wayne as president – in opposition to those who were being incriminated.

The Academy of Motion Picture Arts and Sciences (AMPAS) had to find ways of showing they were on the right side, too. Incredibly, they awarded Oscars to people who had no rights to them, which was in complete accordance with their decision not to give awards to anyone who refused to co-operate with HUAC – or with anyone who had been branded a Communist sympathiser. This ruling was not rescinded until 1959. Carl Foreman and Michael Wilson, who wrote the memorable screenplay of the 1957 *Bridge on the River Kwai,* for instance, suffered the indignity of seeing an Academy Award go to the original book's author, Pierre Boulle – who couldn't even speak English, let alone write it. Larry Adler, who wrote the haunting soundtrack score of *Genevieve* (1953) watched painfully as the Academy nominated the film's music for an Oscar in the name of Muir Mathieson, the musical director, who hadn't actually written a note. 'I was delighted when it didn't win,' Adler, who like Foreman and so many other blacklistees went into exile in Britain, told me.

The miracle was that the movie capital did not die of shame, although for a long time it was apparently terminally ill. And so much more was at stake. As Fredric March said: 'They're after more than Hollywood. This reaches into every American town or city.' And every walk of life, March was one of the most respected actors of the 1930s, 40s and 50s and worked right through until 1973. At the time of the hearings he had just made *The Best Years of Our Lives*, about the difficulties of war veterans settling into civilian life. This was construed by HUAC as being pro-Communist. The fact that he also played Willie Loman in Arthur Miller's *Death of a Salesman* in 1951 didn't exactly endear him to the committee either. Quite suddenly, Communist influence was seen everywhere in a virtual mirror image of what was going on in Moscow. Just as in Russia, where modern art was considered not so much as decadent, as the Soviets had it, but insidiously pro-capitalist, Hollywood films were condemned for displaying left-wing influences.

The screenwriters were accused of inserting Communist propaganda into their scripts. 'Quite ridiculous,' writer-director Melville Shavelson told me. 'It's hard enough to get a script accepted, with all the changes that have to be made, without anyone thinking they could insert anything devious into the story – even if they wanted to.' He added: 'It did influence the content of motion pictures. You had to be careful what you put in a screenplay. Writers were always criticised if they were anywhere near honest.'

On the other hand, Jean Porter, widow of Edward Dmytryk, insists that another writer, John Howard Lawson, who was accepted as the leader of the Hollywood Communist cell, did try to get her husband to put propaganda into his scripts. 'He refused. Lawson told him that if he couldn't follow the party line, he was out. [Dmytryk] had thought that the party was the only means of getting people into jobs . . . He wasn't sympathetic to Communism, he was sympathetic to those who had been used.' Lawson has come to be regarded as the *éminence grise* of the California branch of the Communist party. Carol Eve Rossen, the actress daughter of the writer-director-producer Robert Rossen, who wrote and directed the iconic *All the King's Men* (1949), describes Lawson as 'the guru of the Communist Party. He gave up entirely on his career in the name of the party. He was cultural commissar and he called the shots.'

Norma Barzman, too, rejected totally out of hand the charge of inserting 'subversive material' into scripts. 'The idea has been shown to be a totally unjust charge.' You couldn't, she maintained, get anything like anti-racist or pro-women propaganda into films. 'Producers and heads of studios would never have let anything get by.' On the other hand, Dan Bessie, the son of Alvah Bessie, one of the Hollywood Ten jailed for refusing to tell HUAC who were members of the Communist party, thinks it *did* happen in a minor way. 'I don't think he ever tried to do what the Un-American Committee accused him of – inserting Communist propaganda in films – because he couldn't have done it. It would have been impossible. But they tried to incorporate, for example, black or Mexican characters in situations where those people would naturally be in a situation. I think they tried to promote a general working-class ideology or attitude in terms of dialogue and things like that, wherever they could. This was during a time, of course, when the whole country was, generally speaking, anti-fascist and so – especially during the wartime movies that were made – you had a lot of obvious anti-fascist propaganda in many, many films. I think that was a very deliberate and conscious thing to integrate that kind of thinking into scripts.'

Spies were everywhere – frequently troublemakers who had influence in the studio community. One was Ginger Rogers' mother Lela, who with a metaphorical microscope examined the script for her daughter's next film, *Tender Comrade* (1943), a World War Two story about the wives of servicemen, written by Dalton Trumbo – a man who before long joined the long line of scriptwriters facing the committee. The script contained the line, 'Share and share alike, that's democracy.' Both Ginger and her mother decided the line was Communistic. Ginger refused to say it.

Chris Trumbo, Dalton's son to this day denies that his father was much of a Communist. He told Barbra Paskin: 'Joining the Communist party was like joining any other political party. The idea of party discipline, that would get nowhere with him.' This was proved, he said, when the family sent for Dalton's FBI file. 'He seems to be the maverick member of the Communist party. The FBI tried to turn him into an informer . . .' But they didn't stand a chance. Trumbo puts it down to his father's 'independent American mind.'

Dan Bessie said that politics in his family came from seeing injustice in Vermont, where he was born. 'My mother and father had gone there during the Depression because they couldn't get work and they saw that A and P, the local chainstores, controlled the prices. They'd come back one year and give the farmers a good price and the next year wouldn't give them anything. So that kind of got him [my father] thinking about what was going on politically.'

Then, in 1936, the Spanish Civil War broke out. Bessie, who had been working on the *Brooklyn Daily Eagle*, joined the Spanish Information Bureau and then decided to actually go to Spain to fight on the Republican side. 'The left wing was actively recruiting people and he signed up to go.' Dan remembers the letters his father sent from the Spanish front, even at a time when the writer and his wife were planning a divorce. 'He wrote all the time. And he also sent us a couple of Loyalist militia hats and little Spanish Republican flags.' Back in America, after his activities in Spain, Bessie became chairman of the Warner Bros studio chapter of the Screen Writers Guild. Like several others, he was accused by Jack L Warner of organising a strike at the studio. 'He and Howard Koch [one of the three writers of *Casablanca*, 1942] . . . were fired soon after,' says Dan. It was a strike that revealed much about Hollywood and the people working there – like John Garfield, a name that will crop up in this story later on.

'My father,' recalls Dan, 'described picketing the gate when Garfield drove up in a convertible with a blonde and my father approached him to talk to him – and Garfield waved him off, saying, "Alvah, don't say anything. She doesn't know anything about this".' 'This' being Garfield's participation in left-wing activism, not his fear of others finding out that he was being caught with a woman who was not his wife.

'They don't exactly fire you,' Dan Bessie now remembers, speaking in the present tense – a demonstration of how real and sore it still feels. 'They just don't pick up your option.'

Being fired from a studio had a much bigger impact on Bessie's position than it did on that of Koch, who nevertheless was later blacklisted. Dan now remembers: 'He wasn't one of the big writers like Dalton Trumbo or other people of that calibre. He was definitely a minor writer. He got up to $600 a week, some of those guys were making $2,000–$3,000 a week at one point. But he was certainly influential in the Guild and among his compatriots.'

The Communist Party, it has to be emphasised, was never declared illegal – although, surprisingly, Hubert Humphrey, later a Democrat Vice President of the US and a presidential candidate – did try to introduce a bill to make it so; ironically, the bill was written by Arthur Schlesinger Jr, the 'Camelot' insider who would become John F Kennedy's intellectual guru. But it never got further than the floor of the House. The very Constitution of the United States – so sacred a document that virtually any person in the streets of your average American city, town or village can recite it – upholds the right to free speech as part of its First Amendment. Even so, the so-called Smith Act resulted in several Communist Party leaders being put in jail for being Communists – until the Supreme Court ruled otherwise. When people hauled before HUAC tried to invoke that amendment or the more famous Fifth, reasons were always found to rule them out of order.

One of those people was Paul Robeson's wife Eslanda Goode Robeson, who uniquely also sought refuge not under the First or Fifth Amendment, but under the *Fifteenth*. She appeared before Joseph McCarthy himself, who told her that the Fifteenth only applied to voting rights. 'I am a Negro, you know,' she told the Senator. 'I have been brought up to seek protection under the Fifteenth Amendment as a Negro . . . I always understood it has something to do with my being a Negro and I have always sought protection under it.'

McCarthy used terminology which probably surprised many of the people he had before him: 'Negro or white, Protestant or Jew,' he said, 'We are all American citizens here and you will answer the question as such. The question is "Are you a Communist today?" If you feel the answer will tend to incriminate you, you can refuse to answer.'

'What confuses me a little bit about what you said,' Robeson countered, 'you see is, I am a second-class citizen in this country and, therefore, feel the need of the Fifteenth. That is the reason I use it. I am not quite equal to the rest of the white people.'

McCarthy: 'You are being ordered to answer whether you feel a truthful answer will tend to incriminate you.'

Robeson: 'Under the Fifth and Fifteenth Amendments I refuse to answer.'

McCarthy: 'You are ordered to answer.'

Robeson's husband had his passport revoked to prevent him from protesting outside the United States, where he would find a more ready audience than at home. He had faced a constant campaign of public vituperation. In the infamous Peekskill riot of September 1949, he was forced to cancel his concert when vigilantes began attacking members of the audience. They set fire to a cross and threw rocks as cars departed. The folk singer Pete Seeger – who was to perform with Robeson – was in one of the cars that was hit and he and his son were injured by flying glass.

Accusations of anti-Americanism were thrown around like rice at a wedding. Or perhaps, more appropriately, like clods of earth at a funeral. Some of them were deadly – Julius and Ethel Rosenberg were sent to the electric chair for spying. The Rosenbergs came to epitomise the Cold War and the American fear, encouraged by HUAC and McCarthy's committees, of Communist infiltration. They were a couple of undistinguished Jewish parents of two young sons. Ethel was accused of helping her husband give secrets of the atom bomb to the Soviets by typing letters. They were charged with operating a Communist spy ring, although both denied ever being Communists and maintained to the end that they were set up by the FBI – a fact still claimed by their defenders.

They were 'shopped' by Ethel's brother, David Greenglass, who admitted he had actually supplied drawings of the bomb to Julius but cleared his name by saying that his brother-in-law was the one who had passed the sketches to Russian agents. The judge who sentenced the couple, Irving Kaufman (a Jew who had been assigned the case to avoid any suggestion of anti-Semitism) described the couple's 'crime' as being 'worse than murder'. Undoubtedly, they were used as an example to anyone else who contemplated what was considered as treason. As they went to the electric chair, Julius first and then Ethel immediately following her husband (while his spent urine was still being mopped up from under the death chair; just one of the examples of unparalleled torture), they still protested their innocence.

They remain the only Americans executed for treason in peacetime. Less seriously – in fact, quite hilariously – the patrician Secretary of State Dean Acheson was accused of being a Communist. So was Lucille Ball, who admitted she had joined the party just to please her grandfather. But she had not once attended a meeting and had no idea what the party stood for. 'The only thing red about Lucy,' said her husband Desi Arnaz, 'is her hair and even that's not legitimate.'

But people accepted what they were told. As Ed Asner told us for this book: 'It was part of the subtle control that the government generates through the media, through its Congress, over the people. It's a democracy, but not always democratic.'

In 1999, the 8,000 pages of documents about the blacklist were published by the US Government. They revealed that even Shirley Temple, in adult life a right-wing conservative US ambassador, was named by HUAC in 1938 – when she was 10 years old. Some things couldn't be laughed at. When Whittaker Chambers produced incriminating documents, which had been hidden in a pumpkin, exposing State Department official Alger Hiss as a spy, Hiss went to jail.

The American Army was about to be indicted *en bloc*, until in June 1954, their lawyer, Joseph N Welch, was prepared to stand up and say to McCarthy, 'You have done enough. Have you no sense of decency, Sir? Have you left no sense of decency?'

That was the point when people began coming forward to condemn McCarthy and McCarthyism as they had never dared to do so before. The Wisconsin senator was cowed; the bullying elephant had become the toothless tiger, but not a pussy cat. Nobody now loved the man whose briefcase was found to contain not important papers, but booze.

Edward R Murrow, the most influential television journalist of his day, helped to hasten McCarthy's political demise with a scathing attack in his *See It Now* programme. It was difficult for the Wisconsin bully to recover from that.

In December 1954, McCarthy was censured by his fellow senators and he became to all intents and purposes a non-person – the only member of the Senate not invited to a White House dinner. But HUAC stayed in business.

Ed Asner recalled listening to those Army hearings – the first nationally televised congressional inquiry which was taking place at precisely the same Army fort where he himself had trained after being drafted – and gleefully noticing that 'by this time McCarthy had become totally a fascist dog and I kept cheering for the other side.' People were being affected by the hearings as though by osmosis. The charges made by the committee began to stick in the public's minds simply because they had been made in the first place.

The US Presidents, those all-powerful leaders of the free world, had an ambivalent attitude to something that was undoubtedly a product of the Cold War. The Democrat President Harry S Truman, seen always as the plucky ex-haberdasher who looked after the working man (after having decided to drop the atomic bomb) described McCarthyism as 'the Big Lie'. Right wingers denounced Truman because he acquiesced, so they said in the Communist domination of half of Europe – not that, short of a nuclear war, he could have done much else.

Yet he instituted the Truman Doctrine, which called for Communism to be resisted everywhere, to say nothing of those loyalty oaths in all government departments. More significantly as far as the American voter was concerned, Truman gave his blessing to the setting up of the loyalty boards in all government departments. A 'Civil Service Loyalty Board' was established and 1,400 government employees were purged. In one particular year, 16,000 employees were investigated – and not one of them was found to be a Communist. But Truman was also the man who dismissed the Alger Hiss espionage case as a 'red herring'.

More significantly, he vetoed the McCarran Act (officially the Internal Security Act), which in 1950 authorised the creation of concentration camps 'for the roundup of subversives in emergency situations.' But the Senate overrode him – and passed the act by 89 to 11 votes. J Edgar Hoover had said 20 years earlier that he had lists of people who could be arrested as subversive. The fear of those camps, the ones, it was suggested, which had been used in the infamous rounding up of Japanese Americans early in World War Two, was one of the over-arching factors of the period. Jean Butler, wife of Oscar-nominated screenwriter Hugo Butler, said: 'We were terrified that the McCarran Act would be put into effect. It would allow [the arrest and imprisonment] of suspected spies or saboteurs. We heard they were refurbishing the Japanese camps. There was no way of knowing what was going to happen. We were convinced that the camps were being refurbished.' As it happened, the camps were never used for that purpose.

President Truman didn't say much about Hollywood, even when the second round of hearings began in 1951. These began with the full support of the studios, and of the unions, which to their members was the most crushing factor of all. The previous October, HUAC had revealed that it had asked the Screen Writers Guild for all its records. The Guild complied. The following April, it released a list of star names, men and women who had connections with Communist front organisations. Among them were Marlon Brando, Judy Holliday, José Ferrer and Lee J Cobb. Brando was one who was not called to give evidence.

Anti-Communist feeling, fuelled by the recent Korean war, was as strong as ever. When Dwight D Eisenhower took over in January 1953, McCarthyism had a brief resurgence of popular appeal. Red-baiting was as strong as ever. The Government people who had been dismissed were forced on to the breadline – more of them than at any time since the Great Depression two decades earlier.

In Hollywood, no one was willing to give work to men and women who had so recently been huge money-earners. People with big houses and two limousines in their garages – a very rare thing in the 1950s – sold up and were forced to look for small apartments. Some, as we shall see, went into exile. Others stayed and continued to write – under the names of other writers or sometimes just those of relatives who had never picked up a pen or pressed the keys of a typewriter before in their lives. It became known as 'The Front', the later title of a Woody Allen movie about that terrible time. Allen played a restaurant cashier who became too big for his cash register as he demanded more and more cash for the scripts of brilliant blacklisted writers forced to accept mere percentages of the fees being paid for their own work.

But Hollywood, as the source of the most significant art form of the twentieth century, suffered along with its blacklistees. The studios which had produced thought-provoking movies like *The Best Years of Our Lives* in 1946 and *Crossfire* were forced to go for lighter inoffensive fare – unless it was to make films with titles like *I Was a Communist for the FBI* made in 1951, which, in a reflection of the times, was actually nominated for an Oscar. Between 1947 and 1954 about forty anti-Communist movies were made by the Hollywood studios. None of them had any artistic or even commercial merit. The truth was that the studios were self-censoring to the extent that every time an executive looked at a script, he did so with one eye cast over his shoulder – just in case a secretary in the adjoining room or the engineer checking his intercom was actually a spy for the committee.

When McCarthy, who had been drinking a quart of alcohol a day for years, died of a cirrhotic liver on 2 May 1957 at the age of just 48, it was hoped by many that McCarthyism had died with him. Yet the Hollywood blacklist took a long time to disappear. In fact, it never officially came to an end. But one day in 1960, Kirk Douglas decided that the name of Dalton Trumbo, one of the Hollywood Ten, should be officially recognised as the writer of his movie *Spartacus*, and it began to fade away.

It was a good year for Trumbo himself. It was also in 1960 that Otto Preminger did the same as Kirk Douglas, crediting Trumbo's script for his film, *Exodus*. Preminger, a congenital non-conformist in many ways, was used to controversy, breaking with what everyone else in the film industry considered convention. Seven years earlier, he had flouted film code rules and faced Supreme Court action with the release of his 1953 movie *The Moon Is Blue*, which dealt with the taboo subject of extramarital sex.

If not the moon, certainly the air in Hollywood was pretty blue as a result of those 1960 decisions. Which to some people made a great deal of difference from the recent era tinged with red.

Chapter Two
HUAC

Most fair-minded Americans hope that this committee will abandon the practice of merely providing a forum to those who, for political purposes or otherwise, seek headlines which they could not otherwise obtain.

President Franklin D Roosevelt, October 1938

The HUAC hearings weren't all confined to the big rooms which so closely resemble the American court scenes in a thousand Hollywood movies. Yet, in most cases, the scene was familiar – the defendant involved in an unruly shouting match with the prosecutor while the judge bangs his gavel for order. At the committee hearings, the judge and prosecutor were the same person – the middle-aged John Parnell Thomas, an angry-looking man running to fat. Except that he wasn't a judge, just the committee chairman. The 'defendant' wasn't that either – just a moviemaker, who had broken no law, but who, in 10 notable cases, went to jail just the same.

The intimidation, for that was what it was, went beyond those few rooms in Los Angeles and Washington DC. There were insidious pre-hearings. One of them was in a public toilet. That was the venue for the first assault on the late David Raksin, composer of over 200 movie scores. Raksin's most famous and successful work was the haunting score for the 1944 *film noir* movie *Laura*, which became the second most-recorded song in history – and more famous than the picture itself.

Just before his death, Raksin told me what happened: 'I was down in the Federal Building and went to the john. A man came and stood next to me. He was head of police at MGM, Whitey Hendry, a nice guy. Quite casually, he said to me, "David, did you know about so-and-so?" Sure, I knew about him, but I wasn't going to tell him. He asked me if I could [name him]. I said "Of course not." Of course, the guy had been a member of the Communist Party but I was not about to say that. I knew there was no way.' Actually, the way that there was, the way that things were, Raksin would later be rather more intimidated inside the courtroom at that Federal Building. This was one of the things few people could believe possible. That in the United States of America, of all places, a person's own political views could land him in prison. This was clearly no police state – or was it? The FBI was close to rounding up those they considered to be 'subversive' elements and HUAC was their chief instrument.

Many of the people who faced what David Raksin called 'one of those star chamber places' were immigrants or the children of immigrants who had come to America believing it to be the land of the free. Now, in the course of exercising their constitutional rights, they were being condemned. Not one suspect was proved to be trying to bring down the government. No meaningful legislation ever resulted from the committee which was an arm of the United States Congress. Raksin was not alone in seeing a resemblance between HUAC and the Court of the Star Chamber used by medieval English kings to enforce their will above the law – it was particularly useful to Henry VIII, who used the corrupt members of the court to pass sentences and make decisions outside the normal concept of justice.

HUAC had been set up in 1938 in the wake of the Soviet purge trials and in the midst of the Spanish Civil War. There were members of Congress who were genuinely concerned about the possibility of the infiltration of communists into the fabric of the United States. There were others who, listening to the anti-Semitic ravings of Father Coughlin and Gerald K Smith, and mindful of the increasing membership of the German–American Bund and the America First movement, were worried that fascism was just as likely a threat.

The truth of the matter was that the fascist danger was barely considered. Among HUAC's other strongest supporters was James Scott, Imperial Wizard of the Ku Klux Klan, the James Scott who went on record as saying, 'The programme of the committee mostly parallels the programme of the Klan.' Scott also said: 'Every true American – and that includes every Klansman – is behind you and your committee in its effort to turn the country back to the honest, freedom-loving, God-fearing American to whom it belongs.' That was all that needed to be said about HUAC – until, that is, things got a lot more complicated.

Right from the very beginning, HUAC made Hollywood and the theatre targets, ostensibly because it believed that the performing arts and, in particular, the cinema, by far the most potent communications medium of the age, were being abused by communists and their sympathisers. The first Chairman of what was officially known as the Special Committee on Un-American Activities was Congressman Martin Dies of Texas, a man with a mission – his determination to show that he was going to root out what he saw as the red menace wherever he found it. He immediately declared that there were 'not less [sic] than 2,000 outright communists and party-liners still holding jobs in the government in Washington.' Three years later, he modified his charge to '1,200 subversive officials.' On the other hand, Dies admitted that there was no 'credible evidence of Communist activity in the movie industry.' It was Martin Dies who established the notion of haranguing witnesses, a practice later adopted by his successors, and most notably by Joseph McCarthy himself.

The strange thing is that HUAC wasn't laughed out of court right from the off. Their early findings (not least the one alleging that 10-year-old Shirley Temple was a Communist) were close to ludicrous. In one of its first 1938 hearings, the committee turned its attention to the Federal Theater Project, which had been set up under the Roosevelt New Deal's Work Progress Administration (WPA), principally to find work for unemployed theatre workers and to bring the theatre to people for whom it would otherwise have been a distant world of which they knew and would know nothing. HUAC determined that this was an institution overrun by Communists. Martin Dies was unflinching in his accusations that the whole notion was a Communist conspiracy.

From his initial investigations, Dies met a number of writers and actors who were afraid they were about to be smeared. But, after numerous pressures, he backtracked. He issued a statement immediately afterwards, clearing them. In 1940, Fredric March and Humphrey Bogart were named as communists – only to have the allegations struck down. The Screen Actors Guild came to their support and to others being named by HUAC (among them, James Cagney, Franchot Tone and Jean Muir). A statement from the SAG declared: 'To smear prominent persons without any reliable evidence is to play into the hands of Hitler and Stalin by confusing the innocent with the guilty.' Later, the Guild would totally reverse its stand, much to the chagrin of members who really needed its help.

The real controversy over HUAC all started when an ex-Communist, a former police agent who had infiltrated the local Communist Party, John L Leech leaked testimony which he was making to the committee in camera about the party's infiltration into the film capital. SAG announced: 'The American people like fair play. We are confident they will characterise as the real enemies of America those guilty of these tactics.' They wouldn't take that attitude for long.

Hallie Flanagan, the head of the Federal Theater Project, was subpoenaed to appear. Far from performing left-wing propaganda, she explained, they were providing a distinct emphasis on the classics, like the Elizabethan playwright Christopher Marlowe. The lead inquisitor Joseph Starnes read out an article written by Flanagan and then said: 'You are quoting from this Marlowe. Is he a Communist?'

In July 1938 Congressman J Parnell Thomas, later to be HUAC chairman, added his ten cents worth when he announced that both the Theater and the Writers' Project were hotbeds of Communism infested with radicals from top to bottom. 'Practically every play presented under the auspices of the Project,' said Thomas, 'is sheer propaganda for Communism or the New Deal.' Chairman Dies said he agreed.

The committee seemed to base its ideas on its assumption that every 'decent American' regarded the Soviet Union as the common enemy. Then, in 1941, two things happened that changed everything, two momentous events in world history. In June of that year, Hitler's armies invaded Russia in its Operation Barbarossa. Six months later, on 7 December, Japanese planes bombed Pearl Harbor. ('A date that will live in infamy,' said President Roosevelt, who quite suddenly had been given the excuse he wanted to enter World War Two.)

Suddenly, the wind was taken out of HUAC's red, white and blue sails. Russia was now an ally. 'Uncle Joe', the kindly nickname of Josef Stalin, became the loveable rogue of a statesman with whom both President Roosevelt and Prime Minister Winston Churchill could do business.

The Special Committee at this stage of its life wasn't totally made up of right-wing Republicans. There was, for instance, the Democrat Jerry Voorhis, who said that he was opposed to Communists but wanted more investigations of fascism in the US (as well as searches for Communists). He was joined by two other members from his side of the House, John Dempsey and Joseph Casey. But between 1942 and 1943 all three left the committee in frustration at being constantly outvoted by right-wing conservatives. When the Democrats asked for the Ku Klux Klan to be investigated, the idea was thrown out. It was Voorhis who instituted the only important piece of legislation to result from HUAC. The Voorhis Act of 1940 required organisations representing foreign governments to be registered with the US Government. The United

States Communist Party was never one of those, but the Act specified groups connected not just with the Soviet Union but principally also with Nazi Germany and Japan as well as, ironically, with China and the United Kingdom.

This wasn't the busiest time for the committee, however. It didn't exactly shut up shop, but its activities, like a delicious meal to be eaten later on, were put on something of a low light. But it did take notes. It was incensed that Hollywood could make pro-Soviet films like the 1944 *Song of Russia* or *Mission to Moscow* made the following year, the latter based on the memoirs of former American ambassador to the Soviet Union Joseph Davies; or *North Star*, Lillian Hellman's 1943 movie about how a Russian village defends itself against the Nazis, which won an Oscar nomination for best screenplay. *Mission to Moscow*, featuring some wonderful lookalikes of Roosevelt, Churchill and Stalin, the Big Three who were about to save the planet, had been made by Warner Bros at the precise request of President Roosevelt – a fact that Jack L Warner, head of production at his studio, later chose to cover up.

Each of these films was symptomatic of Hollywood's attitude to its duties in helping the war effort. Eric Sherman, son of Humphrey Bogart's favourite director Vincent Sherman, told me of a conversation he had had with the writer Howard Koch, who, together with Julius and Philip Epstein, had written *Casablanca* in 1942, the year before scripting *Mission to Moscow*. Jack Warner, he said, ordered him to write *Mission*. 'Howard looked at the basic story and said, "But this paints Stalin as a friend to the US and he's obviously a monster." Warner said: "You're doing the script and you're keeping Stalin as a friend." Howard said: "Why?" and Warner said: "Because he's against Hitler and we have to stand up against Hitler . . ."' So, under protest, Howard wrote the script which portrayed Stalin as a friend of the US. Later on, Koch was interviewed by HUAC. A piece of evidence used to prove his anti-Americanism was this portrait of Stalin as a friend. He told them "but Mr Warner ordered me to do it". But Warner would not defend Howard.'

There was another film, written by Lester Cole, one of the celebrated Hollywood Ten, that today his son Michael Cole sees as just as 'subversive' by HUAC's definition – *The Romance of Rosie Ridge* of 1947. Today, the younger Cole teaches film and that movie in particular. 'I've read it as the novella that McKinley Cantor wrote and I looked at my father's treatment of it. And I can tell you what's subversive about it and the same with other films: working-class people turn up in them. There's nothing in the story that says working-class people have to be in it. It's not the topic of the film. But the lives of working-class people are represented in the film . . . He did this insane thing: he made it all about literacy. So this Northerner comes down South and he knows how to read and write.' He adds, 'The Ku Klux Klan figure in the screenplay, although there is none of that in the original book. Is any of that subversive? In what sense is it subversive? Was the social content in American movies subversive? Hell, no, it wasn't!'

But HUAC decided it was. It was enough to make the committee wary of Mr Cole – especially since, in 1944, he had made a film about the Holocaust, *None Shall Escape*. Cole was of Jewish origin, but his son says 'he was absolutely not practicing and not interested in being a Jew one way or another.' HUAC didn't care. It was a good, if flimsy, excuse to strike a black mark that would lead to a black list.

Later, Lester Cole would tell a writer for a publication of the Screen Writers Guild: 'Being cut off from my craft was more than a financial loss. I loved movies. I loved seeing a good motion picture and if I wrote it, I loved it even more. I wanted the work, but more than that, I always felt that I could write what I wanted to write. I could get to more people through the screen than in any other medium.'

Insidiously, HUAC watched and prepared to pounce. They principally eyed writers and actors going to meetings of what they believed were of the Communist Party – a body that had 4,000 members in Los Angeles. Being seen to actually purchase the Communist newspaper the *Daily Worker* was enough to be included in a list of people subject to special investigation, when the time came.

That time came in 1946, months after the end of World War Two, with the triumph of the Republican Party in that year's midterm elections for the House of Representatives. Thanks to Congressman John Rankin, a man whose name will recur in our story, the Special Committee was renamed the House Un-American Activities Committee, HUAC. It was made a permanent Congressional investigating committee – 'enjoying unique subpoena powers.' J Parnell Thomas, who had been a member of HUAC since its inception, became its chairman in 1947 and instantly looked for ways for it to make his career. And he knew how to do it. Unbeknown to Thomas, the vice chairman and later co-chairman of the original committee, Samuel Dickstein, would later ironically be named as a Soviet agent.

Among the earliest members of the reconstituted committee was a certain Richard Nixon Milhous who remained a member until 1950. It served as a useful apprenticeship for his distinctly right-wing political activities.

In May 1947, six months after HUAC's inception, the trades, the daily organs of the film industry, announced the arrival of the committee in town. HOUSE GROUP STARTS RED PROBE, declared *The Hollywood Reporter*, which boasted on its masthead, 'Today's Film News Today'. It turned out to be the post-war American version of the Spanish Inquisition. The committee announced it was going to prove that 'card-carrying party members dominated the Screen Writers Guild, that Communists had succeeded in introducing subversive propaganda into motion pictures and that President Roosevelt had brought improper pressure to bear upon the industry to produce pro-Soviet films during the war.'

The film they had in mind was, of course, *Mission to Moscow*.

Nobody could have anticipated the resulting effect of the news summarised by the *Reporter*. 'Washington's long-threatened probe of Communists in Hollywood got under way yesterday with the arrival here of the sub-committee of the House Committee on Un-American Activities.' It immediately led to charges that the only un-American activity anyone knew about was that very organisation. To emphasise the point, anti-HUAC activists began to conveniently shorten the name still further and call it, simply and conveniently, the 'Un-American Committee'. J Parnell Thomas, who was principally aided by his fellow Republican congressman John McDowell of Pennsylvania, declared that Hollywood was a hotbed of pro-Russian propaganda – which meant it was un-American. 'I have been besieged by demands to investigate this situation,' he said. 'And the whole committee has been besieged by demands.'

One thing was for sure: HUAC's activities made things simple for a lot of people – it helped them work out for themselves the difference between left and right. Millions of non-political people were coming to the conclusion that right was right and left was . . . un-American. The studios appreciated HUAC, too. They reckoned the committee could do a lot of its dirty work for them. Now, it seemed, informing was an acceptable activity.

Like many of his friends, Hollywood Ten writer Alvah Bessie always believed that his psychiatrist revealed to the FBI what had been told to him from the supposed confidentiality of the leather couch.

The committee set itself targets to find not only Communists but also

Communist organisations – and if it couldn't quite make that charge stick, it would call them 'Communist front' bodies. The late bandleader and clarinetist Artie Shaw was hauled before HUAC because, the committee said, he had joined a peace foundation that was a communist front. 'I told them,' he said to me in 2004, 'if they could find a Republican peace foundation, I'd join that.' He said that his attitudes were formed by 1945. 'The atom bomb changed everything. It was scary. We learnt we had a bomb that could destroy a city. I belonged to a lot of organisations like the Committee for Far Eastern Democratic Policy, peace organisations. They suddenly became very unkosher.'

Shaw said that his announcement that he would happily join a Republican peace organisation 'gave them pause. One of them said, "Well, these well-meaning people were deceived."'

The questioning was familiar. 'I belonged to several organisations at this point. "Why did you join the peace conference?" That's what they wanted to know. "They had people from other countries." The chairman said, "You realise that it's a Communist front organisation?" I said, "If you know of a Republican peace organisation, I would join that." That didn't go down too well. It did give them pause. My whole attitude was that I would join any organisation that promised peace. If they wanted to blow up City Hall, I wouldn't want to do it. I joined organisations that I believed in. A peace organisation was a good idea and still is. I never regretted any of those things. I don't have any regret at all.'

He was immediately put on the blacklist. 'I would do late-night television. I guess they thought that people were inoculated by then.'

Shaw might also have been mystified by the US Establishment's own knowledge (or lack of it) of what Communism stood for. Sometimes, it was difficult to take that knowledge seriously. Some years later, the United States Court of Appeal for the District of Columbia Circuit ruled that the 'Communist Party of the United States [is a] Communist action organization.' Which many people must have been glad to have cleared up. Truth to tell, people only had to sign a petition, which they soon forgot about, or – sin of sins – march in a parade pressing for world peace to be called before HUAC and suffer the consequences, which frequently meant blacklisting and the end of their careers.

There were two main probes into Hollywood, in 1947 and again in 1951, which were virtually ongoing until 1955 and finally in 1957 to 1958. It was the 1947 hearings that caused the ball to really roll – with 24 'friendly' witnesses called, 19 of whom were deemed to be 'unfriendly'. More witnesses were called in the second series. HUAC issued reports in 1952 and 1953, stating that 212 individuals were named as Communists by friendly witnesses.

Dalton Trumbo, who was emerging as one of the great stars of the HUAC proceedings, became famous for declaring that both sides of the friendly/unfriendly fence were victims. Even so, he would say that he felt 'uncomfortable' in the company of people who had testified as friendly and admitted that he would 'rather not associate with them.'

HUAC chose its witnesses carefully. The ones they liked best of all, the ones they listened to most intently, were the former Communists who had now declared themselves to have seen the light. Every renegade was proof that the reds were wicked and that any sensible person would get out of their clutches as soon as possible. It was intended that the 'friendly' witnesses would dominate the hearings – nice, white, clean-cut, well-dressed men, like the moguls Jack Warner and Walt Disney, and stars such as Gary Cooper, Ronald Reagan, Adolphe Menjou and Robert Taylor. If they said they hated Communism, so would all their fans. Of course, the studios totally approved. With their stars appearing before HUAC, they were advertising their movies.

The friendly witnesses were allowed to read statements, especially when they were ready to name names. The unfriendly witnesses were not allowed to do so. Not all those who had no names to name but were considered unfriendly were to be totally blacklisted. Edward G Robinson, for one, was put on a 'grey list', despite his voluntary appearances before the committee to persuade them of his non-involvement with Communists. He wasn't unemployable, but it was years before he had anything like a starring role. Suddenly, one of Hollywood's most distinguished actors was relegated to minor roles in even more minor pictures. The only serious charge that seemed to stick was that the parts he played were mostly unsavoury and, therefore, un-American. But he was known as a leftish liberal. Charges that he had any connection with Communism couldn't be made to stick.

It was the start of the television age and J Parnell Thomas took advantage of the fact as though he had been given a valuable new present tied up with a blue ribbon. TV, particularly in the Los Angeles area, covered most of the hearings and he and his committee became household names to the very few who had sets. The film industry watched too, quaking in their hand-made, soft leather shoes, as careers were destroyed. Radio, together with the print press, was by far the main news medium, along with the cinema newsreel.

There were other points of visible interest. On the same day in 1953 that the HUAC investigators arrived to continue their latest round against Hollywood, the Atomic Energy commission announced the start of a new series of atomic tests in Nevada, about 75 miles from Los Angeles. For the duration of the HUAC hearings in Los Angeles, locals could witness bomb flashes and feel the tremors caused by the explosions. The physical reminder of the atomic menace, coupled with daily updates of nuclear tests in the local papers, gave the hearings an additional urgency in the minds of many.

They had a lot to fear. The blacklist was filled with names of people who passed through the portals of the Federal Building in downtown Los Angeles and answered the subpoenas that spelt a strange form of death. The blacklist, however, was not a HUAC product: the studios themselves instituted it all on their own.

The studios looked after their own if it suited them, though. Judy Holliday, the not-so-dumb blonde who had starred in *Born Yesterday* in 1950, was set to be Columbia's most potent box-office force. When Harry Cohn, one of the studio's founders and a feared iron dictator of Columbia, discovered that she was a former Communist Party organiser, he did a deal with Thomas to keep her away from the witness stand (or rather, the table at which those under investigation sat with lawyers, who were rarely allowed to make statements on behalf of their clients).

Deals were very much on the committee's agenda – even after J Parnell Thomas himself had been jailed for corruption in 1950. Arthur Miller, who had his moment before HUAC in 1956, was told that nothing would happen if the then chairman Francis Walter could be photographed with Miller's wife, Marilyn Monroe.

The triumph of the climate of fear engendered by HUAC had a great deal to do with simple cowardice. If the studio heads had gathered together to say they wanted nothing to do with the committee, or if the agents had threatened to pull their clients out of every television series in which they were involved, the rocket that ravaged Hollywood would have become a mere damp squib. The surprising thing is that more people, more lawyers in particular, who had no personal vested interest, didn't protest. 'Taking the Fifth,' a phrase that appeared in newspapers every day during the hearings and those of the McCarthy committee, was seen as an admission of guilt.

Bernard Gordon, a writer who was among the last to be summoned before HUAC, explained: 'Some of the liberal lawyers who worked with our people who were not Communists didn't like us to take the Fifth

Amendment because, although the principle of the Fifth is that you're not guilty, there's an inference of guilt.'

The Constitution laid down in its Fifth Amendment that nobody should be forced to incriminate him or herself. As a chemist named Clarence Hickey – who had been summoned before Joe McCarthy – put it into perspective: 'I don't think you understand the whole purpose of the Fifth Amendment, Senator. That Amendment was put into the Constitution to protect the innocent man from just this kind of star chamber proceeding you are carrying on.'

But HUAC and Joe McCarthy interpreted it differently. Not only that, time and again, 'taking the Fifth' was no protection against incrimination. Naming names was what the committee ordered. Failing to do so was contempt of Congress.

Dan Bessie says that his father, Alvah Bessie, was recommended not to take the Fifth because it would imply guilt and would result in those taking that course being fired from their jobs. HUAC didn't bother about truth or ethics. The more outrageous the charges – and we shall see that the charges were more than merely that – the more newsworthy they became. And that's what the Committee wanted – coverage in the newspapers, in the cinema newsreels and on radio, which had huge numbers of listeners in an age when so few had a TV set, and later on television itself.

The magazine *Newsweek* reported that as a result of HUAC, the public was becoming 'wiser about the ways of the Kremlin.'

The victims became wiser still about the power of HUAC.

Chapter Three
On the Way

*Before every free conscience in America is subpoenaed, please
speak up. Say your piece. Write your Congressman a letter. Airmail
Special. Let the Congress know what you think of its Un-American
Committee. Tell them how much you resent the way Mr Thomas
is kicking the living daylights out of the Bill of Rights.*

Judy Garland, 1947

Betsy Blair knew it was happening because FBI men gatecrashed the
parties she and her husband Gene Kelly gave every Saturday night.

Ben Barzman and his wife Norma were tipped off by a magnificently
beautiful blonde whom years later they realised was Marilyn Monroe.
As Norma told me, her neighbour Groucho Marx didn't approve of
what they were doing – for the moment at least.

The actor Jeff Corey, who was with the Group Theater in New York,
heard about it on the radio. He said afterwards, 'I knew something was
up about a year before the Hollywood Ten were called to testify before
Congress.' It was when the California Un-American activities
Committee started subpoenaing members of the Group Theater that the
first sightings of the Red Light were made. It was when the accusations
were made, Corey said, that the real worries began to surface. He felt
that the sin seemed to be that they put on plays by George Bernard
Shaw, Sean O'Casey and Chekhov. 'I could see the handwriting on the
wall at that point . . . I felt a little doomed after the experience of
the Ten. For me it was simply a matter of time before I'd be called in.'

Madelene Gilford, wife of character actor Jack Gilford, and a close
friend of actor Zero Mostel was tipped off while sitting in a restaurant.
And always, strange figures lurked in the shadows, although sometimes
they sat quite openly in cars outside people's homes or were spotted
manning cameras with long-distance lenses from the windows of houses
opposite those under suspicion.

In their grey flannel suits and snap-brim hats, so unusual in sunny California at any time, the FBI men seemed to be pursuing their own happiness and enjoying their work thoroughly – which is hardly surprising when you learn that they were not spending all their time sitting in cars or looking through camera viewfinders. Part of their job was to go to the best restaurants and gatecrash Gene Kelly's parties.

This wasn't some fictional police state, so beloved of some film makers of the time. It couldn't be in a country where the Bill of Rights promised everyone their right to free speech, free association and the privilege of the 'pursuit of happiness'. Neither should you get the impression that it was some kind of Gestapo or even the newly re-formed KGB. When suspects – for that, indeed, was what they were – eventually came face-to-face with those men in hats, they found them polite, sometimes charming, occasionally sympathetic. But their quarries knew that in their hands they carried a pink piece of paper that could spell life or death to their careers, perhaps even to their lives and, most insidiously of all, to their families.

The 'pink slips', as everyone called them, were invitations to meet the members of HUAC, or more accurately and officially, subpoenas to give evidence as unfriendly witnesses. They all knew that was how they would be regarded. They would have been called 'hostile' in a court of law. But this was no court and what they were going to be accused of was breaking no law. As Larry Adler, the world's most accomplished mouth-organ player, was told by Senator Joe McCarthy's principal henchman, Roy Cohn, 'go fight City Hall.'

Most of the subpoenas were to attend not City Hall, but a building that HUAC had rented on the corner of Hollywood and Vine – one of the most iconic map references in Hollywood lore. Some of the suspects, however, were required to go to Washington DC. The whole situation was bizarre. Paul Jarrico, the writer who in 1941 had been nominated for an Oscar for the screenplay of the film, *Tom Dick and Harry*, was one of the central characters in the whole blacklist story. He actually *asked* the FBI to come and subpoena him, inviting the press along to watch the whole process. Bill Jarrico, the writer's son, told us: 'He arranged to be subpoenaed in front of reporters, so they came to the house. He stood in front of the house and there was a picture in the *Los Angeles Times* the next day of Paul getting his subpoena with our address – in case anybody wanted to write to him.'

It provided the backdrop to a wonderful sense of community around and about that address. 'The people on our block really were very friendly to us. One lady brought us a cake. Without saying anything. Everybody was very friendly.'

Paul's wife Sylvia has as many stories as anyone else involved in the arrival of the FBI G-men. 'Our living room was a very long room and there were windows at the front and windows at the back. So the investigators who sat outside in front could see right through the whole house. We didn't do anything to hide that. We just went about our business. We had some curtains. There were a few dreadful people who would come and sit there in their car at high noon and have their lunch, and then throw the dirty boxes on the lawn and the crusts of their sandwiches to show their contempt.' Sometimes, when the cars pulled up, Jarrico would go out the back door and take a walk. 'Or,' said his wife, 'go to work. I answered the door all the time.'

What weapons to use against these intruders? One of the most effective turned out to be a sense of humour – a characteristic not possessed by the men in snap-brim hats. But certainly Sylvia Jarrico had it: 'This was the time when there was a Red Cross campaign throughout the city and I'd always had a soft spot for them because I was in a flood as a child and they came and helped. So whenever they had a campaign every year, I would go out and say this is time to contribute to the Red Cross. I wanted to see who these people were who behaved so badly in the parked car. So I came out with my Red Cross box and I said, "I'm accepting contributions for the Red Cross and I'd be very glad to accept one from both of you." I felt very nice about it. They just looked at me and sneered, like, "Are you kidding?" They were different people stationed there in the cars all the time.'

And the sort of people they were? Says Sylvia Jarrico: 'They were not enjoyable to me. They were cold; they were contemptuou; they were dressed up like FBI persons. They had on suits and they wore hats and there were many blue-eyed people among them. They were tall.' As she added: 'These were very scary times.'

Bill now admits that as he stood next to his father, he hoped that the caption writers would recall the image of the son 'standing by' his old man. Instead, they said that the young boy was 'by his elbow'. Before that happened, there were FBI visits and, before them, meetings with people likely to be called before HUAC – and then to be blacklisted.

'I used to wander into these meetings which were right outside my bedroom door,' Jarrico now remembers about those sessions. 'It wasn't hard to find them and sometimes I'd sit and listen. On one occasion, somebody said – I don't know that these meetings were secret or that

34

anyone thought I understood them really – to my parents, "Do you really want your kid to be sitting here hearing all this?" My father was perfectly happy for me to hear that.'

Sylvia remembered her husband discussing the matter with their son. 'One of the conversations I remember especially – Paul was saying there were various democracies in the world and the Soviet Union had its democratic principles – for example, "it's against the law to be anti-Semitic in the Soviet Union." And so Bill said: "Is that democracy? Is that freedom of speech? That it's against the law to be anti-Semitic?" And Paul answered, "What is your hurry to be smarter than your father?" and Bill said, "That's the purpose of life, isn't it?"

Jarrico himself might have considered that part of the purpose of his life was to make a statement to HUAC which stated his whole philosophy: 'I should be happy to help this Committee uncover subversion,' he stated, 'but one man's subversion is another man's patriotism. I consider the activities of this committee subversive of the American constitution. I believe this country was founded on the doctrine of freedom, the right of a man to advocate anything he wishes – advocate it, agitate for it, organise for it, attempt to win a majority for it. And I think that any committee that intimidates people, that makes it impossible for people to express their opinion freely, is subverting the basic doctrines of the United States and its constitution.' Thus the screenwriters took advantage of their articulate advocacy skills.

Avoiding the FBI before it got to that point and trying to miss their pink slips was a tremendous test of character – or at least of personality. Those who faced 'the G-men', as they became known in the James Cagney movie, with an element of bravado were not necessarily braver than those who showed their fear – and nor were their wives or families. Joan Scott, who later married one of the Hollywood Ten, Adrian Scott, said that when she heard that the FBI had come to her office, 'I shook so much I couldn't dial Adrian's number. I said I wanted to come up there [to his home] and he said no. That was the worst place for me to be. They had it staked out and [there were] photographers . . . The papers were already filled with Red Scare headlines and he didn't want it to be the "Laurel Canyon Red Love Nest".'

By the time she appeared and was firmly on the blacklist, Joan says she felt there was a huge C branded on her forehead.

Jean Butler recalled her husband, the writer Hugo Butler, saying, 'he had tried the army and knew he wouldn't like jail.' His overwhelming fear was jail and the blacklist. 'It was while we were having dinner the night that the doorbell rang. There were two men in hats – in Southern California no one ever wears a hat. I was so terrified I was almost in tears.' She had to explain her appearance. 'I said we had had a disagreement and off they went. I was in a panic. Our two best friends were in jail: Dalton [Trumbo] and Ring [Lardner Jr] [both members of the Hollywood Ten].' The Butlers realised they had to get away – so they took a trip to the local laundry 'to legitimise our exit. We never went home; we just bummed around.'

There were other meetings. A group of actors who feared the clutches of HUAC, if not the blacklist, used to meet in a desert motel. Paul Jarrico would join them. His wife Sylvia remembered: 'He liked [the actors] and one was a very special friend. So he went down and took Bill with him. They drove into the desert to this motel where the friends were and they started having a discussion about how dispiriting it was that old friends would actually get up and be informers about activities that they themselves had participated in with pleasure and pride, and to turn that into something to attack people with.

'And that it was very, very disturbing but what can you do if you're called before the committee? You do what you can, but the overall situation was very discouraging. So Bill was there, listening to the conversation, and he said to Paul, "You don't even read the titles in your own library," and Paul said, "What title are you thinking about?" And Bill said, *"No Voice Is Wholly Lost"*.'

Sylvia remembers the association with Dalton Trumbo, one which constantly crops up in this story. 'He had great admiration for Trumbo's work. Trumbo was amazingly productive and always was a functioning writer. And he was exciting in conversation.'

Not everyone was quite so understanding. Jarrico was to have the distinction of being blacklisted, not just in America but also behind the Iron Curtain. Sylvia told us: 'Some writers in Hollywood and some writers in New York got together a protest against the treatment of certain writers in the Soviet Union. They were very much disturbed.' Hence Paul's name being added to a list in the Kremlin to match that drawn up in Los Angeles.

Bill Jarrico recalled his babysitter – 'so I was young enough to have a babysitter' – not being too sure about copies of the Constitution and the Bill of Rights which he had on the walls of his bedroom. She looked at them and said, possibly as a joke: 'Ah, subversives.' It may have been a joke but it was an indication of the climate of the times.

As for Paul personally, Sylvia Jarrico says: 'He knew from the very start that this was a committee that had to be resisted. There was a very grave, even frightening, infringement on freedom. So Paul never had a moment's hesitation. He knew he was going to make as strong as possible a statement to the committee challenging their right to ask the questions. He developed a statement – the one about his father being a Russian Jew, a poet and a fighting man.'

The fact that he had been named was of no surprise to him. 'He was not a man to hide his politics,' his wife now says. What might have surprised him was that among the people who named him was Richard Collins, a man who had been his own writing partner and one of the original Hollywood Nineteen. 'Paul had gone to see him. He'd heard that Richard had taken a lawyer who represented a number of people who were informers. So he went to see him to make sure he was not so frightened he'd be considering such a thing.'

It was not a satisfactory meeting. 'Richard said, "Well, what do I do? I have no feeling about being a Communist. I've changed my political orientation. I have nothing to protect."'

It was one of those statements that was calculated to make blood boil. Jarrico told him: 'You have a committee to confront, a committee that's a more serious challenge to American liberties than we've faced in a long time and there's very good work to be done there. The committee needs to be challenged.'

Collins testified against his old friend and partner. Jarrico wasn't the only person he named. As Sylvia Jarrico recalled for this book: 'There was a lot of contempt about Richard Collins because his career had been quite bumpy until he started working with Paul.'

Another who knew nothing about Collins but believes she suffered because of him was the popular film star, Marsha Hunt. 'I never met Richard Collins,' she said, in 1995. 'But when he was in some executive post on *Bonanza*, a friend of mine knew him slightly. At one point, when I was recommended for a script, she was astonished to hear him say, "Don't bother bringing up Marsha Hunt to me. As long as I am connected with this show, she will never work on it."'

That was how powerful the influence of the blacklist was for someone who had never even been subpoenaed to appear before HUAC. Hunt recalls: 'When I returned from New York to Hollywood in 1951, it was a changed place. Now it was armed camps. I do remember a couple of guests at our house getting up and sweeping out when another couple arrived. They would not be under the same roof with "those people". And "those people" had apparently informed at HUAC hearings.'

Harry Rapf was an important name in Hollywood – practically Hollywood royalty. He was one of the founders of the movie capital's most glamorous studios, MGM. But that fact wouldn't help his son Maurice, a cameraman who came under the HUAC lens. Maurice wasn't working for MGM. Nevertheless a studio executive warned him to 'stay away from politics'. According to his daughter, Joanna Rapf, 'He was very active in the Communist Party in Hollywood . . . That was a very, very scary time. My earliest memory of something being strange was when we left Los Angeles in 1948. We moved to New Jersey and then to Vermont. I was much too young, because I was only 7 or 8, but I was very much aware that my parents were outsiders and things weren't quite right.'

So not right that it was simpler to suggest that anti-Semitism was the reason for that situation rather than politics. That gives some idea of just how serious a crime it now appeared to be of the wrong political and perhaps religious persuasion. 'What they told us was that people didn't like us because we were Jewish. I remember my parents weren't allowed to vote. The reason given was that we were Jewish, but [now] I don't think it was that. They didn't talk about the politics. We were very aware, at least my sister and I, that things were strange.'

Today, it is a memory Joanna would rather suppress, perhaps because her parents used alcohol as a means of trying to escape from the conditions HUAC's politics had wrought. Her sister, she says, 'remembers the FBI coming to the door. I remember finding my mother on the floor with a black eye. I think she fell. My sister remembers this whole period as everyone being drunk. People drank a lot and my mother certainly did. I remember finding her on the floor. And it was just part of the general horror of the time.'

Another part of the personal horror was one that no child would ever forget. 'Our parents disappeared . . . they went into hiding so they couldn't be served a subpoena.' A woman named Helen looked after the Rapf children in her house. 'We didn't know where our parents were, and obviously they wouldn't tell us – and when the FBI came to the door, we couldn't tell them where they were.'

So where were they? 'I now know they were in a boat with several other blacklisted couples off the Maine coast somewhere, but we didn't know it then.'

For all that, there had to be explanations. Rapf went back to to basics and taught his children about the origins of Communism. Says Joanna, 'That one word "Communist" . . . it's still denigrating. I remember as a kid – I guess I was 11 or 12 – wanting to know about Communism from my parents. So much so that my father gave me the *Communist Manifesto* to read and it was so wonderful! So utopian! It was just this fabulous, "From each according to his ability, to each according to his needs." What a wonderful idea, I thought it was great. I loved it, I thought, why are people so afraid of this? My father couldn't even begin to explain it to me.'

The pink slips were the dreaded pieces of paper that came like news of the death of a son in action, delivered by men in particular uniforms. But if there were no pink slips, there could be no appearances, friendly or otherwise. The principal object in the life of the unfriendlies was to avoid the FBI men and their pink slips. They didn't all succeed. If they had done so, the story of America in the early post-war years and of Hollywood output and legacy until the 1960s would have been very different.

Sondra Gorney, wife of lyricist Jay Gorney, the man who wrote the national anthem of the Depression, 'Brother, Can You Spare A Dime?', and who later discovered a little girl called Shirley Temple, said of her husband and the G-men: 'We didn't want him to have to be before the committee – so he wasn't there when the FBI came with a subpoena. They gave me one instead. They had one for me, too. I was very active myself. And then our attorney made a deal with them – that Jay would accept his subpoena if they took mine back because we had two little children – and we didn't think it right to jeopardise both parents in the family of two little children, so they took mine back and Jay accepted his.'

Jay Gorney eventually appeared before McCarthy's Senate committee at the courthouse on New York's Foley Square. It was there that something strange happened. Sondra told us about an encounter with Senator Kit Clardy, from Michigan.

'When the courtroom was recessed for lunch and we were going down the steps . . . this senator followed him and said, "Jay, Jay, I want to talk to you" and we were scared. He said, "You graduated from the University of Michigan, didn't you?" and Jay said, "Yes." He said, "Why don't you come to our alumni club some time?" Jay was so shocked! Here was the guy who had practically crucified him and now he was inviting him to come to the alumni club. That shows you the shallowness of some of these political characters.'

As she went on: 'They were doing it for publicity. That's why they attacked all the Hollywood people, because that gave them press. That's what McCarthy did. He attacked big people and he got the press and he made himself important that way. It was a terrible time. It really was because there was such insincerity in what they were doing. I don't think they really believed that we were enemies of the people. Not at all. It was a whole show. They had no consideration about hurting artists and families. They just wanted the attention, the publicity that made them feel important.'

The amazing thing is that it took time for the pennies to drop. Early in 1947, before HUAC set up shop, Communist party members continued to hold meetings, so-called 'progressives', at which people who had no intention of joining the party congregated for drinks at the homes of friends who did hold membership cards. When it became obvious that the FBI were on their trail, there was shock and consternation. Many felt that there was comfort in numbers. Joanna Rapf recalls poker games in which blacklisted writers took part 'and it would rotate from house to house. That was a big part of the social life and it involved Ian Hunter and Ring Lardner, Zero Mostel, Sol Kaplan, Jay Gorney, all of those people who were involved in this poker game. They socialised all the time.' And so easily formed a cast list for that blacklist.

Throughout the period, more and more ways were being sought to dodge the visit by the unfriendly neighbourhood FBI men. Impressions of the G-men vary from blacklistee to blacklistee, but they certainly inspired a great deal of fear. Says Sylvia Jarrico: 'There was a time when I felt very anxious. I had a free-floating anxiety which developed at that time . . . they were very scary times.'

What is apparent from a cursory glance through the testimonies of each of the victims of HUAC is that their experiences and situations were unique. They may have shared similar backgrounds and worked in the same industry, socialising together, sending their kids to the same schools and living in the same neighbourhoods, but there was not a stereotypical blacklistee.

A lot of knowing how to deal with the call from the FBI was auto-didactic. Michael Cole recalls the time when he and his now wife Sheila were courting. 'She and I started dating when we were kids practically and we would hear "click-click" on the phone and we'd just laugh about it and say, "Oh, the FBI is listening on the phone." We knew it was for real. But what were the consequences of our lives? We weren't doing anything wrong. We never felt we were ever doing anything wrong. We'd go to folk music things of left-wing groups out in the Valley. It scared the shit out of my mother, because I was 13 or 14. But we never did anything wrong. We didn't drink. Compared to what's going on around now? Nothing. Zero.'

Michael does remember how scary it could be. And he, like everyone else involved in the beginnings of what would soon become so apparently a witch-hunt, was struck by those uniform hats – each of which represented the dreaded knock of the FBI. 'They wore trench coats and hats. Nobody wore hats. This was West Hollywood. Nobody dresses like that. Once, Burt Lancaster came round. I remember he kind of looked like one of these FBI guys and I said, "I'm not sure who this person is."'

When the real FBI men called, Cole remembered for journalist Barbra Paskin how 'they said: "Wouldn't you like to talk to us now?" and the answer was "No, I have nothing to talk to you about."'

He remembers his parents being 'terrified'. As he said: 'I think probably some of these guys might have been talking with people from Russia. But I have no idea.'

Ben Barzman, a 36-year-old Canadian-born writer and his wife Norma saw no reason not to hold meetings at their Beverly Hills home with its sweeping front lawns on Sunset Plaza Drive. They were sitting there one beautiful spring evening drinking gin and tonics when an aged Cadillac convertible drew up and a beautiful blonde girl got out.

She said, wasn't it lovely to be able to sit on a lawn, drinking cool drinks? 'We offered her one,' Norma told me. 'She loved it and decided that gin and tonic would from then on be "my drink."'

Then she told the story. There had been men stopping cars going up the road. Was she going to number 1290? No, she wasn't, she said, and then asked Norma, 'Isn't this 1290?' It was. The Barzmans were planning a Communist meeting and, despite all the rumours, all the stories of thwarted gatherings, it was going ahead. 'My name's Norma,' said the girl. 'So's mine,' said Mrs Barzman.

What the girl then told them was all the information they needed to make up their minds to cancel the meeting. More grateful than they were to have a certain neighbour around. Every day, Groucho Marx, who lived nearby, would walk past the house and go and chat to them if they were outside. On that very day, he was less forthcoming, with none of the usual jokes or wisecracks which he used to hand out as freely as the tips to his favourite waiters. He was wheeling a pram with his baby daughter Melinda inside. It was a hot day made all the more so by hot winds. *He* thought it was hot, at least. Groucho also said he knew it must be 'doubly hot' for the Barzmans. 'He was behaving very strangely,' Norma remembered. 'Then he said it: "If you needed help, I wouldn't give you anything but ice cubes."'

Strange comment that from Groucho, whose son Arthur Marx told me he was a committed Democrat who subscribed to the left-wing press. 'He didn't approve of blacklisting and all that. But he was very political, although he didn't want to belong to any of those organisations. I think he made a speech and was called a "Cadillac liberal."' Perhaps it was a case, as he said so often, of not wanting to belong to any group that would have him as a member.

Joan Scott doesn't list Groucho in her list of favourite people. 'He would answer the phone as his Japanese houseboy' – which you might think was nothing less than typical among stars who did their best never to answer their own telephones. Another reason could be that Groucho knew that Joan was usually ringing asking for money or for a signature on a petition. 'He was an egomaniac. I think he got a kick out of being difficult.'

The Barzmans didn't tell the visiting blonde about Groucho's statement about the ice cubes. She was on her way to a party at Judy Garland's house nearby, which she was attending because her agent thought it would be good for her career to be seen there.

'Two years later,' Norma Barzman told me, 'in Paris, we were sitting in a café on the Champs Élysées. My husband was reading the *Herald Tribune*. He let out a yelp. "Oh my God, that blonde who warned us, that was Marilyn Monroe,"' Née Norma Jean Baker.

Some of the schemes to avoid the FBI were ingenious. The Barzmans conspired with a friend to thwart the G-men with a simple but temporarily effective scam. Ben, Norma and their children – they would eventually have seven of them – simply swapped homes with their friend and fellow writer Bernard Voorhaus, who had been a member of the Hollywood Anti-Nazi League, which was considered a Communist front organisation. (Even the Bundles for Britain programme – which sent food and other items to the UK – was considered a Red group.) Barzman was writing feature films, Voorhaus B pictures. But they were both known Communists and so was Norma.

The idea was that when the FBI men came to call, the men in the two families would open the door to them, look at the subpoenas in their hands and politely say, 'it is not for me.' The agents would then walk away, mystified. 'It was not something that the FBI men who came knocking on the doors had expected,' Norma Barzman told me. As Voorhaus himself explained: 'They had to touch you with the subpoena. If [Ben] knew they were going to his house he would phone me to say get out – and vice versa.'

It worked because both the Barzmans and the Voorhauses lived in similar properties and had children of a similar age, who, when spotted about the house or swimming in the pools, could confirm the illusion of confused identity. The men knocked on the door of the Voorhaus home, introduced themselves and said they had something for Mr Voorhaus. 'I am NOT Mr Voorhaus,' said Barzman and nothing the men could do could convince anyone otherwise. The same charade was being enacted in reverse at the Barzman's house. 'You understand it is an offence to lie to a United States marshal,' Norma recalled the man saying. 'Yes,' her husband replied. At which point, the marshal emphasised that he, Mr Voorhaus, was in serious trouble. 'But I'm not Mr Voorhaus,' Barzman said, and closed the door in the Government man's face.

He was one of those who chose to go abroad, into exile: 'The community that I knew had broken up so much in the blacklist period. It was a marvellous period I was in. They were making films with social content. This wasn't it any more.'

Dalton Trumbo, perhaps the most famous of the blacklistees, didn't go as far as swapping identities. His daughter Nikola Trumbo now remembers: 'We did move from one house to another and I think that was in anticipation of ultimately moving to our ranch outside of Los Angeles, in the mountains, . . . so the timing of the move may have been to stall or delay a subpoena as long as possible.'

They might have, for a time, succeeded in avoiding a subpoena, but not the eagle eyes of the G-men. And that went for her and her younger brother, Christopher. 'We were followed,' Nikola told us. 'As kids my brother and I used to make fun of the FBI, of what we termed was the FBI's stupidity. We drove a huge black Packard sedan, a brand new one that was totally unmistakable anywhere. This was in 1948 or 1949, I guess. Anyway, we found as we were driving from Los Angeles to our ranch, which was about an hour and a half drive, when we got up to the ranch we discovered there was a piece of white sheet tied to the bumper. We guessed that this was the way the FBI was trying to keep track of us.'

And like everyone else, the Trumbos knew that their phones were being tapped. 'You could hear the clicks. It was a fairly primitive technology back then.' Children were not allowed to use the phone for that reason. No one could be sure they wouldn't let cats out of bags. Her parents couldn't have 'normal' telephone conversations with friends either. Microphones were planted in private houses. Says Nikola: 'I think they'd watch a house and if owners left the home for any length of time, they could come in and plant something. I don't know if one was ever found.'

If anything, the FBI men were more feared than HUAC itself. Norma Barzman, in her memoir, *The Red and the Blacklist*, remembered her Russian-born mother-in-law, who had escaped the pogroms being convinced that the marshals were nothing more than Cossacks. Like many of the previous generation of Jews who had faced the Cossacks, the Barzmans packed their bags and crept out of the Voorhaus home to sail on the Queen Mary for England. The Voorhauses made a similar journey.

Oliver Crawford, one of the few to recover his career after the blacklist, was another Hollywood writer who dodged FBI men and US marshals, although with little obvious subtlety. Even so, he escaped being served with a subpoena. 'I would spend most of my time locked up in my home. I always made sure that my wife opened the door,' he told me. 'It was as simple as that. They couldn't mail [a subpoena] to me either. I would see them sitting in their cars and I'm sure they occasionally waved to me when I just had to go out.'

Sometimes, Oliver had to leave his small house in Los Angeles, close to what is now the Beverly Center in West Hollywood. 'I would go after five o'clock when the men who were watching my house all day long would go home. One time, they came through that door,' he said, pointing to his outer screen. 'I wouldn't open the inner door. They asked if I would testify. I said "No". I asked who named me. They couldn't answer me. They wouldn't tell me. They were pleasant enough. And then they left. I was pretty well a prisoner in this house. When I did escape, it was to sneak out at night.'

The men were nothing if not persistent. 'They came one more time. Again, I refused. I expected them at any moment to break down the door, but they didn't try anything rough.'

Crawford was fired by Burt Lancaster's production company. 'I was called by a producer and told that the only way I could survive would be to give evidence about being a Communist and give names of other Communists. I was out and I knew it.' He had just finished writing the screenplay of Lancaster's spirited 1955 Western saga *The Kentuckian*, for which he was to receive no screen credit. As we shall see, that was to be the fate of dozens of others, not all of whom managed to avoid the subpoena servers.

Always, it affected their families. Joanne Crawford, Oliver's daughter, told me of the problems of having to move home because of the FBI chase. Michael Cole, son of Lester Cole, the writer who was one of the first to be handed a pink slip, said his family would move, not so much to escape the men in hats but more because their money was draining away. 'My parents moved houses more often than I would have liked to move houses,' he said. 'There wasn't any running away. When the FBI came to the door, we would just say, "Hello." '

He himself wasn't told what to say if he opened the door to them. 'No. What were we going to say? A 10-year-old kid, what were the FBI going to say, "What is your daddy doing today?" "I don't know, he's back in the study writing."'

That was rather more open than the reaction of Will Geer, whose notable career ground to a halt because of the blacklist but then, years later, he found renewed fame in old age as Grandpa Walton in the long-running TV show, *The Waltons*. Geer always said that the reason he was on the FBI list was because his wife's grandmother was Ella Reeve Bloor, a pioneer union organiser – and a devout Communist. Will was never a member of the party, but he worked for left-wing causes. The day that the FBI men came to call, he hid. As his daughter Ellen Geer told Barbra Paskin: 'There was a knock-knock-knock at our door and there was a man with a pink piece of paper. Pop hid in the closet. I couldn't understand why, but he said it was because he wanted to finish a film project.' Mom was holding the baby, Thad. She said: "Who are you? What is it? What do you want?" And then said Pop wasn't there. It wasn't like Mom to lie. The man left and then Mom and Pop suddenly told us to go away and we heard them whispering in the living room . . . Talk, talk, talk. And it felt so serious. And Mom crying and trying to figure out what to do.' What they decided to do was to buy land in Topanga, in the hills above Malibu.

Most of the children of those served subpoenas tell a similar story – of suddenly being excluded from family discussions where previously they had formed a part. 'No, they didn't want us in the room, they needed to deal with this,' Ellen Geer recalls. 'I had the baby and went upstairs with Kate, my sister. And then suddenly we were told we were going on a wonderful trip.'

At that point, something strange and very unusual happened. The subpoena was served – but not, as the law appeared to insist, on Geer himself. According to Ellen, his wife took it, saying her husband was away on location. It changed everything for the Geer family. Said Ellen: 'As a child, I didn't know things were off track until that day they whispered in the living room. I just knew happiness.'

Geer's wife, actress Herta Ware, was at first more worried than her husband, who, unlike others in his situation, wasn't continually looking over his shoulder. 'He was an optimist. Mom, who was so childlike and so sunshine like, sometimes she would say, "Pop, this is serious. This is really going to be a problem in our lives." Pop, I don't think he believed it could ever be that way. He was such a piece of true Americana. He couldn't believe it, even when it was happening to him.'

Especially when the family moved – and split up. 'I went to live with Poppa in New York City. That's when I learned about it because I was 15 and my sister and I went to live with him on the Lower East Side. And yes, the FBI would come to the door of that place on 18th Street. A couple of times. He opened the door to them, but he kicked them out.'

It was so often simply a matter of politics. Lester Cole always insisted that he never even knew if he ever had a party card. 'He was damned well an active member of the Communist Party,' says his son. 'But I don't think he thought he was doing anything subversive. I think he was doing what he thought was in the best interests of the United States. But not running around spying for Russians. Nobody's ever accused him of it.' On the other hand, Lester Cole welcomed the Nazi-Soviet pact. 'He thought it was a great thing,' his son remembered for us. 'That was a load of crap. It wasn't a great thing and we know that in retrospect. He believed history was on our side. His faith that the Soviet Union was a decent place, it was quite amazing.'

Screenwriter Bernard Gordon had been working on a film called *The Lawless Breed* in 1953, to star Rock Hudson. He and colleagues would talk about the HUAC proceedings while they were being broadcast. Some people, he told us, knew that he had friends in the party, 'and that I was obviously interested in what was happening. Privately, we'd talk about it – but not publicly because they didn't want to point the finger at me, but they were happy I was still working as a scriptwriter. I remember the guys next door saying, "Come on, Bernie, come and listen, this is very interesting." And I'm sitting there thinking, "Jesus Christ, leave me out of this."'

He was not invited to the sneak preview of the movie, but went anyway, paying for his own ticket. By then, the process servers, as he called the FBI men, had done their job. 'My wife and I did our best to avoid them,' he said. 'We lived in a miserable little apartment. A man in a nice Oldsmobile would come and park outside and knock on the door. Neither of us would open the door. Our housekeeper was told to say we were out. So was our 4-year-old daughter, who loved to go and open the door. We told her that a man was trying to sell us magazine subscriptions which we did not want. I told her it was not nice to hurt the man's feelings. Just say I'm not at home.'

Eventually, Gordon *was* at home. He was subpoenaed to appear in Room 518 at the Federal Building in Los Angeles in September 1952. But he didn't actually face the committee. His evidence was postponed twice, while he sat in the Federal Building waiting, nervously, to be called.

'To this day, people come to me and ask if I was really subpoenaed. I want to kick them in the nuts.' Simultaneously, it appeared that his career was taking a giant leap forward. 'Unexpectedly, I got an invitation to go to Warner Bros for a job and I went there and I wrote a treatment that they liked and were talking to me about a contract. But under the circumstances, I had to take the subpoena. Within a day I was called to Brynie Foy's office. [Foy was head of B pictures at Warners. They called him 'King of the Bs'.]

'I was surrounded by those thugs who ran security at Warner Bros. They were very nice and said, "Come on, Bernie, you know why you're here. You have a great future here."' Which meant that he had to go to the committee and be friendly.

'Otherwise,' they told him, 'you'll be fired.' And fired he was.

Gordon had a statement ready for his testimony for HUAC which he knew he would never be allowed to deliver.

Jeff Corey had been decorated in World War Two. 'He was a combat cameraman,' his wife Hope recalled for this book, 'and he had been cited, not for bravery, but for making a particularly good film and especially a particular shot of a kamikaze which was coming in to attack the ship, *The Yorktown*.'

When Corey heard his name mentioned on the radio in connection with the coming hearings of HUAC, the action was no less frightening. 'I cried,' Hope recalled. 'It was not much fun. It was pretty awful.'

There would be no dodging the subpoena server for Jeff. 'Everyone who was political expected [to be served].' He didn't actually belong to the Communist party. 'But that was beside the point,' says Hope. Like many others, at that time he was not political, because 'he didn't like what was going on in the Soviet Union.' In other words, the committee had suspicions and were determined to nail anyone who aroused them. The actor made up his mind: he was going to take the Fifth Amendment.

Actors were, inevitably, heavily caught up in HUAC's activities. In their attempts to avoid having to give testimony – as much as anything because they knew it would mean going on to the list that producers kept locked away in their desk drawers – they also undertook elaborate schemes to avoid receiving the pink slips. However, simply attending a party or being seen with an undesirable character was enough to set the ball rolling.

Few actors were as gilded as Gene Kelly and his young wife Betsy Blair, both with enviable reputations. They were among the most attractive people in the Hollywood community. Gene was the pride of MGM, a dancer who could mesmerise his international audience. They were splendid actors. They were also wonderful hosts, as the whole movie community knew. That included everyone who knew that on Saturday nights the doors of the Kellys' Beverly Hills home were open for the finest parties in a town where parties are a way of life. Gene would sing and dance and every other star who had ever appeared before a camera and was still around would come and sing for his gourmet supper – or act or tell jokes. Gene and Betsy knew everyone who came, from the young piano playing André Previn to Fred Astaire singing Gershwin. Occasionally, someone would slip in, but the Kellys always assumed these uninvited guests were brought by someone who, in turn, might just as easily have been brought by someone else.

The FBI men who did sneak in – and to this day, Betsy Blair is not willing to swear to it, but is pretty sure they did – came totally uninvited. Their intelligence network was such that it told them that the parties were being held and the information they would produce could be a gold mine. And not just FBI men, with or without their customary uniform. As Betsy told me: 'There must have been an informer among our friends. I think now there was, maybe more than one, because there were people who did give names who were informers.' But it happened in every group in Hollywood.

The glitzy parties put on by the Kellys were important events in the Hollywood social calendar. As Betsy told me: 'The big evenings. We had an evening for the NAACP [The National Association for the Advancement of Coloured People]. Paul Robeson was guest of honour and we would invite 100 people. It was organised so that Gene spoke, introduced Robeson and Robeson sang. Ruth Conte (wife of Richard

Conte) and I collected the cheques. At a party like that I am sure there were informers. There were gatecrashers. The door was open. It wasn't like now. There wasn't security or body guards, or checking anything. People brought somebody, we didn't know who they were. We didn't think to ask.'

According to Ms Blair: 'Now you can say this, the FBI had done their job. They were completely stupid in many ways, but they did know what they were doing, too. They would call anyone whom they suspected of being a Communist – and then they could send them to jail, make them lose their livelihood at least. But they wouldn't have called someone like me, who was what they called a fellow traveller.'

Betsy never joined the Communist Party, although she at one time wanted to do so. 'I told my friend [the actor] Lloyd Gough that I wanted to be a member of the party. One day, he drove me up to the Hollywood Hills and said no, I shouldn't. I was married to a very important man and it was better not to have couples divided like that.'

Kelly himself was a left-leaning Democrat, but not a Communist party member. 'He was a complete Democrat. He was a Democrat. He was a socialist. He believed in unions and equal rights – everything that goes with the left, the best part of the United States. He was a serious artist, too.'

A serious artist who realised the advantages that his wife had. 'He wasn't as available as I was. He was a more serious thinker than I was. I was completely enthusiastic. There just had to be someone and I said yes, I could telephone people, send out things. I was very useful and hard-working. He never interfered with what I wanted to do. He never lost his principles. He always supported me, helped people get jobs. He was a good man.'

But he didn't believe that either he or his wife should be members of the Communist party. 'He said he didn't think I'd make a very good Communist because I didn't like people to tell me what to do or what to read or anything,' she told me. 'But at the time, I thought I'd make a *very* good communist. That was the future, it seemed. I know I was deluded. It all became clear, as long ago as 1956 when Khrushchev made his speech about Stalin. It wasn't as idealistic or beautiful as I thought. I should have read George Orwell or Arthur Koestler.'

Sondra Gorney remembered that her family suffered as a result of friends who turned informer. 'Some dear friends of ours named us. They were screenwriters and the man was working for a studio and didn't want to lose his job – so he named those who he thought were leftists, to save his job. It happened through the House Un-American Committee. People turned against their best friends to save their own positions.'

Their children suffered in a different way, she recalls: 'Jay was a hero at [their son] Daniel's school because he'd written the school song. Danny was so proud . . . but after Jay was up in front of the committee, the newspaper ran a front-page story about his position and the school pulled the song. They no longer used it as an assembly song, because thinking Jay was a Red, they couldn't use it. It was ironic, because it was such a sweet song.'

That wasn't all. 'Teachers were being mean [to Danny] and he didn't even want to tell me about that. But the day after Jay's appearance and the newspapers had come out, I was at work and I got a call to come home, Danny's been hurt. I rushed home and sure enough, Danny was home with a bandage on his head. He'd gone to an after-school playgroup and several of the older boys knocked him down and hit his head against the stone because they said his father was a dirty Communist.

'And of course he didn't understand what that was at all, but when I asked him, "Who did this to you, Danny?" He said, "Uh uh, I don't name names." So he got the gist of what was happening in the hearings of naming names.'

Screenwriter Gordon Kahn was among the more notable and frequently quoted people at this time. Before going into exile in Mexico, he wrote a letter to his wife, explaining why he had taken a stand against naming names. In doing so, he was, in his own way, illustrating the folly of giving way to blackmail. 'If now, in full flight from any principle I possess, I went and recanted everything and every decent thing I believe in, it wouldn't be enough. They'd want to know "Who else? Now that you are purged, who else? Give us names, dates and places." Do you think I could live with myself for a minute after I did a thing like that? Or with you? Or could face my children? If this is a decent world when they grow up, they'd spit on me and be perfectly justified in doing so. No, I've got to hang on to something and if I can't be the most prosperous writer, I want to be able to hold my head up among the people of America and the world.'

Larry Parks had given his testimony and Kahn had no intention of doing the same thing, of crawling through the same mud. So he never answered his subpoena but fled the country instead. His son Tony Kahn remembers the time of the subpoena being one of fear, even though he was so young: 'I was about 3 years old. No one sat down and said "Let me give you the word for what's going on in the household right now, the fear. But I certainly, like any kid, was filled with emotion and I sensed that people around me were very scared – and also, as a little kid, I probably, very egotistically or egocentrically, thought it was my fault or at least up to me to make the fear go away . . . I assumed the source of this really scary stuff that was going on was *in* the house. And like a 3-year-old, it took the form for me of some sort of a monster and a monster that probably lived in the living room of our house, which was the largest room and also the least used. It had been the place where a lot of entertaining had gone on. It was a dark room, the lights weren't on, there was a kind of a gas fireplace in there that was never turned on.'

This extended itself into what was currently happening. 'I must have got a sense maybe through conversation that people had been betraying each other, that so-and-so who'd been a friend had suddenly become an enemy because of what they had done before the committee. I'm guessing that I picked this up somehow. All I knew was that if I was picked up by the police, they would probably want to ask me questions and they'd put me under a very strong light that they used for interrogations. I must have got that from a movie.' This was more than just childhood fantasy. What was undoubtedly true was that it was all totally relevant to the world around. 'I didn't know what to do because I knew it was wrong to betray somebody, to say something bad about them while they weren't there but I also wanted the police to like me because I was afraid of the police. So I would really just not be able to finish the fantasy because I didn't know what I would do, whether I would give them the information they wanted or not.'

For police read FBI, the people who made his father flee their home and who parked outside the house even after he had gone, the people whose presence his mother explained. 'She'd talk about what it was like to return to the house in Los Angeles after my father had fled, because when he fled there was very little planning and after she recovered from surgery, when she came back, it was after my father had already left and FBI agents were coming to the door asking if she knew where he was. She remembers that very clearly.'

The question to ask is how it was that so many people in Hollywood, so many of them incredibly wealthy, living in big houses with big swimming pools, driving big cars, became members of what was regarded as the proletarian party. Betty Garrett says that she and her husband Larry Parks joined simply because they found the party the only organisation in the post-Depression 1930s that seemed to be concerned with social welfare. 'I first came to New York,' she told me, 'as part of a very socially conscious group. I became aware for the first time about racial discrimination, poor housing and such like, which made me feel I wasn't doing enough as a citizen to right these wrongs. It seemed at the time that the Communist Party was the only one doing anything for these things. So I marched in parades for better housing and against racial discrimination.'

At one time, she stood on top of a truck parked on Broadway in New York, speaking passionately about the curse of the age – lynching. That was on behalf of an organisation called the Urban League. When the Spanish Civil War broke out, she was in the vanguard of young people calling for help for the Republican cause, opposing the rebellion initiated by General Francisco Franco. 'I gave money to Civil War orphans. These were all causes that seemed to be for social justice. A great many people were involved for that reason.'

These good deeds focused HUAC's attention against her. Like many, she and Larry would become disillusioned with the Communist Party. Larry said he left in 1945, after four years of membership, but Betty is not sure. 'Dear God, I don't remember,' she told me. 'I think a lot of people were very disillusioned by the Hitler-Stalin pact and that kinda turned people against the whole idea. I don't even remember any particular time. We just lost interest in it. I still believe in a lot of those things – getting unions formed, anti-discrimination.'

None of those things was terribly popular among the people who regarded themselves as the Hollywood Establishment. As Betty Garrett says: 'There was always a political element.' It was spearheaded by that arch-conformist, Louis B Mayer. Actor-dancer George Murphy got Ronald Reagan involved, for instance. 'There was a great deal of proselytising to come over to that very conservative view.' These were the early days of HUAC's investigations – Betty arrived at MGM in 1946, the year that her husband had his first triumph in *The Jolson Story,* and three years before her own big impact with Frank Sinatra and Gene Kelly in *On The Town.* So right from the early days, the swords were drawn, ready for a battle between right and left. Or, as the gentlemen from HUAC might have put it, between right and wrong. The difference between the two factions was that HUAC had the Government behind them.

Larry Adler put it to me like this: 'Everybody was suspicious of everyone else. The question was not what you were doing, but who you were doing it for. If you were held to be too friendly to Russia, it counted against you.'

According to film producer Stanley Rubin, who had spent the war years as part of the Forces United Motion Picture Unit – the first unit of the United States Military to be made up entirely of motion picture personnel – it was all too easy to see. 'People in this business tend to be anti-war. In the first years of the Cold War, leading up to the 1950 Communist invasion of South Korea, that was not always considered a patriotic stance to take.'

David Raksin knew why he wanted to be a communist – and why he decided later that he didn't want to be one at all: 'I had a friend who was a member of the party,' Raksin told me. 'One evening, he persuaded me to join and I did. I joined and went to a branch meeting. I've always thought since then that if people really intended to embarrass those who joined, they would only have to go to a Communist party meeting. We did the unforgivable. We sat around in the evening and discussed *Das Kapital*. If you could think of anything less gratifying, I would like to know about it. Anybody who knows about that has got to know that we were idiots of creation. There we were, earnestly discussing the world and the world was burning up around us.'

He hadn't anticipated that. 'I joined in 1938 and got out in 1939,' he told me. Not *entirely*, he would admit, of his own volition. 'It was suggested to me tactfully and kindly that I should get my rear end out of there because the lady who talked to me about this said, "I know you're a decent guy because you're always raising issues that have nothing to do with us." I said it had everything to do with us – although people were saying it's not going to be our war. I didn't like it when they said that. She told me I should get out of the party and I did.'

As he said: 'I realised that my weak stomach did not permit me to be anything but a person of good intentions regarding the future and what was right and wrong. I suddenly realised that this kind of fastidiousness was not getting us anywhere.'

For Betsy Blair, everything was conditioned in a rather contrary way by her environment and the people who constituted it. 'The people I knew were all wealthy, with contacts with the studios. At the same time, the background for most people wasn't very wealthy at all. Many of the people had immigrant parents who had seen life you wouldn't see if you were born and bred in Los Angeles, unless you were Mexican. It was probably unconscious, but the attitude was "We are so well off, we have to share it. We have to care for others." For me it was that. Why should

I have this beautiful house and garden and there are people who don't have enough to eat?'

As for her husband, 'Gene was an absolute. Gene absolutely shared all the political beliefs and social conscience that I had.'

The Kellys arrived in Los Angeles on 7 December 1941, the day Pearl Harbor was bombed. She was quite suddenly thrust into a new situation and a new awareness. 'I learned from Gene and from his friends. I didn't even know there had been a war in Spain. Gene was a more serious thinker than I was. I was completely enthusiastic. When I was told there had to be someone [to pass the Communist message] I said yes.'

And that was what seemed to be the feeling among those who would later be grouped together as blacklistees. The actor J Edward Bromberg died while in exile in Britain. 'He died of a broken heart,' his close friend Theodore Bikel told me. His death had a resounding effect on the Left in the theatre and in Hollywood, too.

The actress Lee Grant, seemingly on the threshold of a brilliant career after co-starring (and gaining an Oscar nomination in the process) with Kirk Douglas in *Detective Story*, was a speaker at the memorial service for Bromberg soon after the 1951 movie. It led to her own apparent destruction. But only led to it. *Detective Story* was written by Arnold Manhoff (although his name didn't appear on the credits). 'We became romantically involved,' Lee told Barbra Paskin. 'It led to me being a pillow Communist. I had no idea what Communism was, but all around me, people I adored, like Bromberg, were being felled like being in front of a firing squad. For me it was a question of what side are you on? Arnie said at a certain point that the people he knew were uncomfortable with me being outside the party because the FBI was tapping our phone, stopping me on the street – who do I know? When did I know them? Arnie felt that his friends would be more comfortable knowing that I was part of the party, rather than outside, since the forces were so strong in trying to get people to talk. My joining the party was saying OK to him – and that was it.'

She was not the only one being unexpectedly thrust into politics, not the only pillow Communist. She certainly was not the only one who would have been incapable of taking an exam in Marxist theology. 'I never read Marx, never read Engels. I had many, many disagreements with what I saw to be the change in Russian arts, the tractor movies I was seeing, seeing the wheat fields, which to me was being on a platform. We had those disagreements.' Manhoff, whom she later married, was her mentor. 'I was a tremendous disappointment as a student. Nothing made sense to me. I was very stupid. I knew shopping and I knew acting. That was pretty much it. My whole education was Julliard to the Neighbourhood Playhouse. Entering into an area of the kind of intellect that my husband had was beyond my capacity and wasn't where my brain goes.'

Her philosophy was simple. 'I knew what was fair and what wasn't fair.'

Chapter Four
Such Friends

You know we have to ask questions to get the facts. Who's judging us? Who is in charge? Who is the House Committee on Un-American Activities?

June Havoc, actress, on the radio programme Hollywood Fights Back, 1947

First, they went for their friends. The members of HUAC, led by the vicious J Parnell Thomas, with the anti-Semitic, anti-Black John Rankin and the articulate, young, dark-complexioned Richard M Nixon at his side, set up their stall in Los Angeles in May 1947. Forty-three subpoenas had been delivered, including those to their putative friendly witnesses.

Thomas, Rankin and Nixon turned the fashionable Biltmore Hotel into a court house. They chose well. The Biltmore was one of the great buildings of downtown Los Angeles. Since 1923, the 11-storey structure had been one of the places that visitors, particularly government people and businessmen, had chosen time and again for its cathedral-like public room ceilings, its opulent conference rooms and its swimming pools. HUAC knew its activities were going to be in the public eye. Except that they weren't planning any confrontations. Apart, that is, from one witness, the composer Hanns Eisler, whose brother, Gerhardt Eisler, was described by HUAC as 'a shadowy figure, the real head of Communism in America.' Another appellation applied to him was 'the key Kremlin agent in America.'

Gerhardt had been living in America since 1941, after being in a Nazi concentration camp, and had fought in the Spanish Civil War. A former journalist, he appeared before HUAC in February 1947, before it turned its attention to Hollywood. The chief HUAC investigator, Robert Stripling, set up Eisler as a target. The fact that he was represented by a lawyer, Carol King, who had defended the Communist union leader, Harry Bridges, only confirmed the fact that he was a dangerous man, as far the committee was concerned.

Eisler denied charges that he was a spy. What's more, he claimed he was being held against his will as a political prisoner. Coming before HUAC, in a way that would pre-empt what would happen to the Hollywood Ten, he asked to be allowed to read a statement. As in the later cases, this was refused. After all, how could the committee allow a man who had been dubbed 'the boss to all the Reds' to spout his pro-Communist propaganda?

On the other hand, had HUAC actually answered the questions, what would have been wrong? The Communist Party was not illegal. By answering, it could have been argued, the Committee was merely confirming the fact and giving additional credence to it – in the face of all the propaganda to the contrary which so many people believed. For, by the mid 1940s, very few average John and Jane Does would have accepted the legality of the party.

Stripling was playing hard ball. His trump card was Eisler's sister, who not only gave evidence against Gerhardt, but also their brother Hanns, who became HUAC's first Hollywood victim. Hanns never denied he had been a Communist, but no evidence of pro-Soviet or pro-Communist activity in California had been proved or was to be proved during the year-long hearing. When called before the Committee, Hanns had been writing film scores at his Malibu home for various Hollywood studios. His appearance was grist to HUAC's mill. At last, they could find someone who would provide proof that the film capital was riddled with Communist influences. Not only was Hanns Eisler the first victim, he was the catalyst for the success of the rising star of Richard Nixon, then in his first term as a United States Congressman. To him, Eisler's case was 'perhaps the most important ever to have come before this committee.'

It turned out that Hanns had been at the end of the FBI's telescope – and in the sight of the black cars driven by men in raincoats and fedora hats – since 1935. Which gives some idea of how long the anti-Communist scare had been fermenting. The G-men hounded Eisler until he appeared before HUAC and was subsequently forced to leave the country under a voluntary deportation.

He refused to be intimidated by HUAC, whose tactics he dismissed as 'hysterical'. Nevertheless, his appearance was enough to start a massive campaign against him, particularly in the press. The New York *Journal American* brought in a 'former Communist' – always a useful device for spreading suspect intelligence – who said that Eisler was 'more than just a member of the Communist Party – he was one of the real top policy makers in the field of music, movies and the arts.' As the former member said: 'Hanns would outline plans to be followed in Hollywood to recruit movie stars, to place Communist propaganda in screen scripts and in general was the commissar of the West Coast Party activists on the movie front.'

The FBI began tapping his phone – even though their records failed to uncover any conversations on Communist activities. Hanns had also written music for the plays of his friend Bertold Brecht, although these could have been seen more as anti-fascist than pro-Communist. He left America under pressure – unlike Brecht, who was fed up with the American cultural scene and whose subsequent appearance before HUAC resulted in his settlement in East Berlin. Eisler, on the other hand, was friendly with Charlie Chaplin, Clifford Odets, Artie Shaw and Ava Gardner and loved being in their social circle.

His appearance, according to Stripling, would be the start of the Hollywood investigations. He later wrote: 'Chairman Thomas, Representative McDowell, Investigator Louis Russell and I went to Hollywood in the spring of 1947. Our primary task was to uncover and subpoena Hanns Eisler.'

(The bluff English-born actor Charles Laughton was a close friend of both Bertold Brecht and Hanns Eisler. When told they were both Communists, Laughton said: 'That's ridiculous. [Eisler's] music is just like Mozart.' Later, Laughton realised the associations could be dangerous for him. In 1956, when Brecht died, Laughton was invited to a memorial service. The invitation scared him out of his wits. He immediately rang the FBI to say he had nothing to do with getting the invitation.)

This was before any association with witnesses would be considered dangerous for those not yet called. Support was on hand from the composers Leonard Bernstein and Aaron Copland (they were known to have left-wing sympathies; Copland was called before the Committee, Bernstein was not), who appealed for any investigations to be stopped. They formed a defence committee – and had petitions signed by, among others, Albert Einstein, Thomas Mann, Pablo Picasso and Henri Matisse. There was a benefit concert sponsored by Igor Stravinsky. Stripling added: 'With Eisler served and heard in a short executive session we began calling in key Hollywood figures.'

The 'key figure witnesses' they were then calling had all been dubbed friendly. They were some of the most attractive, best-known faces in the world, stars who they knew would be at ease surrounded by the heavy black-and-white newsreel cameras of the era. In addition, the moguls of Hollywood would be represented. All of them were being assembled to say how great was the idea of rounding up the Reds who had wormed their way into the film business. *Newsweek* magazine said: 'Don't look for any so-called corrective legislation to result from the forthcoming Un-American Activities Committee investigation of Communism in Hollywood. Primarily the committee is fishing for headlines. By citing specific examples of Communist influences in movie scripts, the group hopes to alert the public to them.'

It was a clever move on HUAC's part. But it wasn't as simple as that. The faces being paraded through the crowds would command huge audiences, particularly in the Los Angeles area. If the committee was after publicity for all they were doing to save the nation, there couldn't have been a better way to do it. This was a public relations dream.

Except that these would be private preliminary hearings, rehearsals for what would be later held in Washington. As Stripling wrote: 'We obtained enough preliminary testimony to make a public hearing imperative.' These were 'soundings', sorties before a sub committee who wanted to find out what these friendlies would say and what they could be persuaded to say.

But the faces alone weren't enough. There would be plenty of those, along with unimaginable drama, in the months to come. The Washington hearings that followed later in the year offered far more. Here, in the initial hearings, the public could see, were a group of reasonable men, treating these glamorous witnesses with a great deal of respect. Who could possibly object to that? Witch-hunts? This was a group of American congressmen who were carrying out the business of America – to protect its citizens. No one could draw any parallels with all the terrible things that were happening in Soviet Russia.

And the idea of this being a trial has been knocked down by experts. No one doubts that Hollywood itself was on trial from the moment the Ten arrived in Washington. But the hearings? The committee members liked to play both prosecutors and judges, they wanted the witnesses to seem to be like defendants, who were suffering like anyone else threatened with jail, but there was no 'due process': you might have a lawyer by your side, but he had no rights to object. In fact, there were no rights at all. Witnesses couldn't call witnesses themselves.

The stars were called and they shone brilliantly, particularly for the Washington cameras. But not shining, it has to be said, with any intellectual brilliance. It is possibly another reason why people like

Robert Taylor and Gary Cooper were called. They made the committee members look highly intelligent.

And all of them, including a young activist by the name of Ronald Reagan and the handsome Robert Montgomery, were poised to say that Hollywood was riddled with Communists and welcomed this chance of getting them off the block. No one mentioned 'blacklists'. The word hadn't yet been coined, but you didn't have to be too clever to work out the result. As Robert Taylor turned towards the big microphone in front of him, women all over Southern California held their breath. They did so in other parts of America when they saw the newsreels a few days later.

More than 1,000 women clogged the caucus room, sweating under the harsh klieg lights of the newsreel cameras. Not only were the women mobbing the stars and begging for autographs, they were so hot, they were disrobing in the process – as much as could be conceived to be decent. This was before the time when shows could be bounced from one part of the States to the other, let alone across the Atlantic, so the scene of frantic crowds was enjoyed mainly by those in southern California. Taylor, elegantly turned out, his greased hair shining as much as the big black car that brought him to the hotel, his widow's peak perfectly styled, was every bit as handsome as he had been in 1940's *Waterloo Bridge, Magnificent Obsession* five years earlier, and – now there was some explaining to do about this – *Song of Russia* in 1944. He didn't say a great deal, although he said he hadn't wanted to make the movie, but he was under contract to MGM and Mr Mayer was not someone you could trifle with. What did come out of his mouth was carefully engineered to indicate how much he hated Communists. Then came the important moment: would he be kind enough to name names? The idea was novel in May 1947. Yes, he said, he would be so kind.

Did he recall the names of any members of the Screen Actors Guild – already tainted by the committee as a pro-Communist and therefore anti-American organisation – who were Reds?

He had been primed and was waiting for that. 'Well, one chap I am thinking of currently is Mr Howard Da Silva that [sic] always has something to say at the wrong time. Karen Morley also usually appears at the guild meetings.'

He also said about those meetings: 'There's always a certain group of actors and actresses whose every action would indicate to me that, if they are not Communists, they are working awfully hard to be Communists.'

*

At his preliminary hearing, Gary Cooper could have been re-enacting a scene from *Mr Smith Goes to Washington* (1939), even though Mr Cooper went no further than the hearings. He was asked: 'Do you believe as a prominent person in your field that it would be wise for us, for the Congress, to pass legislation to outlaw the Communist Party of the United States?'

He stumbled for the words, smiled, just as Gary Cooper always stumbled for words, and smiled in his movies. 'I think it would be a good idea,' he said, 'although I don't know. I have never read Karl Marx and I don't know the basis of Communism, beyond what I have picked up from hearsay – and what I have heard I don't like because it isn't on the level.'

Muted cheers could be heard at that. Gary Cooper, the all-American guy, the Sgt York who had killed all those Germans and remained a simple hillbilly, was clearly one of them. The committee smiled more widely and praised Mr Cooper more loudly than the audience for what was a consummate performance. What none of them suspected, however, was that he was to prove a man of independent mind with his own sense of justice. Five years later that sense of justice would save his film classic *High Noon* from destruction.

Others who were deemed friendly witnesses included Robert Montgomery, George Murphy, the director Leo McCarey and the union leader Roy Brewer, who had organised the famous Warner Bros strikes and now declared himself an enemy of Communism.

Cooper was plainly respected. That was not the situation with another actor who has come to define the HUAC hearings, Adolphe Menjou. His was a name that made the committee cheer and a goodly section of the more progressive side of Hollywood shiver. Both appeared again when in October, they were called to testify in Washington. Dapper with a small moustache, Menjou, who liked to call himself of American-French descent, was known as the best-dressed man in Hollywood. Menjou had specialised in playing slightly unpleasant, self-serving business executives. He had played a mogul in the original 1937 version of *A Star Is Born* and when he appeared before the committee, he was speaking on behalf of what could only have been described as the employer class.

He praised the 'vigilance' of the right-wing organisation the Motion Picture Alliance for the Preservation of American Ideals set up in 1944 to counter what its members believed was Communist influence. Among its principal activists were John Wayne and his fellow right-wing actor

Ward Bond and, at its head, Samuel Grosvenor Wood, the director. When HUAC announced it was going to hold its inquiries into what they believed was going on in Hollywood, the MPA furnished the friendly witnesses. It was well known that the alliance had been set up with the blessing of most of the studio heads. As far as Menjou was concerned, it had stepped in to prevent 'an enormous amount of sly, subtle, un-American class-struggle propaganda from going into pictures.'

What was more, 'We find crackpots everywhere. We have them in California – political idiots, political morons, dangerous Communists.'

Given his way, Menjou said, if the Russians came to America, he'd send them all to Texas so that the Texans could kill them on the spot. Not all the studio bosses approved of the man, while lauding his efforts to keep the film capital Red-free. Dore Schary, head of production at MGM (and soon to be head of the studio in place of Louis B Mayer) described Menjou as a 'creep'. Schary's daughter Jill Robinson Shaw told me: 'He was furious with that man. Nobody liked him. He was a right-wing, fascist monster. He wasn't very bright, but then, as my dad said, you didn't expect movie stars to be very smart.'

But Menjou was articulate and what he said was good to hear – if you were a HUAC member. He declared: 'I'm a Red-baiter. I'm a witch-hunter if the witches are Communists.'

But it was not surprising there were Reds in Hollywood. 'We find crackpots everywhere. We have them in California, political idiots, political morons, dangerous Communists.'

Which was not something said at the time about Ronald Reagan, who had declared two months earlier on his election as Screen Actors Guild president: 'Ninety-nine per cent of us are pretty well aware of what is going on and I think we have done a pretty good job in our business of keeping those people's activities curtailed.' But he took the wind out of the sails of one of HUAC's main charges: 'I do not believe the Communists have ever at any time been able to use the motion picture screen as a sounding board for their philosophy or ideology.'

To Robert Montgomery, a former president of the SAG, there was an ever-growing Communist threat in the film capital. The Guild was experiencing it at first hand. There was, he said, 'an organised minority' there, people who were establishing a 'very active Communist front organisation' within the industry.

But the Association of Motion Picture Producers could not agree. Their president Eric Johnston gave evidence in which he said there had been an 'overwhelming defeat' whenever anyone tried to insert propaganda in scripts, so there was no need for studios to fire anyone who might be thought to be a Communist.

Such a forthright and unequivocal statement was seemingly destined to create a crack in a major plank in HUAC's platform. But the committee's influence was stronger than many assumed. John Rankin went as far as to say that there were coded messages in dozens of Hollywood films.

During World War Two, the writer Melville Shavelson said, 'I actually wrote for something called the Hollywood Writers Mobilisation, which was preparing shows that were going to the Army camps. I was called up by Harry Cohn, the head of Columbia Pictures, because it was supposedly a Communist front organisation. Why that was, I don't know.'

As for getting pro-Communist, or even anti-Allied propaganda into a movie, the idea was 'ridiculous. I never heard of any occasion when the Communists integrated propaganda into a film. It's too difficult to make a film in the first place.'

Eric Johnston the President of the producers' organisation the Motion Picture Association, was trying to ride two horses at the same time and falling off the saddles of both of them. While there was no Communist influence, he also said later in 1947 that the studios would refuse to employ 'proven Communists' if by doing so, there would be that Red influence.

That wasn't what the studios wanted. Communist writers and actors were still giving the paying customers what they thought they desired. Eddie Mannix of MGM said there would be no searching for Communists who otherwise did their jobs particularly satisfactorily. MGM didn't need any help in making sure that its films were not being infiltrated by propaganda. It was a stance backed by other producers – but only for a very short time.

Memories of the 1940 investigations were still in people's minds. The earlier hearings had been abandoned after the Screen Actors Guild, behaving much more courageously than they would 7 years later, declared: 'To smear persons without any reliable evidence is to play into the hands of Hitler and Stalin by confusing the innocent with the guilty. Certain actors have been Communist, without proof, in a manner that allows them no effective challenge. The American people like fair play. We are confident they will characterise as real enemies of Americanism those guilty of these tactics.'

Not that the committee gave up that easily. The Joint Fact-Finding Committee on Un-American Activities of the California legislature decided to get in on the act the following year. Its chairman, Jack Tenney, opened his own investigation of what he called 'Reds in Movies'. But Russia had been invaded and the mood was much more conciliatory towards the Soviets, so there was no co-operation from the Hollywood Establishment who, in any case, wanted to be thought of as reflecting public sentiment (not to do so would seem unpatriotic). After just a couple of days, the hearing packed up.

The HUAC 1947 hearings at the Biltmore were held in private – or, appropriately, considering the business these people were in, in camera. It was intended that they lay their goods on the stall and prepare themselves for the public brouhaha which would convene in Washington that September. The chance for summer holidays would, HUAC believed, allow the witnesses to feel fresh enough to give the evidence they wanted.

The man chosen to represent the moguls was Jack L Warner, head of the Warner Bros studio (although his brother Harry was chairman, Jack was head of production). At the earlier hearing he had named as many names as he could think of. He was considered not totally reliable because he had made *Mission to Moscow*. Jack L Warner appeared in the huge Caucus Room adjoining the Capitol building on 3 November 1947, looking every inch the big business boss, complete with an immaculate suit cut by Schmit, the by-appointment Hollywood tailor, and florid expression on his face, which betrayed the twin facts that he was a great success and also very pleased with himself.

On the same day, the actor Adolphe Menjou gave evidence. They were not quite singing from the same sheet of music. As Menjou said: 'I don't think *Mission to Moscow* should have been made. It's a thoroughly dishonest picture.' A charge that Warner denied vociferously when he appeared before the committee. 'I always turn my back whenever I see one of those Reds coming,' he declared.

Unlike what would happen when the unfriendlies took the stand, these friendly witnesses were given full rein to make what statements they liked and speak uninterrupted in giving their evidence.

This was heaven-sent to Jack Warner, who loved most of all to appear as a comedian (and imitator of Al Jolson, his idol) on his own radio station, and to give swanky dinner parties to visiting celebrities – like the time he greeted Albert Einstein with the words, 'You know, Professor, I have a theory about relatives, too – don't hire 'em.'

Like Menjou, Warner had a small moustache and was a dapper dresser. Unlike the reputedly anti-Semitic Menjou, he was Jewish. Also unlike Menjou, Warner never took himself totally seriously. 'Ideological termites have burrowed into many American industries,' he declared. 'Wherever they may be, I say let us dig them out and get rid of them. My brothers and I will be happy to subscribe generously to a pest-removal fund. We are willing to establish such a fund to ship to Russia the people who don't like our American system of government and prefer the Communistic system to ours.'

Jack was, it has to be said, the only Warner brother not born in Russia, although he was probably conceived there. His birth was in Canada, on his family's way to the United States. He went on in a statement that he was allowed to read in full: 'If there are Communists in our industry, or any other industry, organisation or society who want to undermine our free institutions let's find out about it and know who they are.' With that one sentence, Jack L Warner gave notice that if HUAC pressed studio employees to name names, he, and by implication, the other moguls, would be right behind the committee. As he said, he wanted to co-operate because 'Communists inject 95 per cent of their propaganda into films through the medium of writers.' It was an incredibly precise percentage figure and what did it mean? No one could be sure if he were saying that 95 per cent of writers inserted propaganda into films or that the un-American details in a script were inserted by the same writers.

Warner also cut to the chase – the chase of studios that actually had made what conceivably could be considered pro-Russian films. So what was Warner's answer to all those complaints about *Mission to Moscow* in 1942? In many ways it was treading old ground. The filming of the memoirs of America's ambassador to the Soviet capital, Joseph E Davies, followed the movie it had made in World War One, *My Four Years in Germany*, an account of the service of the US envoy to Berlin. 'It was made when our country was fighting for its existence, with Russia as one of our allies,' said Warner. 'It was made to fulfil the same wartime purpose for which we made such other pictures as *Air Force*, *This Is The Army*, *Objective, Burma!*, *Destination Tokyo*, *Action in The North Atlantic*, and a great many more.

'If making *Mission to Moscow* in 1942 was a subversive activity, then the American Liberty Ships which carried food and guns to Russian allies and the American naval vessels which convoyed them were likewise engaged in subversive activities. The picture was made only to help a desperate war effort and not for posterity.'

He was right there. The film has rarely been seen since then – and certainly not during the investigations.

The chief investigator, Robert E Stripling, asked if the film was accurate. Warner rallied to that. 'I am on record about forty times or more that I have never been in Russia. I don't know what Russia was like in 1937 or 1944 or 1947. So how can I tell you if it was right or wrong?'

Wasn't he on dangerous ground, then? 'No . . . there was a war on. The world was at stake.'

If Warner thought he was being put through it as a friendly witness, both in the private May hearings and the ones that followed in October 1947, he could have no idea what would be faced by the so-called unfriendlies a few months later.

Louis B Mayer, who regarded himself not just as emperor of his own fiefdom at MGM ('Makers of Great Musicals' was virtually as justified as its correct title, Metro Goldwyn Mayer) but the paterfamilias of a large, all-American family. He firmly believed in wrapping himself in the Stars and Stripes as chairman of the Republican Committee of California – guardian of everything that was holy in the life of the United States – embodying the American Dream. It was a phenomenally long way from his early struggles as the son of immigrants trying to make a go of his scrap-metal business. He saw his films as showing the beauties of American life and could be relied upon to say just what the HUAC members wanted to hear.

'During my 25 years in the motion-picture industry I have always sought to maintain the screen as a force for public good,' he declared.

That, it would later turn out, was also the motto of his competitors in the film industry. The other moguls were keeping an eye out for films that were 'for public good'. Or rather, those that were not 'for public good'.

The later blacklisted writer Bernard Gordon recalled a strike at the Paramount studios – when the bosses had cameras trained on the picket line so that they could pick out each of the protestors for future use.

'On the second floor of the main building at Paramount studios, there's a large corner office and it's full of thirty or forty filing cabinets in which they've stored synopses or full scripts of everything they've ever bought or paid to have written. I think someone once counted and said there were 1,600 stories and scripts, many of which had never been used.' One of them was by a certain J Edgar Hoover. 'I happened to be up there,' Gordon told me. 'There was a camera and it was hidden from the people outside, but it was filming the pickets who were down below. One of the cameramen was doing a pretty good job of recording the faces of everyone who was down on the picket line. What were they doing with the names of any of them? It gave them a record of who the bad people were who were picketing.' Bad people who really shouldn't be making nice, wholesome movies.

No one could argue with that. But what Congressman Thomas most wanted to hear was to come soon afterwards – after, that is, Mayer's confirmation that the motion-picture industry 'employs many thousands of people. As is the case with the newspaper, radio, publishing and theatre businesses, we cannot be responsible for the political views of each individual employee.'

But then it came: 'It is, however, our complete responsibility to determine what appears on the motion-picture screen. It is my earnest hope that this committee will perform a public service by recommending to the Congress legislation establishing a national policy regulating employment of Communists in private industry. It is my belief they should be denied the sanctuary of the freedom they seek to destroy.'

It was as if the Committee had directly hired as a PR man the figure who was undoubtedly the most powerful of all the moguls. But then came a piece of information that was highly instructive. 'There were a number of representatives of the government who made periodical visits to the studios during the war. They discussed with us from time to time the types of pictures which they felt might assist the war effort. They were co-ordinators and at no time did they attempt to tell us what we should or should not do. We made our own decisions on production. We are proud of our war efforts and the results speak for themselves.'

But did Mr Mayer have an Achilles heel? Was *Song of Russia* his *Mission to Moscow*? He worried about that – and so did the committee, who needed to show from the outset that they had friends; that the friendlies were just that.

The 1944 film starring Robert Taylor and Susan Peters was written by the soon-to-be-blacklisted Paul Jarrico and was derided from the start. It was the story of an American symphony orchestra conductor who goes to Russia and is overcome with admiration for how the Russian people coped with the problems of facing enemy action. *Newsweek* magazine said: 'MGM performs the neatest trick of the week by leaning over backward in Russia's favour without once swaying from right to left.'

That took a little interpretation, but Mr Mayer said he remained proud of the film which, he said, 'seemed a good medium of entertainment and at the same time offered an opportunity for a pat on the back of our then ally Russia. It also offered an opportunity to use the music of Tchaikovsky.' As Mayer added: 'We mentioned this to the government co-ordinators and they agreed with us that it would be a good idea to make the picture.' It was made, he said, at the time that the Soviets were fighting the battle of Stalingrad and when the US Ambassador in Moscow, Admiral Standley, had appealed for "assistance, second only to the supplies being provided by the US fleet."'

Besides, *Song of Russia* was, according to Mayer, 'little more than a pleasant musical romance, the story of a boy and girl that, except for the music of Tchaikovsky, might just as well have taken place in Switzerland, England or any other country on earth.'

Was LB suggesting that no one played Tchaikovsky in Switzerland, England 'or any other country on earth'?

Bill Jarrico, son of the writer of the film, Paul Jarrico, says he was not sure if President Roosevelt had specifically asked for the film to be made, but: 'The OSS was interested in Hollywood's making pictures that affirmed the collaboration in this war against fascism.' *Song of Russia*, he said, was 'made to be friendly. In 1938, we made *Ninotchka* and shortly thereafter *Comrade X* [1940] with Clark Gable. Both these films kidded Russia.'

A little too much according to the writer Ayn Rand, who wanted to define what propaganda amounted to. You wouldn't find any, she said, in her book and soon-to-be 1949 film script, *The Fountainhead*, which would star Gary Cooper, an actor of whom she distinctly approved. She thought, however, that both *Song of Russia* and *The Best Years of Our Lives* were rank with left-wing implications. The committee wanted to hear all it could about *Song of Russia*. They did not, however, intend to listen to any songs about *The Best Years of Our Lives*, starring names like Fredric March and Dana Andrews, an archetypal story of the difficulties war veterans faced when trying to adjust to civilian life. It was a popular movie and HUAC were sensitive to just how well liked it was. Go all out against popular taste and there was a risk that the committee would lose public support at just the time when they were beginning their work – and, more significantly, just when America seemed to be behind them. Indeed, had anyone troubled to take a public opinion poll on the subject, it is fair to say that a majority would back J Parnell Thomas and his work. In the public perception, propaganda had taken on the mantle of being a dirty word.

Rand contended, when she appeared before the committee on 20 October 1947, that she was opposed to 'anything that sells people the idea that life in Russia is good and that people are free and happy.' That is what *Song of Russia* did, she claimed. Mayer, who would have sung 'The Star-Spangled Banner' into the Tannoy speakers at Culver City every morning if he had been asked to do so, was apoplectic that such an accusation could be made against anything that came out of his All-American studio.

Ayn Rand, though, warmed to her theme. She had been born in St Petersburg, and refused to call it by its then current name, Leningrad, as it had been when she left in 1926. In fact, she practically burned to her theme with indignation. Robert Taylor's conductor was not her idea of a pro-American character. 'He starts playing the American national anthem and the national anthem dissolves into a Russian mob, with the sickle and hammer on a red flag very prominent above their heads. I am sorry, but that made me sick. That is something which I do not see how native Americans permit and I am only a naturalised American. That was a terrible touch of propaganda. As a writer, I can tell you exactly what it suggests to the people. It suggests literally and technically that it is quite all right for the American national anthem to dissolve into the Soviet.'

Such was the extent of the opprobrium that the committee wanted to hear about wicked Commie Hollywood. But there was more to come, a lot more to come. Not only was she willing to make her statement, but Rand asked for time to say more about *Song of Russia*. It wasn't the Russia she knew: 'The streets are clean and prosperous looking. There are no food lines anywhere. You see shots of the marble subway – the famous Russian subway out of which they make such propaganda capital. There is a marble statue of Stalin thrown in. There is a park where you see happy little children in white blouses running around. I don't know whose children they are, but they are really happy kiddies. They are not homeless children in rags, such as I have seen in Russia. Then you see an excursion boat, on which Russian people are smiling, sitting around very cheerfully, dressed in some sort of satin blouses such as they only wear in Russian restaurants here. Then they attend a luxurious dance. I don't know where they got the idea of the clothes and the settings that they used at the ball.'

As for village life portrayed in the film: 'You see the happy peasants.' Inevitably, she mentions the tractor, which so often symbolised the Russia of Stalin's day. Terrible, she thought. 'How could it help the war effort?'

The Republican senator on the committee, John S Wood, asked her why she thought the film had been made. Her answer: 'I ask you what relation could a lie about Russia have with the war effort? I would like to have somebody explain that to me.' And then, cuttingly, she noted that in the midst of a concert being performed on screen, there was a scene featuring the Soviet border and a close-up of the sign declaring it to be the 'USSR'. 'I would just like to remind you that this is the border where probably thousands of people have died trying to escape out of his lovely paradise.'

She didn't hold back on her strictures. 'Look,' she said at one stage, 'It is almost impossible to convey to a free people what it is like to live in a totalitarian dictatorship. I can tell you a lot of details. I can never completely convince you, because you are free. It is in a way good that you can't even conceive of what it's like. Certainly, they have friends and mothers-in-law. They try to live a human life, but you understand it is totally inhuman. Try to imagine what it is like if you are in constant terror from morning till night and at night you are waiting for the doorbell to ring, where you are afraid of anything and everybody.'

She could not have known that that was precisely what the men and women awaiting subpoenas to appear as unfriendly witnesses were feeling as they tried to avoid the men from the FBI. It was a term coined by the *Hollywood Reporter* but 'unfriendly' hardly said half of it. They were unfriendly in the way a mountain lion would be to a hunter aiming for one of its cubs. They were getting more and more unfriendly towards their own guilds, which were worrying about the influence of the right wing – and showed it by being more right than they were. Telegrams to apparently recalcitrant members were signed by the Screen Actors Guild President on 19 August 1947: IMPERATIVE THAT GUILD RECEIVE AT ONCE SIGNED AFFIDAVIT RE NO AFFILIATION WITH COMMUNIST PARTY IN ORDER THAT WE MAY FILE FRIDAY FOR ELECTIONS. RONNIE REAGAN. Reagan was the designated spokesman for all the good – or should that be friendly? – actors working in Hollywood who were not actually called before HUAC. Two years later, he, along with the Guild secretary, Jack Dales, would make a statement to *Variety*: 'We are just a few of the many loyal Americans in Hollywood who have helped bring about the complete frustration and failure of the Communist Party in the motion picture industry.'

By then, the media had done its best to show that the party was destroying the American people's favourite entertainment medium and had been doing so for years before HUAC started its inquiries.

Early in 1941, before the raid on Pearl Harbor brought the country into World War Two, newspaper magnate William Randolph Hearst declared Orson Welles to be a 'Red'. He had seen *Citizen Kane* that year and rightly saw it as a parody of his own life. But Ayn Rand at the HUAC session she addressed was doing her best to show that she was doing her best, too. She wanted the committee to know that making that one movie was symptomatic of how Communists were running Hollywood. She also said: 'I fully believe Mr Mayer when he says that he did not make a Communist picture. To do him justice, I can tell you, I noticed by watching the picture, where there was an effort to cut propaganda out. I believe he tried to cut propaganda out of the picture, but the terrible thing is the carelessness with ideas, not realising that the mere presentation of that kind of happy existence in a country of slavery and horror is terrible because it *is* propaganda. You are telling people that it is all right to live in a totalitarian state.' With this one statement, she was showing both how easy it was to widen the issue of Communist infiltration and to make that a yardstick against which subsequent hearings would be measured. The right-wing press loved it. HOLLYWOOD CRAWLING WITH REDS, declared the *Des Moines Register,* a newspaper with bigger fame and influence than the city from which it stemmed.

If *Song of Russia* was a seemingly strange subject to discuss in a Congressional committee, it paled into insignificance in comparison with the 1933 cartoon *The Three Little Pigs*. That came up when Walt Disney, who had a reputation for being even more right-wing than some members of the committee, appeared on 24 October 1947. He told the HUAC hearings in Washington that his films were distributed all over the world – 'except the Russian countries.' That was because 'we can't do business with them.' The Soviets had bought *The Three Little Pigs* 'and used it through Russia. And they looked at a lot of our pictures and I think they ran a lot of them in Russia but then turned them back to us and said they didn't want them. They didn't suit their purposes.'

But had Disney ever made propaganda pictures? Surely not.

'During the War we did,' said Disney. But not the sort of propaganda the committee had in mind. 'We made quite a few, working with different government agencies. We did one for the Treasury on taxes and I did four anti-Hitler films. And I did one on my own for air power.' He said he would never allow propaganda to feature in films in this post-war era. Were there, Mr H A Smith asked, any Communists or fascists working in his studio? 'No,' he replied firmly. 'At the present time, I feel that everybody in my studio is 100 per cent American.'

But there had been Communists employed by him in the past. And it was they who organised a strike at his studio. 'It proved so with time – and I definitely feel it was a Communist group trying to take over my artists and they did take them over.'

It was at this point that Walt Disney named names – or at least, one name. 'It came to my attention when a delegation of my boys, my artists, came to me and told me that Mr Herbert Sorrell . . .'

Smith: 'Is that Herbert K Sorrell?'

Disney: 'Herbert K Sorrell was trying to take them over. I explained to them that it was none of my concern, that I had been cautioned to not even talk with any of my boys on labour. They said it was not just a matter of labour. It was just a matter of them not wanting to go with Sorrell and they had heard that I was going to sign with Sorrell and they said they wanted an election to prove that Sorrell didn't have the majority.' Disney said that Sorrell had told him, 'You can't stand this strike. I will smear you and I will make a dust bowl out of your plant.'

According to Disney, it almost happened. 'When he pulled the strike, the first people to smear me and put me on the unfair list were all of the Commie front organisations. I can't remember them all, they change so often, but what is clear in my mind is the League of Women Shoppers, *The People's World*, the *Daily Worker* and the *PM* magazine in New York . . . They smeared me. Nobody came near to find out what the true facts of the thing were. And I even went through the same smear in South America – through the same Commie periodicals in South America and generally throughout the world all of the Commie groups began smear campaigns against me and my pictures.'

The use of the word 'Commie' showed Disney laying all the cards on the table. Disney, who was later charged with being both anti-labour and anti-Semitic, was singing music to the ears of HUAC. His evidence and the story it told was a fascinating commentary on conditions in 1947 and the political climate. How, he was asked by John McDowell, did that word 'smear' show itself?

'Well,' Disney replied, 'they distorted everything. They lied. There was no way you could ever counteract anything that they did. They formed picket lines in front of the theatres and, well, they called my plant a sweatshop – and that is not true and anybody in Hollywood would prove it otherwise. They claimed things that were not true at all and there was no way you could fight it back. It was not a labour problem at all because – I mean, I've never had labour trouble, and I think that would be backed up by anybody in Hollywood.'

At that point, the chairman, J Parnell Thomas, said he wanted to ask a question: 'In other words, Mr Disney, Communists out there smeared you because you wouldn't knuckle under?'

'I wouldn't go along with their way of operating,' he said to a committee which was very happy with the way Walt Disney was operating. He mentioned other names. There was an artist called David Hilberman. 'I looked into his record,' said Disney, 'and I found that, number one, he had no religion and, number two, he had spent considerable time at the Moscow Arts Theatre studying art direction, or something.' Which was enough to condemn him, plainly.

Then there was William Pomerance. 'They are all tied up with the same outfit.' An outfit, he said, that he didn't believe was a political party. 'I believe it is an un-American thing. The thing that I resent the most is that they are able to get into these unions, take them over and represent to the world that a group of people in my plant, who I know are good, 100 per cent Americans, are trapped by this group and represented to the world as accepting all of those ideologies and it is not so. And I feel that they really ought to be smoked out and shown up for what they are – so that all of the good, free causes in this country, all the liberalisms that really are American, can go out without the taint of Communism.'

Disney said there were many reasons why the Communists wanted to take over the movie business. 'But I don't think they have gotten very far and I think the industry is made up of good Americans, just like in my plant, good, solid Americans. My boys have been fighting it longer than I have. They are trying to get out from under it and they will, in time, if we can just show them up.'

J Parnell Thomas told him: 'I want to congratulate you on the form of entertainment which you have given the American people and given the world and congratulate you for taking time out to come here and testify before this committee.'

Most of those called as friendly witnesses received the same sort of approbation. Sam G Wood talked about the Motion Picture Alliance for the Preservation of American Ideals, of which he was director. His own films included some of the most important that Hollywood had yet produced, like *Goodbye Mr Chips* in 1939 and *For Whom the Bell Tolls* four years later, a movie about the Spanish Civil War, which it could have been suggested was distinctly left wing. He told the committee: 'We felt there was a definite effort by members of the Communist Party to take over the unions and guilds.'

'Do Communists run schools?' he was asked.

'Yes, youngsters go there to study – and we see them in theatres.' He mentioned the People's Education Centre. 'Edward Dmytryk teaches there.' His was a name forever after associated with the HUAC hearings. There were other names recorded and written down during what were meant to be private meetings, or at least sessions for members only. Bernard Gordon recalls speaking up at a meeting of the Conference of Studio Unions. He wanted to negotiate for members to get sick leave. But nobody else spoke up. 'I saw a guy was drawing something and he knew perfectly well what my politics were. He passed the piece of paper around to his confrères and I realised he was doing something in the Red-baiting department. Afterwards, somebody told me he'd actually drawn a hammer and sickle and pointed it to me – indicating that I was the hammer and sickle fellow.'

Gordon told his wife about it, about what he feared would be the beginning of the end for him. The mystery of how people came to be named was . . . well, a mystery. Certainly, there were no strict rules or protocol. Looking back with the benefit of hindsight, it is not only strange how some people were handed the dreaded pink slips, but also how others escaped. Not that they were dangers to the nation, not that they had held Communist party cards, but they were seen at the same innocuous events or had been in the company of the same so-called 'subversives' that led others to be called before the committee.

Bernie Gordon was never actually named, but he received his subpoena. An aspiring producer at Universal – 'a real shit, by the way' – who had named his own wife as a Communist, put the boot in. 'This is a man who knew my background, he'd been very sympathetic and had been on my side,' said Gordon. 'But when it came to the problem of what was going to happen, he sneakily told me a subpoena was out for me, "but for God's sake, don't tell anyone I told you." He wanted to be on my side, but not to be known to be on my side.'

These were not uncommon circumstances, as there were plenty of people who behaved as double agents, trying to ingratiate themselves with the committee and its supporters as well as the victims. It turned out that this 'real shit' had been told by the executive producer of the unit in which Gordon had been working. 'There was no big secret, but naturally nobody said anything to me. But eventually the secret was out when he told me. And I was terminated at the studio.' Terminated after he'd just finished the biggest project in his life to date. He had written the script of the 1953 Rock Hudson movie, *The Lawless Breed*. His script was then rewritten by someone else. Gordon remains bitter to this day.

Bitterness, to one extent or another, was an emotion every victim of HUAC felt, even though some of their children now like to think that was not so. Could there be a better reason for that emotion when a writer, even one under investigation, was nominated for an Oscar – even while in the process of being investigated and even after a subpoena had been 'safely' delivered? As we shall see, this actually happened.

Bernie Gordon knew that apparent success was not sufficient protection. He assumed he would get the dreaded pink slip, although he remained, for a time, optimistic. 'There was always a sense that you might fall through the cracks if you weren't actually subpoenaed. I didn't want to be named publicly. I had just finished two scripts that they were very enthusiastic about and they were talking about giving me a contract at Universal. There was always the hope that I might survive in some curious way. Some people did.'

Gordon's situation reveals another unexpected aspect to the story. Studios had their own police departments, whose main function was to keep uninvited people off the lot as well as to investigate thefts, from props to scripts. More often than was made known by that other studio police force, the publicity machine, the police force which would break up illicit affairs which could be conceived as damaging the studio reputation. With the arrival of HUAC, they had a new function – to weed out the Reds. Gordon was called before the head of the studio police department, 'a notorious sonofabitch.' If he were to be called before the Committee, he must agree to be a 'co-operative witness' – not necessarily a 'friendly witness', which was an entirely different animal. 'They said, "Look Bernie, all you have to do is answer a few questions and you have a career before you and we want to give you a contract, and you have a wife and new baby. Just answer a few questions."'

From that moment began the job of hunting the subpoena server – or rather, avoiding the subpoena server. No matter how he tried and how he persuaded his housekeeper and his daughter not to answer the front door or phone, eventually the subpoena was served. And there was the question of the telephone. As Gordon now says: 'You didn't have to answer it or if you didn't know who was calling and they asked questions, you just hung up on them. You were under no obligation to talk to them. Generally speaking, you avoided picking up the phone, because you didn't want to say "He's not here" or something.'

The fear of the telephone was ever present. When friends or family phoned, there was always the worry of who might be, not on the other end, but in a car or an office bugging their conversations. 'We were very conscious of it and we were very careful about what we said on the telephone.'

Not so much Dalton Trumbo. He was one of the rare sufferers of diphtheria at the time the FBI was hounding him. His daughter Nikola recalled to me: 'He was actually delirious and he'd be on the telephone talking with someone and then he would curse the FBI who were listening.'

Children were unavoidably caught up in all this. In 1952, Joanna Rapf wrote in her own diary: 'Everything is crazy in our house. We jump every time the phone rings. I won't write any more in this because someone might read it some day.' What she did write about – and she was just 10 years old at the time – was how she was constantly living under a cloud of fear, as she now remembers, 'like jumping every time the phone rings or a glass smashed.' She recalls men coming to the house and, like everyone we spoke to, the image of these men is ingrained in her memory. To her, they were 'tall men . . . tall men in suits.'

Bella Stander, whose father, the actor Lionel, was to make an important, some would say historic, mark on the committee, describes the FBI hunters as one of the most intimidating features of the whole period. 'I think it was the most ghastly time of his life. And he was literally being tailed by the FBI 24 hours a day. At one point, they were watching him from an apartment opposite ours.'

Already, Hollywood itself had gone on trial. Dalton Trumbo was one of 10 men to go into history as 10 families were thrown into disruption. It's unlikely they appreciated what was really in store for them. Chances are they did not. What is certain is that it was a frightening prospect. The night before, Trumbo and Lawson had tried to cover their anxieties with a big party at a Manhattan penthouse, courtesy of a wealthy sympathiser. The following morning as they drove up to New York's Penn Station, they were greeted by hundreds of supporters, all carrying banners. People were brave in the autumn of 1947. The tragedy was that comparatively few would remain so. Holding banners would be reason enough to be interviewed by the FBI. Failure to name names would be all that was necessary to be thrust on to the professional scrap heap. They didn't know that – or if they did, most tried to hide their fears – when the two men took the night train to Washington.

Chapter Five
The Hollywood Ten

President Roosevelt called the Un-American Committee a sordid procedure and that describes it pretty accurately. Innocent people dragged there through the mud of insinuation and slander. The testimony of convicts and subversives accepted and given to the press as though it were the gospel truth. Reputations ruined and people hounded out of their jobs.

Actor Robert Ryan in 1947 radio broadcast Hollywood Fights Back

(Hollywood Fights Back was the title of a two-part radio broadcast paid for by the Committee for the First Amendment (CFA), a group of stars and others in Hollywood and the entertainment business to protest at the hearings in Washington DC of 19 men summoned before HUAC. Those taking part flew to the American capital to protest in person. As we have already seen, it was indicative of how they felt that several of them, like Robert Ryan quoted above, liked to refer to HUAC as 'the Un-American Committee'. Whether Congress itself saw the significance of that is not known for sure.)

The traumas began the morning of the arrival at the courthouse of John Howard Lawson and Dalton Trumbo, two of the Hollywood Ten, as they were now dubbed by the press, and by everyone who took an interest in the tragic change that was coming over America. They were interviewed by the press, cocky, confident and funny Dalton Trumbo, talking about how much money he had made as a screen writer (a boast, but also a statement of how being a Communist did not mean one had to be broke and jealous) and the phlegmatic John Howard Lawson.

Lawson's son, Jeff, remembers a day when he climbed those steps with his father and brothers. 'They were interviewed [and] a lot of newspaper people came. And then we went to the jail. I've seen pictures of myself on the courthouse steps a few times on TV. Then we went in and there were some proceedings and the lawyers were there and then they were taken away. And I went that afternoon and visited him in this jail and I remember it was like this blue glass and he was behind it and he was . . . I could see he was . . . pretty tense. He was telling me people to call and things to do. It was like he was still on the outside.'

What HUAC was there to prove was that they were anywhere but. No matter how strongly it could be denied and despite protests that it was all going to be simply an investigation for the benefit of the nation – and, in particular, of that part of it who were influenced by the movies – it was going to be a show trial. Nothing that J Parnell Thomas had indicated at that point would make quite the same impression. 'It was looked on as a fight,' Jeff Lawson says, 'and they were not spies or saboteurs. There, in the huge caucus room adjoining the Capitol, [Thomas] banged his gavel and refused to allow the men before him – mostly writers – to speak, except to answer his one oft-repeated question, "Are you now or have you ever been a Communist?"' Or, it has to be said, give answers to any of the other questions he and his investigators wanted to ask and which remained unanswered.

Whether the witnesses, who had been subpoenaed to appear in this marble-pillared room, were impressed by the surroundings as they walked up the steps leading to the building one has reason to doubt. Hundreds of Hollywood films had featured similar if not equal grandeur in a building that was designed in 1903 to house the 'caucuses', party sessions to discuss policy in forthcoming debates. But since 1938, it had widened its functions – as a centre for House investigations – inquiring into the activities of labour unions, foreign spies, fascist propagandists and, as now, what HUAC described as subversive activities in America.

The architects of the building, John Carrere and Thomas Hastings, anticipated that with its marble columns and chandeliers, it would be the centre of one of those dignified political hearings so proudly boasted of by senators and congressmen. After all, it was in the caucus room that Congress had held its inquiries into the sinking of the Titanic. Instead, it more closely resembled a cattle market. As the Hollywood group of unfriendlies entered, they could only wonder what was going to happen. Not only was each one alone, apart from his lawyer, facing a platform of antagonistic committee members and investigators, but row after row behind and in front was filled with congressional advisers, members of the public, the press and, above all, with the film newsreel cameras and radio microphones which were looking after the national interest in what seemed to be the most important event since the end of World War Two.

John Howard Lawson became totemic of the battle between HUAC and the accused – although, almost laughingly, they were not officially being accused of anything. They were mere witnesses. However, the investigator, Stripling, fired at one of them: 'You are being charged with being a Communist', an accusation that would come back to haunt Thomas himself during the House contempt hearing against Albert Maltz. As Lawson tried to make himself heard, Thomas again and again knocked his hammer and said, 'No, no, no.'

'It is very unfortunate and tragic that I have to teach this committee . . .'

He could get no further. The inquisitor interrupted, sounding like a frustrated vaudeville straight man. 'That's not the question . . . that's not the question.'

If it wasn't so unfortunate and tragic, it could have been a scene from Neil Simon's *The Sunshine Boys*. But there was little that was sunny about the hearings which opened in Washington in October 1947, with castigated writers and directors and the sympathetic Hollywood people attending those same hearings. As we shall see, a group of dedicated Hollywood personalities tried from the beginning to show their support for the men who were forced to go to the capital.

His statement would have castigated the committee for its own un-American stance. No American, he wanted to say, would be safe if HUAC were not stopped in its illegal enterprise. Later, he did manage to read part of the statement on radio and newsreel.

For those who weren't there, *Newsweek* described the scene: 'The hearing room by now was in turmoil. Thomas, Stripling [the investigator] and Lawson were all shouting at once. His face and neck flaming red, Thomas kept banging his gavel, but the screen writer ignored him. The four hundred men and women in the audience booed and cheered. The six newsreel cameras hummed. The thirty newspaper photographers scurried around, exploding flashbulbs.'

Nineteen unfriendlies had been sent subpoenas at the same time as 24 friendly witnesses, the Hollywood people who were willing to condemn the industry being in thrall to the Communist Party and, by implication, the Soviet Union. The committee said it was going to prove that 'card-carrying party members dominated the Screen Writers Guild, that Communists had succeeded in introducing subversive propaganda into motion pictures and that President Roosevelt had brought improper pressure to bear upon the industry to produce pro-Soviet films during the war.' There was one film they had in mind: Warner Bros' *Mission to Moscow*.

Lawson had been credited with writing *Algiers* in 1943, *They Shall Have Music* the following year, *Action in the North Atlantic* in 1943 and *Sahara* the same year. He had been the first president of the Screen Writers Guild. The others subpoenaed were:

Alvah Bessie, writer of *Northern Pursuit* (1943) and co-writer of *Objective, Burma!* which could be said to be the most patriotic pro-American film ever made – so patriotic that it was banned in Britain until the mid-50s. The movie, starring Errol Flynn, gave the impression that the Americans won the war in the Burmese jungles, completely ignoring the British 14th Army, who would say it did all the dirty work in that country. Bessie had been awarded a Guggenheim fellowship in creative writing in 1935.

Herbert Biberman, director of films like *Meet Nero Wolfe* (1936), *One Way Ticket* (1935) and *The Master Race* (1944). He had been in Hollywood since 1935 and had written and been associate producer of *New Orleans* (1947), which starred some of the finest jazz musicians of the era.

Lester Cole, writer of screenplays including *None Shall Escape* (1944), *Blood on the Sun* (1945) and *High Wall* (1947), which starred Robert Taylor. He was also the co-writer with Alvah Bessie of *Objective Burma!*

Edward Dmytryk, director of films such as *Confessions of Boston Blackie* (1941), *Seven Miles From Alcatraz* (1942), *Hitler's Children* (1943) and, most memorably, *Crossfire*.

Ring Lardner Jr, eminent writer of the 1942 Oscar-winning *Woman of the Year* starring Katharine Hepburn and Spencer Tracy. The Academy Award was for Lardner's screenplay. He also wrote the scripts of the anti-Nazi films, *The Cross of Lorraine* (1943) and *Tomorrow, the World!* (1944). The highly controversial – mainly because of the revealing necklines – *Forever Amber* (1947) was written by him in collaboration with Philip Dunne.

Albert Maltz, who wrote, among others, *This Gun For Hire* (1942), *Pride of the Marines* (1936), *The House I Live In* (1945), a tribute to multi-cultural America, and *The Naked City* (1958).

Samuel Ornitz, screenwriter of *The Man Who Reclaimed His Head* (1934), *Three Kids and a Queen* (1935), *Two Wise Maids* (1937) and *Three Faces West* (1940).

Adrian Scott, who wrote *Mr Lucky* (1943) and produced, among others, *So Well Remembered* (1948) and *Crossfire*.

Dalton Trumbo, writer of the Ginger Rogers' film *Kitty Foyle* (1940), *Thirty Seconds Over Tokyo* (1944) and *Our Vines Have Tender Grapes* (1945).

All were called before HUAC in Washington in October 1947, along with Bertold Brecht, the German writer who had been in Hollywood when he wrote *Hangmen Also Die*. The 1943 film dealt with the assassination of the Nazi overlord of Czechoslovakia, Reinhard Heydrich. After giving evidence, he fled to East Germany.

In addition, subpoenas were issued against Larry Parks; the writer-director Irving Pichel, who had written the 1946 films *Tomorrow Is Forever*, *OSS* and *The Bride Wore Boots*; Gordon Kahn, writer of *The African Queen* released in 1951; Robert Rossen, best known for writing, producing and directing *All the King's Men*, based on the story of Hughie Long, corrupt governor of Louisiana, as well as writing *The Roaring Twenties* in 1939, *A Walk In the Sun* (1945), *Edge of Darkness* (1943), *Body and Soul* (1947) and the uncredited (because of his Communist background) *Treasure of the Sierra Madre* in 1948; Richard Collins, who wrote *Song of Russia* as well as *Thousands Cheer* in 1943. He would later name names; Lewis Milestone, who had directed the Oscar-winning indictment of World War One, *All Quiet on the Western Front* in 1930; Howard Koch, screenwriter and playwright who in addition to his work in *Casablanca* had adapted *The War of the Worlds* for Orson Welles's Mercury Theatre radio broadcast, which had caused panic all over America. He was also uncredited as the writer of *The Best Years of Our Lives* in 1946, the archetypal story of the problems of American Servicemen adjusting to civilian life; Waldo Salt, who wrote *Mr Winkle Goes to War* in 1944, *The Flame and the Arrow* six years later.

After examining Brecht, the committee packed up. There is a story that Larry Parks was about to be called, but he was in the men's room when they started looking for him. He went home to face the committee another day – and to make more films until that happened. Among them *Jolson Sings Again*.

With Brecht no longer on the scene, the first 10 men were to become the centre of the most significant *cause célèbre* of the whole HUAC era. They were the Hollywood Ten. They would be held in suspense for more than 3 years. They were dealt with by a committee that was extremely satisfied with the performances of its friendlies and which was now sharpening its knives for the next battle.

Whether they expected it all to be straightforward is a matter for speculation, but when the unfriendlies were called on 27 October 1947, J Parnell Thomas and his principal 'investigator' (in effect, the prosecution counsel) Stripling enjoyed every moment of a game in which all the rules were in their favour.

The purpose of the hearings, said Thomas, was to 'reveal subversive, Communist and un-American influence in motion pictures.' People got wind of what was going on early in the day. Gregory Peck said: 'There is more than one way to lose your liberty. It can be torn out of your hands by a tyrant, but it can also slip away, day by day, when you are too busy to notice, too scared.' When I was writing my authorised Gregory Peck biography he told me: 'I have never been a Communist, but I was, I suppose, left wing. Richard Nixon would think so. He put me on his enemies list. I was never called before the committee, but I hated what they did.'

Edward Dmytryk, who was born in Canada of Ukranian parents, told the committee that he was a naturalised American. He had been a member of the Communist party since 1945, but did not get a chance to tell the committee about that. 'I have a statement here to make,' he said. But he didn't get any further.

'The chair has ruled that the statement is not pertinent . . . .are you a member of the Screen Directors Guild?'

He protested: 'I feel the questions have been designed . . .'

Dmytryk was not allowed to say what he felt. 'It is not up to you to feel how they have been designed. You are here to respond to the question . . .'

'I would like to answer it. I would like to answer it in my own way. This question is designed to weaken the guilds.'

The Chairman took no notice, other than to interrupt with *the* question: 'Are you now or have you ever been a member of the Communist Party?'

He refused to answer in anything but his own way, which was not allowed. 'I feel a question of constitutional rights is involved,' Dmytryk protested. 'I have been advised that there is a question of constitutional rights involved. The Constitution does not ask that such a question be answered in the way you want. I think that what organisations I belong to, what I think and what I say cannot be questioned by this committee.'

He was taking the First Amendment, which guaranteed freedom of speech. The Chair ruled otherwise and he would later be cited for contempt of Congress.

His widow, Jean Porter, told me: 'After they started the inquisition, he didn't know what was happening. Attorneys tried to make appointments with congressmen who might help. But no one wanted to touch it. Truman was President, but no one knew how he felt. He didn't help them at all.'

Nor it appears was there anything like a united front among the Ten. Jean Porter told us: 'John Howard Lawson was so overpowering. He was not very pleasant. He was the leader of the Communist party between New York and Hollywood, and from Moscow to New York. He was Mr Big. John Howard Lawson blasted everybody I know. Eddie just turned white. The committee was taken aback. They were not expecting that kind of fight from our guys.' Which, rather than being a weakness, showed a certain sense of strength. Or at least so it appeared.

Once they knew they would be cited, the die had been cast. The Government might be against them; they could end up in jail. But they thought they had jobs to go back to. 'The questioning was over,' Jean Porter remembers. 'They didn't know they would be fired. He got back home the day before Thanksgiving. They were all fired. All of the money they earned, they put in a fund to go towards lawyers.' The writers could find ways of turning out screenplays. 'Eddie couldn't do that. He wasn't a writer; he was a director.' No one imagined that eventually Dmytryk would become a turncoat.

Ring Lardner Jr also said he had a statement to read. Stripling told him: 'After you testify, you can read your statement . . . Are you a member of the Screen Writers Guild?'

Lardner responded: 'Mr Stripling, I want to be co-operative about this, but there are certain limits to my co-operation. I don't want to help you divide or smash this Guild or infiltrate the motion picture industry in any way for a purpose that seems to be to control that business . . . to control what the American people can see or hear in the motion picture theatres.'

Stripling replied: 'If you refuse to answer the questions, you will not be able to read your statement . . . Are you a member of the Screen Writers Guild? That's a very simple question.'

Lardner: 'It seems to me that if you can make me answer this question, tomorrow you could ask someone if he believed in spiritualism.'

Stripling said he had no interest in spiritualism. The question was put to him again: 'Are you now or have you ever been . . . ?' And he added: 'Any real American would be proud to answer that.'

Lardner's answer was another one for the history books: 'I *could* answer that, but if I do, I would hate myself in the morning.'

Thomas was infuriated by what was clearly – and the Ten agreed with him – a concerted decision not to answer any questions. 'Leave the witness chair!' he shouted. 'Leave the witness chair! Take him away.'

But Lardner didn't want to be taken away. 'I think I am leaving by force. You said I could read my statement,' he declared. Thomas screamed: 'Sergeant, take the witness away. No, you can't.'

But Lardner would say that he went into the hearing certain that he was in the right. He had recently signed a new contract with 20th Century Fox on the strength of which he bought himself a big new house in Santa Monica. His confidence was based on a 1943 judgment of the US Supreme Court, which declared: 'If there is any fixed star in our constitutional constellation, it is that no official, high or petty, can prescribe what shall be orthodox in politics, nationalism, religion or other matters of opinion, or force citizens to confess by word or act their faith therein.'

Lardner would admit that he had been a Communist, but not to a committee which he insisted had no right or reason to ask. He said he had joined because it was a party 'in whose ranks I had found some of the most thoughtful, witty and generally stimulating men and women of Hollywood.' He added: 'I also encountered a number of bores and unstable characters, which seemed to bear out Bernard Shaw's observation that revolutionary movements tend to attract the best and worst elements in a given society.'

Fifty years later, Lardner did get round to reading his statement. He would have talked about the films he wrote for the Office of Strategic Services (OSS) and an animated cartoon called *The Brotherhood of Man*. It exposed, 'the myth that any inherent differences exist among people of different skin colour and geographical origin. It doesn't matter to me what kind of preposterous documents your investigators produce from unnamed sources describing my affiliations under some such heavily cloaked pseudonym. My record includes no anti-democratic word or act, no spoken or written expression of anti-Semitism, anti-Negro feeling or opposition to American democratic principles, as I understand them.'

As for the atmosphere in Hollywood, 'where I have lived for the last 10 years, is considerably different than that of the small segment of Washington to which I have been exposed in the last 10 days. There are a few frightened people there – men like Adolphe Menjou and John C Moffitt throw so many furtive glances over their shoulders that they run a serious risk of dislocation.'

The statement would have gone on: 'What I am most concerned about is the ultimate result that might come from a successful fulfilment of your purpose. On Tuesday, the chairman said that there was subversive material in motion pictures and proposed that it be prevented in the future by an industry blacklist. The motion-picture producers have not indicated that they are gullible enough to fall for such a ruse, but if they ever did, the fact that I might be prevented from working at my profession would be of little account. The really important effect would be that the producers themselves would lose control over their pictures and that the same shackling of education, labour, radio and newspapers would follow. We are already subject in Hollywood to a censorship that makes most pictures empty and childish. Under the kind of censorship which this inquisition threatens, a leading man wouldn't even be able to blurt out the words 'I love you' unless he had first secured a notarised affidavit proving she was a pure white Protestant gentile of old Confederate stock.'

The committee wouldn't have liked that. It might have undone the whole purpose of their operation. Sam Ornitz – described by fellow writer John Bright as 'an elder statesman of the left, although he was not yet forty – was asked when he appeared whether he were a member of the Screen Writers Guild. His answer: 'I wish to reply to that question by saying this involves a serious question of conscience.'

'Conscience?' he was asked.

'Conscience. I say you do raise a serious question of conscience for me when you ask me to act in concert with you to override the Constitution.'

Stripling and Thomas were growing infuriated. In fairness to the committee – and it is indeed difficult to *be* fair to them – they were being manipulated by highly intelligent, extraordinarily articulate men, who had devised a strategy that was designed to frustrate the whole questioning system. There could be no reason to deny membership of the SWG since its membership list was easily obtainable and as an organisation was doing nothing illegal – any more than the Communist Party itself for that matter.

'The witness is through. Stand away.' Those words were heard almost as often as the question about membership of the party. Uniformed guards came to pull away Ornitz by force, but he went quietly if not willingly.

Lardner and the other members of the Hollywood Ten were clearly on the HUAC hate list. Trumbo had also tried to read a statement. He was 35 years old, born in Colorado, a descendant of early settlers and a war correspondent who had joined the Communist Party in 1943. As he later said: 'To me, it was not a matter of great consequence. It represented no significant change in my thought or in my life.' Such a background, to say nothing of his enormous output of novels (including the seminal *Johnny Got His Gun*) and screenplays, made him a feisty opponent. But that feistiness would not be enough.

'Mr Chairman,' he managed to blurt out, 'the rights of American labour to inviolably secret membership lists have been won in this country by a great cost of blood and a great cost in terms of hunger.'

The only witness who answered all the questions was Bertold Brecht, who dealt with everything he was asked – including a denial that he was a member of the Communist Party. Dan Bessie said that Brecht 'was advised to take a careful neutral position because he was, after all, an enemy alien . . . I think they urged him not to defy the committee but just to tell them what he knew and what he didn't want to know. [He] then immediately caught a plane for Europe and Communist East Berlin.' All the others were charged with contempt of Congress and would have their cases heard by the House of Representatives as a whole that November.

On 30 October 1947 the initial hearings came to an abrupt end. Both John Howard Lawson and Dalton Trumbo were physically dragged off the witness stand and out of the building. The following day, Brecht caught his plane out of America. *Variety,* the showbiz bible, famous for its headlines such as WALL STREET LAYS AN EGG at the time of the 1929 crash, headlined this story less imaginatively: COMMIE CARNIVAL CLOSES: AN EGG IS LAID.

What happened next followed the law of the United States, but interpreted with all the subtlety of a Soviet show trial in which the defendants are summarily given the sentences that everyone suspected they would receive right from the beginning. The word accepted by legal experts was that, once the House of Representatives had heard the details – and, it would assume – accepted HUAC's findings, they had to be 'formally tried'.

The next stage was for the matter to be debated in Congress – to decide if an allegation of contempt could be sustained. For no obvious reason, Maltz and Trumbo were the two test cases subjected to congressional debate. J Parnell Thomas was totally dismissive of the rights of either man or of any of the other Ten. No amount of 'fog about constitutional rights and the First Amendment should obscure their political conspiracy against America,' he declared on the floor of the House of Representatives. The congressmen concurred. A total of 347 votes were recorded for citing Albert Maltz for contempt, as against just 17 in his favour. Trumbo only had 16 votes for and 240 against him. The other 8 were voted 'against' by means of an unrecorded voice vote.

On 5 December 1947 a federal grand jury took over the case and indicted each of the Hollywood Ten – but separately. That was an important factor. The Ten all wanted to be tried together. It would have saved on the cost of legal representation. Instead, all had to pay for their own lawyers. Lawson was the first to lose his battle, followed in quick succession by Trumbo and the others. What followed then was the only example of co-operation between HUAC or its representatives and the Ten. The two opposing legal teams agreed that none of the Eight would face an appeals court, but would accept for the Eight the same sentence as would be handed out to the first two. Before that, however, would come appeals for Trumbo and Lawson.

Two funds were set up to pay for the defence, both administered by the Ten themselves – the Freedom From Fear Committee (FFFC) and the Committee to Free the Hollywood Ten (CFHT). Another 100 Hollywood families, mostly with political sympathies in line with those of the Ten, joined the fight. They raised more than $150,000, but it did not do much good.

When the trials opened, despite the fact that it all had to be done over and over again, there was just one answer to the citations. The case was put thus: 'The particular questions put to the defendant . . . violated the rights reserved to the defendant under the First, Fourth, Fifth, Ninth and Tenth Amendments to the Constitution to be protected from official inquisition that can compel disclosure of his private beliefs and associations.'

On 18 March 1948, the defence of the First Amendment (which the Ten regarded as their main weapon since they believed they were merely upholding their freedom of speech rights) was quite clearly no longer viable. The appellate court had by then ruled on an earlier case that Dr Edward Barsky and 16 members of the Joint Anti-Fascist Refugee Committee had been cited in 1946 for refusing to produce the records of their organisation or to answer HUAC's questions, on grounds protected by the First Amendment. But the court ruled that Congress had 'power to make an inquiry of an individual which may elicit the answers that the witness is a believer in Communism or a member of the Communist Party.'

It all went on for a very long time.

Lawson was found guilty of contempt on 19 April 1948 after a week-long trial. Trumbo's guilty verdict followed on 5 May.

There had already been another trial – of Hanns Eisler, the composer and friend of Bertold Brecht. It was his connection with Eisler that led to Brecht being called before the committee and subsequently fleeing the country. The Supreme Court refused to reopen the Barsky case, which was disastrous to the hopes of the Hollywood Ten. On 13 June 1949, the appellate court ruled against Lawson and Trumbo, who were now the two test cases.

The Court pronounced: 'We expressly hold herein that the House Committee on Un-American Activities or a properly appointed sub-committee thereof has the power to inquire whether a witness subpoenaed by it is or is not a member of the Communist Party or a believer in Communism and that this power carries with it necessarily the power to effect criminal punishment for failure or refusal to answer that question.' Lawson and Trumbo were sentenced on the same day that the Rosenbergs heard the conclusion of the government's case against them asking for the death penalty, which before long would be enacted.

But the death penalty was never on the cards for the Ten. Indeed, even imprisonment was going to be for a comparatively short time. But that didn't mean they would not want to avoid going to jail. Their outward demeanour was not one of obvious worry. With Trumbo and Lawson already sentenced, 7 of the Ten arrived at the Washington courthouse, climbing the steps arm in arm. Sanuel Ornitz, determinedly looking ahead, smoking his pipe; Ring Lardner Jr, tall, bow-tied; Albert Maltz, bespectacled; and the balding Alvah Bessie, all smiling. Lester Cole seemed a little more apprehensive, but the tall, elegant figure of Herbert Biberman and the bald Edward Dmytryk were both smiling, too. Adrian Scott missed the hearing and the lineup – he was ill and his appearance had to be delayed. When he finally did appear, chief investigator Stripling was so bamboozled by all that he had been doing that he mistakenly called him 'Mr Dmytryk'. Further from the truth that could not be.

Was there still hope in the Supreme Court? Despite varying rates of success, the Hollywood lawyers believed that the First Amendment would still help them. Their own soundings had shown that there would be a majority of judges on the Supreme Bench who would be sympathetic. They were sure that that court, ultimate guardians of the Constitution, would rule in their favour, safe in the knowledge that the First Amendment was the cornerstone of both that document and American democracy. They wanted to challenge the committee's purpose, indeed its rights to exist.

As Michael Cole says: 'My father thought he was going to win: he didn't do this to lose, he thought he was going to win . . . he won judgements, mind you. He eventually lost and was sent to jail, but there was a period of time where it hung in the balance.' They were legally advised, but as it turned out, wrongly so. They were told that protection of their right to free speech was all that they needed. What if they had taken the Fifth, instead? Few people had invoked that at that stage. The Fifth implied not their rights to free speech, but to say 'I'm guilty, but not saying that as such.' They didn't want anything that implied guilt. No, the First would do it.

So did they ever really have a chance before the Supreme Court?

Two judges whom they had deemed friendly, Justices Murphy and Rutledge, had died in the interim between the hearings (although doubt has been cast by certain historians as to whether their presence on the bench would have really made any difference to the Ten). In fact, the Supreme Court refused even to hear the case. Barsky had set the wrong precedent, as far as the Hollywood men were concerned.

What was more, the court turned upside down most people's idea of what the Fifth Amendment represented. In the end, it had to be invoked now that the First was no protection – which meant that a witness would not be able to defend himself at all. If he didn't 'take the Fifth' – and become what Joe McCarthy called 'a Fifth Amendment Communist' – he could be compelled to name names.

Jeff Lawson is convinced that his father, John Howard Lawson, believed the Ten would win in that corner of Washington. 'He was very surprised they didn't, but he was very radical by that time. He became radical and I think he felt there was a danger of fascism in the country and saw the committee as attacking artistic freedom and he stood up and wanted very strongly to trash the committee.'

It was, he emphasises today, more of a team effort than it has sometimes been given credit for. 'Those guys worked together and they agreed pretty much on what they were doing. Dalton was a humourist, a very funny guy who liked to crack jokes. The morning before they went to jail, he was cracking jokes with the media about how many expensive typewriters he had, impressing them with how much money he made as a writer. And my father was a very serious man who studied history a lot. He was easily the most outstanding intellectual of those Hollywood writers. He wrote books on history, books on film, and one of the greatest books ever written on dramatic theory.' Now he would have more time to develop his intellectual abilities.

On 11 June, Lawson and Trumbo were the first to go to prison – sentenced to a year at Ashland County Jail in Ohio. (According to his son, Jeff, this was not the only indignity suffered by John Howard Lawson: 'There was a certain jealousy and I've been told that, when my father was in jail, [some] of those writers took over the Hollywood Communist Party leadership and they kicked my father out, basically.') These first 2 of the Ten to be sentenced surrendered to a United States marshal and paid a $1,000 fine. Seven of the other 8, knowing there was no way they could win, went to Washington for what Lardner would describe as their 'perfunctory' trial, none of which lasted more than an hour. Adrian Scott was sentenced in September.

Paul Buhl describes Scott as 'one of the most tragic figures' in all the blacklist – because as a producer he could find no other work, not even under a false name, the way many of the writers could.

There were three different judges sitting, and each one of them handed out a different sentence from his colleagues: Dmytryk and Biberman were given six months each and a $500 fine. They were let out after five months in jail. The other six received a year in jail and a $1,000 fine. All those sentenced to a year were allowed two months off for good behaviour. The others were allowed a month respite.

No one further appealed, following their original decisions to accept the verdict of the two test cases. 'It took just a few minutes,' Lardner said. As for the period in jail, 'it was just a little tougher than being in the army. You just wait it out and it's over with.'

The lawyers were not left to their own devices, with the Ten doing exactly what they suggested. After all, the Ten were intellectuals, used to researching, delving and examining details. Herbert Biberman certainly wouldn't have permitted that. He wasn't the most popular of the Hollywood Ten – at least among his fellow accused. Alvah Bessie, in a TV programme about the period called *Tender Comrades*, said: 'Herbert was always a pain in the ass and we used to say in Hollywood, "Herbert is an ass, but he is our pain in the ass."'

Professional rivalries and the pressure of confinement tested friendships to the extreme. After their first drive from Washington to Texarkana with two federal marshals, Alvah Bessie and Herbert Biberman fell out. Later Bessie said: 'I had the misfortune of being in the same jail with him. We left Washington handcuffed to each other in the back seat of a car driven by a Texas marshal and a detective. All the way from Washington to Texarkana. On the way we were deposited in two different prisons, one in Virginia and one in Tennessee. We were sitting in the back seat and Herbert, all the way from Washington to Texas, was giving a lecture to the two gentlemen in the front seat about what our case was all about, what the American Civil War was all about, what the Russian Revolution was all about, the American Revolution, the French Revolution.' On another occasion, he remembered: 'He was boring everybody to death.'

Bessie wasn't sure about his fellow prisoner's attitude at all – particularly when they first arrived at the prison and they were both asked for details about their religion. 'He stood up straight,' Bessie later remembered for a TV programme about the blacklist. 'He was in the National Guard in California, and said "I AM A JEW." I thought, "Oh Christ!" The next day we both got a Hebrew Bible in our prison cell. But Herbert would die in pieces for what he believed in. The man was enormously self-sacrificing. He went out on a limb and did a great job of organising the whole defence of the Ten up until we went to jail. And I grew to like him basically because he was a man of principle, a man of great courage, a man of enormous ingenuity and imagination.'

The Ashland prisoners were not treated badly. They slept in dormitories, rather than cells. Of the other prisoners, Jeff Lawson remembers: 'Most of them were just Kentucky mountain guys who made moonshine gin and whiskey. It was a low security risk jail.' Which puts the HUAC fears into a kind of perspective. Trumbo used to write letters for these mountain moonshiners. He also wrote poetry for his family. 'Say then but this of me;/ Preferring not to crawl on his knees/ In freedom to a bowl of buttered slops/ Set out for him by some contemptuous clown/ He walked to jail on his feet.'

Scott went to Ashland, too. Maltz and Dmytryk served in Mill Point, West Virginia. Ornitz was taken to Springfield, Missouri. Before Lester

Cole was released from the prison at Danbury, Connecticut, to which he and Ring Lardner had been sent, he walked past the federal jail's chicken farm, outside the prison walls. He recognised the man running the enterprise – one J Parnell Thomas, who, since the Hollywood Ten hearings, had been convicted of taking bribes. Thomas had taken the Fifth Amendment. Cole couldn't resist the temptation. 'I see you are still shovelling chicken shit around,' he said to his old tormentor.

There would be no compensation for the Hollywood Ten – even when in 1977, the Supreme Court, led by Chief Justice Berger, over-turned the ruling, in effect saying that the First Amendment should have saved the men. Herbert Biberman decided to face his new life with a fresh kind of determination – or, rather, with the sort of determination that he had shown during the hearings before being shunted off to jail. Hearings that, according to his niece, Ann Strick, had people 'riveted'. She told Barbra Paskin: '[There was] great distress. Great stress and great distress. It ruined the theatrical careers of three people.' Of Herbert and of his actress wife Gale Sondergaard, who before long would find herself shuffled into a starring role in the HUAC hearings, along with her actress sister, Hester.

Biberman, said his niece, 'came out of prison and in typical Herbert fashion decided to go into the business of remodelling houses, which he did with as much zest as he'd ever done in his life; as he'd ever worked in theatre, as he'd ever worked in film, as he'd ever worked in political actions.' Or in prison in Texarkana, which none of his family visited in an age when cross-country travel, and certainly internal flights, were rarely undertaken. 'He wanted to become the best, whatever it was. The best floor sweeper, the best latrine cleaner, whatever. Herbert roared at life and life roared back. That was Herbert.

'There was never a word of complaint literally from any of them about the loss of their theatrical lives or about their financial straits. They were admirable . . . I think they simply felt that they had taken a moral position in which they believed to the core of their beings that it was a position in absolute accord with the best of American intention. And that they were willing to accept the consequences of their unpopular behaviour and position.'

That did not mean there would not be more fights and arguments. The brunette Gale Sondergaard, who had made her name playing attractive but sinister characters in films like *My Favorite Blonde* in 1942 and *Appointment in Berlin* the following year, would be at the forefront.

For the Ten, their agonies had not ended with their hearings. And not for others who were 'interesting' HUAC. 'Once these people went to jail,' said Michael Cole, 'then other people became very fearful. And naturally so.'

The jailed ones became non-citizens, deprived not just of their liberty, but most of their rights, too. Like all convicts, they were, for instance, barred from exercising their previous right to vote. And it could be argued that by merely standing by their constitutional rights, they officially faced the harshest punishment of all: they and hundreds of others in the months and years to come were blacklisted. Nevertheless, jail changed a lot of the men who had previously lived a life not just of political freedom, but for many, of incredible luxury.

Alvah Bessie, who was the only one of the Ten to have served in the International Brigades in Spain, however, was not one of the wealthy ones. 'We didn't have the money to go and visit him,' his son now recalls. 'His wife and my half sister Edith visited him. They went a couple of times to Texarkana.' As far as Dan was concerned, the relationship was confined to writing letters. 'I think he tried to be as good a father as he could from jail. He asked us a lot about things. What we were doing, what our lives were like. He talked a little about his case and attempts to appeal to the Government for clemency and all of the things of that kind. And he also was kind of writing chatty letters about some of the things he was doing in jail, the jobs he had and things like that. He got depressed around the time the whole thing happened. But then, Alvah was always what many people have called a curmudgeonly character. Very cynical, but he was not really a down person. He was usually pretty upbeat most of the time.

He had a mixed 'career' at Texarkana. Part of the time he was employed as a typist, an appropriate function the prison authorities decided for a writer – the armed forces frequently came to the same sort of conclusion – and then he was a truck driver.

He was imprisoned along with fraudsters, convicted bootleggers and counterfeiters. Alvah shared a cell with a con man, who even offered to raise $5000 for a film Dan Bessie was writing. Bessie now says: 'We knew how he'd get it. We said, "No thanks." That was years after the Hollywood Ten years and the con man had become a Bessie family friend.'

Other experiences led to friendships – and to the breaking of them. Bessie may not have initially liked Biberman but he never denied his work on behalf of the whole group, nor his kindness. Just as he was about to be released from his five-month imprisonment, Biberman told Bessie that he would like to serve three months of the other man's sentence to even things up. Bessie checked with a guard. It was absolutely true, but wasn't possible to implement.

Hilda Ornitz remembered: 'He was very contained. So was his wife Sadie. They were not emotional people. Sadie was a very contained person, she did not show her emotions . . . no weeping and wailing. But you could see the affection between them was very strong. Sadie was not like a lot of Jewish mothers who just yell and scream and make a lot of noise . . . I think he wanted to prepare himself [for this reunion] to not let go or do anything uncomfortable.' This was particularly true when he left jail and met his family once more.

Hilda Ornitz, Sam's daughter-in-law, remembers her first meeting with him as he arrived at the Union Station in Los Angeles, after leaving the prison in Illinois. Yet it was an emotional reunion. Not only was he meeting his daughter-in-law for the first time since going to prison, his son and their children, but also Sadie, who also had not visited him at the penitentiary. Nor had they spoken much on the phone. 'This was March 1951 and people did not talk to each other as frequently as they do now on the phone.'

But the family had talked *about* him. Sam's sons Arthur (an eminent cinematographer whose later work included the 1962 *Requiem for a Heavyweight*, *Serpico* in 1973 and *Midnight Cowboy* in 1969), Hilda's husband and Donald, and his own brothers helped keep the couple away from access to the broker's men. They did not talk about it when Sam left jail. In fact, he didn't suffer as much as he might have done. As his daughter-in-law remembered: 'He considered himself a novelist and not a screenwriter. Sam was working on another novel which he finished in jail. He says they were very good to him. He got a job working in the library, became very friendly with the warden. They treated him well and let him work on his book.'

Hilda had lived with Sadie while Sam was in jail. 'She was a really smart person. During the time Sam was away, she ran the Hollywood Women's Club, a political group.' Her husband was not the only one for whom left-wing politics was part of life, but they were always part of each other's lives. 'He was very loving, very kind. He thought he'd let her down, I think, in some way. He never had any regrets for what he'd done. Neither had Sadie. They thought they'd done the right thing. We all thought that. Nobody ever blamed him for what he'd done.'

Joan Scott remembers something quite remarkable about Biberman: 'I think the other inmates called Herbert "Mr Biberman" while he was in jail.' He was hard to take. He was from another time zone and another planet.' As was his brother, Edward Biberman. 'They were either stage actors or trained as stage actors and they spoke like from another world in this very elegant, polished East Coast style of speech. They had this kind of grand manner, too. I don't think they meant to talk down to people but it just sounded like that because of their speech. They're very decent people, all these guys.'

Michael Cole insists that jail did not change his father. 'Oh, I don't think so. When he came out of prison he was 45 years old. He could do an incredible number of push-ups and he had a lot of stories.' And there was one, perhaps surprising, factor: 'I sure didn't know that he was upset coming out of prison and when we visited him in prison, he didn't act unhappy.' Danbury, known as the 'jail on the hill', was close to the Lardner family home, called The Manse, home of Ring Lardner and his family. They would spend time with Lester and then go on to the Lardners' and then take the train back to New York. As for his father: 'I think he used the time well. He did a lot of reading. He was involved in correspondence of various kinds.'

The blacklist followed immediately after those first hearings, and so did its repercussions. Norman Corwin remembered for me: 'The so-called Hollywood Ten who went to prison were accused of having insinuated Communist propaganda into their films. Looking back on it today, it was pathetic and bathetic and very injurious.' It wasn't all that good for HUAC either in the long run. 'HUAC was very proud of its achievements which amounted to nil and the repression was sweeping. They picked Hollywood because their victims were well known.'

Arthur Miller, who would have his own brushes with HUAC – and would immortalise his feelings about the committee in his masterpiece about the Salem witch-hunts, *The Crucible* (although we can't be sure that the HUAC members were bright enough to catch the allusions), was said by commentators to be 'a victim of the paranoid style in American politics'. Miller said his play was not formulated 'until McCarthy'. The Senator's investigations and those of HUAC were 'replaying some of the Hitler garbage.' He said that HUAC in particular demanded people gave them their soul. 'It wasn't names,' he said that they principally wanted, but more to 'degrade the person . . . that was what it was all about.

'These men simply [had] a lust and a love for viciousness . . . [they] enjoyed seeing the suffering they were inflicting. I felt towards them as

96

Czechs in Prague feel toward similar situations . . . I couldn't let myself be deflected from that.' He would say afterwards: 'I have often wished I'd had the temperament to do an absurd comedy, which is what the situation so often deserved. The country had been delivered over to the radical right, a ministry of free-floating apprehension toward absolutely anything that never happens in Missouri.'

Miller said he 'had invested too much of my mind for my contempt for the whole procedure. I appeared as a very dangerous man or else I wouldn't be asked to appear.'

He was the victim of paranoia, so paranoid that two film projects that Miller had on the stocks were shelved and his plays were banned from the American Army's theatrical repertoire (which, of course, didn't impress Senator McCarthy too much, as he soon charged the Army itself with being riddled with Communism).

But it was an old story. As Norman Corwin put it to me: 'This is a thing that happens to many countries – like when you consider the anti-Semitism of France and the genocidal tendencies of African countries. There was a great deal of pressure against anybody who stood up for their rights. For example, I was asked by the Democratic National Committee to produce a programme supporting Franklin Delano Roosevelt. The programme consisted of stars, farmers and sailors, people without names, people who had benefited from the administration of Roosevelt. Farmers had for the first time electricity coming into their farm houses.

One of the stars backed out at the last minute – not because he had changed his mind but because his sponsor on radio was coming down hard on him and threatened not to renew his contract. There was this tyranny exercised by a great many.' I asked him what this said about America. 'What it says about America is what it says about other countries – Idi Amin and the repressions and the academic frenzies that have seized countries from time to time. We had the alien Sedition Acts which resulted in such things as Thomas Jefferson's mail being opened.'

In contemporary American terms, there was another factor. People with no political background suddenly found themselves with immense power. As Corwin said: 'One of them was a grocer who operated a large market in Syracuse, New York, who said he was going to cancel his orders to any company which employed a pinko or a Communist. He achieved quite a lot of power and the captains of the radio industry crumbled. They toed the line, they appointed their own security officers and they operated a blacklist.'

Corwin went on: 'There was a hysteria, a generated, manipulated fear of our adversary in the Soviet Union – and what this committee did was to copy the Soviet repression. This was particularly a Communist manoeuvre to have the state control talent and control thinking.'

Lives were immediately changed, some never to recover. Even the sanguine nothing-gets-me-down Sam Ornitz. 'I think it was very hard on Sam,' his daughter-in-law concedes. 'He was used to being taken care of. Sadie said he wasn't the same after he came back from prison . . . Yes, she was angry, I guess. *He* was still angry. I remember him having arguments with his younger son, with Donald. Sam liked to have political arguments with people. It was as if he had to prove something after he got out. It was just difficult sometimes being around him.'

Christopher Trumbo, son of Dalton, said his father devoted time from the beginning to try to find work not just for himself, but for other writers. 'He liked the idea of concerted political action.' And other writers liked him; at least, they had great respect for him. Paul Jarrico would describe him as 'the Mark Twain of his generation.'

Certainly, he felt better about him than he did about John Howard Lawson, who became a sort of target of retribution. Jarrico has been blamed for principally unseating Lawson from the leadership of the Hollywood Communist Party. He wasn't alone. 'It's partly a generational difference there,' says Lawson's son. 'My father was of the older generation who came to Hollywood from Broadway, most of them, and they had established reputations beforehand, before they came to Hollywood. They came there as successful playwrights or whatever it was. And that's different from Paul Jarrico's younger generation . . . they were more influenced by the 30s . . . and wanted to be broader, whereas my father's generation was influenced by the horrors of the First World War and the 20s cultural revolt and I think he was naturally more suspicious of capitalism than someone like me who was exposed so much to the better things of the New Deal and government support of the arts. My father, I think, was more radical in essence and became more revolutionary.

'They had to blame somebody and my father is the guy they blamed. Liberals now tend to say, "Well, the way you should have been was like Dalton Trumbo," who was not like my father. My father was too militant. And I think it might have been a mistake to have been that militant, but I don't think that's why everybody was blacklisted or why the rightwing wanted to throttle the Communists there.'

The generational difference was not the only thing that set John Howard Lawson on a different path to those taken by the other Nine. He was, it could be said, the only one who blacklisted himself.

It was in 1946 that Larry Parks became an international star with *The Jolson Story*. That is well known. What is much less known is that the film was, to a large part, written by John Howard Lawson. His name appears on no credits for the film, but on the other hand neither does that of Sidney Buchman, who, as co-star Evelyn Keyes told me, wrote much of it, too. Indeed, Buchman steered the picture through, even though the official producer was the newspaper columnist Sidney Skolsky, who had had the original idea for the production.

Only one name appears as the writer of the film – Stephen Longstreet, although, Keyes said, his contribution had been minimal. Could it have been that Harry Cohn, head of Columbia Pictures, had got wind of what HUAC would be up to a year later and was willing to back his new star, who had a great future and was going to bring in a lot of money to his company – but didn't feel the same way about an awkward, difficult writer whose name no one would remember? It is more than possible. His son, however, says that Lawson didn't want any credit – because he was opposed to the blackface act that Jolson adopted and which Parks portrayed (the principal reason why the film is rarely seen on TV any more). He thought, says Jeff Lawson, 'that it was not good for blacks, was insulting to them. And he was always concerned with the position of blacks and discrimination and he refused credit. I don't remember Sidney Buchman saying anything. What I heard him say was that Harry Cohn was furious with him for refusing credit. I know he worked on that for a long time and wrote a lot of it.'

If that were so, then John Howard Lawson was very much ahead of his time. It was only 60 years ago when blackface was still a popular act on vaudeville stages and minstrel shows played on both sides of the Atlantic. Most significant of all, Jolson never had the intention of belittling the black man. His stock character, Gus the butler or the stable boy, always had the upper hand – Jolson couldn't play anyone who did not have that. In one scene from his 1930 film *Big Boy*, the plantation owner points his whip at Jolson and says, 'Dust my boots, boy' – to which he replies, 'I don't dust nobody's boots. I is free.' No other entertainer would have dared to have said that at the time and there is nothing in *The Jolson Story* that gives the impression of him being in the least racist.

*   *   *

Another question arises: Who shopped the Hollywood Ten? Who was it who decided that here was a group of men who would provide HUAC with so much ammunition that their campaign would have enough lifeblood to do whatever it wanted? It wasn't a matter of looking at scripts to find proof of what they would have called activity. As we find so often, looking for Communist infiltration in a Hollywood screenplay was frequently a needle-in-a-haystack search. Chris Trumbo wonders to this day who tried to destroy his father's name.

'It would be nice to know who the informers were. We always assumed that our telephone was tapped by the FBI. The invasion of our privacy. Every once in a while, my father had long conversations with the person at the other end of the line, on and on, and discussed the politics of the day with them. Somewhere on some tape this still exists.'

Michael Cole insists that Lester never attempted to 'dodge' a subpoena. 'That was not the style in our household. They [my parents] believed in what they were doing. They believed that they were absolutely correct to stand on the First Amendment so what was there to dodge? There was something to fight about, but there wasn't anything to dodge. I don't think that going to jail bothered my father, I really don't. If the prospect of it bothered him, I didn't know about it.'

Michael Cole still remembers going to camp in the mountains for two months in the summer when his father was 'away'. One of the people accompanying him was folk singer Pete Seeger, himself to figure in the McCarthyism story. 'There again, I went to camp with David Eliscu and we were counsellors in this camp. So a number again of these connections of sort of former party members or their children and I never knew who was who. People didn't go around flashing party cards or even being worried about it one way or the other. Various friends would come, some of whom were subsequently blacklisted and some of whom weren't. It wasn't like there was a political correctness test for who your friends were. It was more likely to be whether they were good fly fishermen.'

All along, Cole's father's political sensitivities were matters of conscience. He had rich friends, but he had poor ones, too. Black people and Japanese friends would come to visit and stay. 'My father's involvement in politics and in the Communist Party was some sort of combination of a very deep belief that all human beings are created equal . . . that was the way we treated people in our household and the Constitution of the United States and its First Amendment were like holy documents.'

100

The problems created by being in jail were huge. As Chris Trumbo said: 'What the Hollywood Ten faced was this: they were all blacklisted, fired, had two problems, to defend themselves and they must earn a living. They wanted to influence public opinion so that public opinion would be on their side.'

Among those who also found themselves on that iniquitous list – which, from time to time, the Hollywood hierarchy would deny existed – was a group of other stars who rented a plane and flew to Washington in a vain and ill-considered attempt at reversing the fate of the Ten. Vain and ill-considered because they suffered from the deepest cut of all – treachery and sabotage. Before long, many from this band faced HUAC investigations themselves. One of the blacklistees, the writer Albert Maltz, said the Hollywood Ten were heroes. 'If it was a question of choosing to be hero or a shit,' Lardner would rejoin, 'you can't really say the decision not to be a shit is heroic.'

Chapter Six
Hollywood Fights Back – Almost

This malicious propaganda has gone so far that on the fourth of July, over in Madison, Wisconsin, people were afraid to say they believed in the Declaration of Independence. A hundred and twelve people were asked to sign a petition that contained nothing except quotations from the Declaration of Independence and the Bill of Rights. One hundred and eleven of those people refused to sign that paper – many of them because they were afraid that it was some kind of subversive document and they would lose their jobs or be called Communists.

Harry S Truman, 29 July 1951

President Truman, who had refused to order HUAC to pack up its files and its bags, finally realised that matters had gone too far. A group of stars, directors and producers came to the same conclusion almost four years before – when the Hollywood Ten were being investigated in the Caucus Room adjoining the Capitol. But not all maintained that position.

Stage one: they hired a plane and flew to Washington. There, they were the cream of Hollywood – 26 of them, including the *Bogarts*; Humphrey and Lauren (Betty) Bacall, two years after their first film and their first meeting together in 1944's *To Have And Have Not*; *John Huston*, who since the 1930s with masterpieces like *High Sierra* in 1941 and *The Maltese Falcon* the same year and most recently with his *Treasure of the Sierra Madre* starring his father, Walter, was about to prove yet again that he was more than the old man's son; *Larry Adler*, who earned a black mark (which entitled him to a place on the black*list*) for entertaining Russian troops in the war, was one of its conveners and was photographed with this veritable who's who of Tinseltown in a celebrated photograph with the Capitol dome in the background.

There was *Danny Kaye*, about to become the sensation of the London Palladium, the favourite of Princess Margaret and one of the shiniest of shining stars in the Sam Goldwyn stable; there was also *Marsha Hunt*, who always displayed a sort of naughty beauty in her MGM and Paramount pictures, and was once described as Hollywood's youngest character actress. She was also a big radio star in the days when this was the big medium in America and would later be featured in a *Life* cover story – bigger publicity than any star could hope for.

They went to the US capital full of hope for they were about to show that Hollywood was behind its Ten. A statement they issued said: 'We're just Americans who believe in constitutional democratic government. We're protesting the nature of this hearing, because individuals have the right to be free from political inquisition. And we resent any attempt by law or intimidation to censor the movies as a medium of free expression.'

They wanted none of the fascism that they thought HUAC espoused. Their determination was clear from the moment they boarded the chartered plane for the 9-hour flight from the West to the East Coast. The aircraft left the Los Angeles Municipal Airport at 7.45 in the morning and stopped halfway at Kansas City to refuel.

Marsha Hunt remembers that stop as well as the eventual end of the journey. 'You know, when we did our flight, we came down in the dead of night and in the pouring rain. There were hordes of people with umbrellas there to meet the stars. They didn't care about Communism. They just wanted to see Bogart and Bacall and the rest of us.'

There was a tremendous sense of optimism. They really believed that the country was behind them. And events were proving just how far beyond the normal left-wing constituency this support was. Howard Hughes, having taken over RKO, was the epitome of both capitalism and the power of the movie mogul, offered to lend one of his own TWA airliners, but the Federal Aviation Agency forbade it. So contributions from all over the movie industry paid for it. Ironically the name of the chartered plane was Red Star. 'Coincidence,' mused Lauren Bacall later, 'or design?'

Support was so widespread that nobody on board could believe that their effort would do anything but succeed. It was the age when movie stars were the most important people in the world – at least, that was how they were perceived by the fans who went often went two or three times a week to the movies. Few were more popular at the time than Danny Kaye. On the flight, he showed he was as well liked by the people in his business as by the general public. He kept the other stars in fits. 'He was wonderful,' Marsha Hunt remembered for me. There he was, tall, thin, red-headed, twisting his tongue with the list of Russian composers that had been written for him by his wife Sylvia Fine, who was on the flight, too. He manipulated his hands like the Walter Mitty surgeon character he so desperately wanted to be, and did the conga along the aisles for his *tour de force* number 'Manic Depressive Presents' just as when he had featured it in his first film *Up In Arms*.

At that stage, everyone knew just how up in arms the group of stars themselves were. Their recorded voices and those of dozens more could be heard on two radio programmes, transmitted in successive weeks called *Hollywood Fights Back*, written and produced by Norman Corwin. There was Bogart, Bacall, Kaye and Hunt, as well as Evelyn Keyes, still riding high from her co-starring role in *The Jolson Story*; Paul Henreid, still a bankable name five years after *Casablanca* and the 1942 *Now, Voyageur*; Edward G Robinson and Lucille Ball, and over a dozen more. Bogart summed up what they all felt: 'Is democracy so feeble that it can be subverted merely by a look or a line, an inflection or gesture?'

With hindsight, some of the things these stars said can seem either incredibly brave or foolhardy. And amazingly prescient. Streetwise tough-guy John Garfield, who would eventually have a somewhat ambivalent role in the whole business, said, 'If this committee gets a green light from the American people now, will it be possible to make a broadcast like this a year from today?' He did not realise that it probably wouldn't have been possible not just the following year, but perhaps even just a month later. Such was the failure of the celebrities' efforts and the power of HUAC's influence. But they would never have guessed it could all change as quickly as it did.

These were stars laying it on a line many of them would, just a few days later, not have wanted to cross. The programmes were paid for by the specially formed committee for the First Amendment, in other words by the stars themselves. The committee had begun with a massive petition signed by about 400 people – including stars like Lucille Ball, Kirk Douglas, John Garfield, Ava Gardner and Orson Welles; music people like Benny Goodman and Ira Gershwin; entertainers Groucho Marx and Frank Sinatra; and four senators. The petition declared: 'We, the undersigned, as American citizens who believe in constitutional democratic government, are disgusted and outraged by the continuing attempt of the House Committee on Un-American Activities to smear the motion-picture industry. We hold that these hearings are morally wrong because any investigation into the political beliefs of the individual is contrary to the basic principles of our democracy. Any attempt to curb freedom of expression and to set arbitrary standards of Americanism is in itself disloyal to both the spirit and the letter of our constitution.'

The radio programmes were broadcast from each coast on two consecutive weeks: the first after the 26 got to Washington on 26 October and the second, following their return to Los Angeles on 2 November. They said much the same thing. They were written, Marsha Hunt remembered for me, by her husband, the writer Robert Presnell with Norman Corwin and Millard Lampbell, the folk singer who worked with Pete Seeger (another blacklist victim), and Woody Guthrie. The production took place 'in the dead of night at those beautiful headquarters of MCA, and as soon as they'd finish typing out one of them, they'd tear it out of the typewriter and give it to me and say, "This goes to so-and-so, here's the address" and I would drive up into Brentwood or Beverly Hills or Bel Air and hand them their parts.' It was part of the process of what she said was fighting fire with fire.

It all started with a lunch at Lucey's Restaurant on Melrose Avenue in Hollywood, just across the road from RKO and Paramount studios and, therefore, a popular haunt for movie people. Sitting around one of Lucy's immaculately-laid tables, joking about the latest Hollywood gossip, were the directors John Huston and William Wyler, the writer Philip Dunne, co-founder of the Screen Writers' Guild, and the actor Alexander Knox. With jokes and gossip out of the way, they agreed that something had to be done to try to help the men about to face HUAC. 'We were principally concerned,' said Dunne, 'with the assault on civil liberties, what to us looked like persecution of the so-called unfriendly witnesses and the reputations of hundreds of others whose names were being slandered.' And so began The Committee for the First Amendment, with a founding ceremony taking place a few days later at Ira Gershwin's home.

Like Howard Hughes only a short while later, some of the richest people in America, living in its most salubrious addresses, were apparently siding with what HUAC and its supporters would have called a Communist enterprise. That was how it viewed the trip to Washington and the big rally that was held at Los Angeles' Shrine Auditorium. The Shrine was an enormous place, later used for Academy

Award presentations, and there was a whole series of meetings held there, always drawing huge attendances, thanks to the cast of stars who would be on show. The meetings were organised by HICCASP, the Hollywood Independent Citizens' Committee of the Arts, Sciences and Professionals (as distinct from the Academy of Motion Picture Arts and Sciences, which awards the Oscars). The HICCASP was originally designed as a vehicle to get Franklin D Roosevelt re-elected. The group soon turned in a pro-Soviet direction. Among its leading lights were Gregory Peck, John Garfield and Jane Fontaine and her sister Olivia de Havilland. They were all fundraisers – with people like Peck and Garfield passing round the hat or making substantial donations. They were organised like a military operation, co-ordinated partly by Joan LaCour, who later married of one of the Hollywood Ten, Adrian Scott. Among others who joined the stars was Henry Wallace, who had been Roosevelt's vice-president before the 1944 election.

People were on hand to make sure that the stars not known for their political instincts, like Katharine Hepburn, showed up on time and knew what they had to do. There was a feeling among the organisers that perhaps too many of them had hearts in the right place, but were not too sure how to express their feelings. When the decidedly left-wing Henry Wallace took the platform, however, there was a roar of applause from people who obviously did know that he was on their side.

Ironically, one of the stars who worked with them in the early days was Ronald Reagan. Joan Scott's opinion of him remains much like that of other people at the time. 'I have never met a more limited man – to put it politely. He was stupid. He was an actor who made a good speaker, but talking with him before and after events, this was a man who simply was not well informed, not very knowledgeable. He was a kind of personable performer.'

Marsha Hunt remembers him both as a left-wing activist and as a bitter enemy of her cause. When he was a liberal, he had been 'boring' – 'He would buttonhole you at a party and talk liberalism at you. You look for an escape. That arch conservatism was quite an about-face.'

No one believed that the stars, so used to having people fawning over them, would get short shrift from the senators and congressmen they were lobbying and petitioning in Washington. But they would. From a sizeable number of America's lawmakers There was no offer of help.

'We sat in the hearings,' Marsha Hunt told me, 'and it was horrific. There was this huge room, with a lot of shouting, very crowded. It was chilling. The Ten were treated worse than if they had been on trial. But this was not a court of law. What you saw were the highlights – or, rather, the lowlights. It was so theatrical. The committee sat on a very long dais behind a table, all of it chaired by J Parnell Thomas.'

By the time the plane landed back in California, after a flight that was as sombre as the outward journey had been vibrant, a new programme could have been broadcast, called perhaps *Hollywood Takes It Back*, although the second broadcast script was not amended to reflect the change in circumstances.

Stage two: one by one, Kaye, Huston and above all, the Bogarts – more effusive than any of the others – recanted. Bogie himself went on record as saying that his participation in the trip to the nation's capital had been 'ill-advised, foolish.' And he added: 'I detest Communism.' In the March 1948 issue of *Photoplay*, normally just a fan magazine but one now taking on the political complexion of the producers who provided all the material to fill the paper, Bogie said he had been 'duped'.

To Marsha Hunt, it was a case of 'astonishment. Because Bogie had been the most vociferous. He was passionately angry about what was happening with the House Committee. It was baffling. And the fact that the whole movement of defending free speech, freedom of advocacy and privacy of opinion, of how you vote, that's what the secret ballot is supposed to be for.'

She says she was disgusted and felt so betrayed and astonished that she never contacted either of the Bogarts again. 'I never came across them ever again – and I'd played opposite Bogart on radio . . . long before any of this trouble. We all felt so close on this flight. It was strange.'

Bogie's *Photoplay* piece went on to describe himself as 'a foolish and impetuous American . . . As the guy said to the warden just before he was hanged: "This will teach me a lesson I'll never forget." No, sir. I'll never forget the lesson that was taught to me in the year 1947 in Washington DC. When I got back to Hollywood, some friends sent me a mounted fish and underneath it was written, "If I hadn't opened my big mouth, I wouldn't be here."'

Bogart was not the only one. John Garfield declared in another piece, written with the help of a friend, Arnold Forster, but never published, 'I'm A Sucker for a Left Hook'. Surprisingly, in the light of what would soon happen, Edward G Robinson was quoted as declaring: 'The Reds made a sucker out of me.' This was later denied by the same man who had stated in one of the *Hollywood Fights Back* broadcasts: 'It has been broadly suggested that Hollywood pictures are un-American when they make the villain a landlord, a banker or a man with a fancy vest. Well, long before people were being slandered by being called Communists, William S Hart was galloping across the movie screen like a ball of fire to pay off the mortgage on the old homestead and the villain was the town banker or a reasonable facsimile.'

These men had been got at by the studios and told that being part of the Committee for the First Amendment was not conducive to a film star's career. No official blacklist yet, but these were the first threats. The names of those who did not heed the warnings were being inscribed on pieces of paper locked into producers' desk drawers. Within days they knew they would not be working again for some time. Or maybe never again. One such victim was Marsha Hunt, the daughter of a staunch Republican family. She never considered herself political, certainly never a Communist. 'It didn't interest me,' she told me. 'I never went to any Communist meetings. Politics didn't interest me until then . . . They never asked me to their party. I never came to it. There were, it turned out, several people who were members of the Communist Party, but they never pressed it on me.'

Three years after the Washington trip she was told she had been listed in a journal called *Red Channels*, which was a pamphlet-style book issued by the right-wing journal *Counterattack*. It consisted of nothing more than a collection of hundreds of names of people and the organisations to which they were alleged to have belonged, plus perhaps the parades and rallies they might have attended. It was all unofficial and unsubstantiated but enough to end careers with a dab of printer's ink. Actually, it was so unofficial that people could pay to have their names removed from *Red Channels*, though by this point, the die had been cast.

Marsha's listing came as a shock. She heard about it in a phone call with her agent after returning to her hotel from dinner with Eleanor Roosevelt in Paris. Several associations with Communist front organisations were listed. 'Some I'd never heard about, complete lies.' It was that, she said, which sealed her fate. 'I was outraged. I had simply reacted to what had been happening to my field of work. I was punished.'

Other groups or occasions in which she had been involved were 'completely innocent . . . viewed with suspicion.' And so was she. People considered to be friends suddenly shunned her. 'I was libelled by the Hearst Press. But she did nothing about it. I was told that if I made a fuss about it, it would be in the papers again.'

Marsha, like those who reneged and others who refused was asked to 'repent'. Her agent read a statement over the phone which he suggested be issued in her name. It was, she said, 'full of *mea culpa* and what an innocent dupe I had been by making the flight which was really masterminded by Commies. But I said, "It's not true. The flight was not masterminded by the Communists." I was told,' Marsha recounted for me, 'that if I said I was sorry, I could work anywhere that I wanted to.'

But she wasn't sorry and wouldn't say that she was. And thus she couldn't work *anywhere* that she wanted to.

For those who refused to be cowed, there was extreme pain at the defection of people like the Bogarts and Danny Kaye who had been not just so supportive, but so much part of the fabric of the operation. As Marsha Hunt said: 'It was a body blow to our movement. The whole climate faded, the climate was rapidly changing to fear.'

Gene Kelly told her to 'Save your fire for when it matters. You're beginning to be heard.' As Marsha told me: 'Those of us who questioned the sudden preoccupation with Communism, we then became suspect and possibly were reported.'

They could not have known that as they set out for Washington airport. Marsha joined the Committee for the First Amendment, took part in the *Hollywood Fights Back* radio shows and flew to Washington because she believed that fair play demanded it. Hunt's husband was 'a far more long-standing liberal than me. He made me a liberal. I didn't have a grasp of anything. I'd been making movies all of my life, right out of school and into Paramount. There was no time out to learn about the world, but Robert opened my eyes and ears to so much that I had never had a chance to discover.

'I was totally distraught by the defection of people like the Bogarts,' she told me. 'There was this feeling of betrayal. It was a sense not shared by everyone. I flew to Washington not about Communism but because my field was under attack. Movies were being maligned. And it was absurd. You couldn't put propaganda into a film without being caught at it.'

Marsha Hunt now looks back on a 'movement [that] was to defend the First Amendment to the Constitution of the United States.' She was convinced – particularly after the stand of the Screen Actors Guild – that America, 'was neither the land of the free nor the home of the brave.' I asked her about the effect of her involvement on her family. 'If you mean my Republican family, they were in pain. I wish I could say that they rallied. It didn't happen. They didn't back me as I would have hoped and expected. They didn't know enough to understand.'

Other right-wingers wouldn't understand either. Particularly Robert Montgomery, with whom Hunt clashed at board meetings of the Actors Guild. Then there was one of the resident bitches of Hollywood, the columnist Hedda Hopper. She said that all the people who had gone on the flight 'ought to be asked the $64,000 question.' The number-one question in the HUAC arsenal – are they now or had they ever been members of the Communist Party?

So what was Marsha's real crime? The writer Glen Lovell was to put it succinctly and accurately: 'Hunt ruffled feathers simply being Hunt: articulate, involved, a passionate defender of minority rights and eventually a Guild activist. Hunt, like others who protested from the wings, became the victim of innuendo, studio smear tactics – and most demoralizing – the Byzantine politics of her own union.'

Byzantine? Hollywood historians were just beginning to realise that what was happening in Southern California was, in its way, as startling as anything in Byzantium.

Chapter Seven
And Unto the Next Generation

It is apparent that the purpose of the hearing is to try to dictate and control through the device of the hearings, what goes on the screens of America. This is no concern of any Congressional Committee. It is the concern solely of those who produce motion pictures. It doesn't require a law to cripple the right of free speech. Intimidation and coercion will do it. Fear will do it. Freedom simply cannot live in an atmosphere of fear.

Paul V McNutt, special counsel for the Motion Picture Association (MPA),
October 1947

While the anxieties of the Hollywood Ten have been regularly documented, little attention has been paid to the families of the men cited and then sent to jail. All the time that the Ten sat, were harangued and tried to argue, wives and children were suffering along with them. Most of the Hollywood Ten had not been friends before, but as the hearings continued, a distinct bond quite obviously has been formed, a bond that extended to the younger generation, too. Chris Trumbo's children and Paul Jarrico's, for instance, were great friends, Bill Jarrico now recalls. They, in particular, felt their parents' anger. Paul Jarrico himself was asked in a TV interview whether he felt angry about being selected for the blacklist. 'I felt righteous anger,' he said. 'But it was mostly a determination to fight back. It was not just . . . "They can't do this to me." '

This feeling was exacerbated by the way he was treated by Howard Hughes and his lawyers – which was symbolic of the lack of humanity demonstrated by adversaries during the pogrom. Jarrico drove up to the RKO studios just after he appeared before the committee – only to be banned from the lot. It took a few days before he could go there to collect his belongings from what was formerly his office. Sylvia Jarrico says that they anticipated it all. 'Oh yes, Hughes being the person that he was, it was very easy to anticipate. And Paul introduced a suit against him as a formality, a suit because his name was taken off the picture that he'd been working on and he wasn't given credit and his contract was cancelled. So he filed suit. The lawyers for Hughes included people that Paul had gone to school with and I remember this very nice man gave the argument that the Screen Writers Guild has already given the right to the producers to take away credit from those who stand in public obloquy. And he said, "Paul Jarrico has failed to co-operate with the committee and in this way he is considered to be standing public obloquy and therefore he has no right to credit and no right to the fulfilment of his contract".'

Dalton Trumbo was as angry as his friend. And like Jarrico he wanted to do something about it. Christopher Trumbo told Barbra Paskin. 'He was trying to adjust to other people's thoughts and ideas.'

The families were affected as much as the Ten themselves. Michael Cole remembered how his father Lester and mother tried to pull themselves together. 'My parents went to a fair amount of trouble, I think, to try and retain a normalcy about life.' His father spent time in his study, writing. But a happy marriage was no longer possible. 'Whatever my parents were losing sleep over, they did not visit it on us. I appreciate they were having marital problems at this point. They sent us to a very nice school, the nicest place you'd ever want to send your kids . . . My father was traumatised because he wanted to work. He wanted to write screenplays.'

Because of the marital difficulties, Michael and his brother were sent to boarding school even before Lester Cole went to jail. 'It's hard for me to imagine them ever being married, knowing their personalities, because they were so different from each other. And knowing my mother was very shy and very uncertain of herself and my father was not shy and he was hard on people, so it was hard for me to put them together. A tough combination.'

Chris Trumbo said that his parents told him about the hearings. He was then 7 years old. Communism, they explained, was a matter of 'each according to his capacity, each according to his contribution.' As for capitalism, it amounted to hiring labour as cheaply as possible. His sister, he said, became a Communist, but he himself rather liked the idea of capitalism. 'My parents' politics really had to do with American populism and almost nothing with Communism itself. They both came from poor backgrounds.' Most of his father's friends were Communists who provided 'intellectual stimulation'.

What is obvious about the Hollywood Ten and their families was that there were no hard and fast rules about what wives and children knew. Michael Cole says today that he has no idea if his mother shared her husband's political views. 'Maybe she was a member of the party, I have absolutely no idea. I never asked her. I don't think it mattered. She certainly was a person who held the family together while my father was going around being a public figure. It was disastrously difficult for her. First of all, independent of any politics, my father was not an easy man. In particular, he wasn't easy on women – and she was a very attractive person and a very competent person.' So competent, in fact, that she ran for Congress. 'She was a very shy person, so it must have been a terribly difficult thing for her to do.'

As for Michael Cole, he found his own way of being involved. 'From a very young age, I worked. At that time, we sold newspapers on street corners and I did that. So I would sell newspapers where my father was in the newspaper. I thought it was great. I always felt it was something to be proud of and not something to be ashamed of.' Not that life was always easy. 'I did get into trouble in school.' And that was not surprising, as young children heretofore home-schooled had accepted their parents' prejudices – as in the Rodgers and Hammerstein *South Pacific* song, 'You've Got To Be Taught.' It was the time when young black or Jewish children would also suffer their first examples of racial abuse, following examples set at home. Cole explained for this book: 'In elementary school there was a period when somebody said: "Your father is a Communist and you're a terrible person," and I got into a couple of fights in school.' And what did he think that child meant by such statements? 'I understood it was un-American.' It was an understanding of the other children's motives, but not an acceptance of them. He was loyal to his parents and nothing would shake that. 'I told [my father] about it but the thing is look at my view of the thing. What was I supposed to ask him – "Why are they attacking us?" And he would say, "Because these are reactionary people who are racist and I have these beliefs that we should have justice, social justice, economic justice in this country – and look around; you don't see it." I think that's what he believed.'

Michael added: 'If you believe what you're doing is right and if you believe that what you're doing is supported by the Constitution of the United States, if you believe that then you should not have lots of poor people who are mostly black. Is that un-American? I don't think so now and I didn't think so then. So yes, it's unpleasant when somebody hits me and taunts me in the school yard, but I . . . thought I had done something right, and I had a social group where I could live my life without having that intrude upon me much of the time.'

Dan Bessie's brother was taunted at school with the word 'traitor'. He and his tormentor got down to basics – a fist fight. 'My brother was very aggressive at that time and he was not going to take any of that kind of stuff. He was very much upset by what people would say about our father.'

Bessie himself doesn't remember being particularly frightened at that time. 'I was never afraid during that period. I was confused. And I think the confusion came out of being 12 or 14 years old during that era. I was fairly unsophisticated politically and I didn't know much about what Communism was or what my father's politics were. I think I found myself defending him both pre-jail and during the time he was in jail to people without knowledge, but out of loyalty to my father – because my father and mother were divorced and I, of course, was always trying to make a reconnection with him in some way and I found myself sticking up for him and talking through my hat about stuff I didn't even know much about.'

He never thought his father was a criminal, however. 'No, I never thought that . . . I just thought he was getting a dirty deal,' he added, 'I remember the day when they went to the airport, when he went off to jail and I had to take his car to the Screen Writers Guild.'

Alvah Bessie had borrowed money on the car from the SWG and had to return it to partially repay his debt. 'He had several glasses of wine before he left and he left me the car to take back. He was pretty sad. He didn't want to go off to jail, but I think he decided he was going to be true to his convictions, no matter what.'

Dan Bessie had a young wife then. 'They were setting up what we euphemistically called concentration camps or internment centres for subversives and I think we were concerned that our children might suffer from that. So we made provisions for our children in case we were arrested during that period. A lot of people were concerned about that sort of thing.'

The families were concerned about the separation that imprisonment brought. Unlike some families, the Trumbos visited Dalton as often as they could. 'Visiting him in jail was for me a treat,' says his son, Chris. 'There was a machine gun which I thought was great; just like the movies.'

At the time Chris discovered a bitter irony that even a 7-year-old child could appreciate. 'On his second day in prison, I went to the movies [to see] *Call Me Madam*. I discovered I couldn't sit in the balcony, because only black people sit in the balcony. I'm visiting my father for un-American activities, while on the other side of the fence, this is going on.'

The children of the Ten are not obsessed by what happened to their fathers, but they can be forgiven for frequently reflecting on it. Like Michael Cole: 'I don't know how they were selected,' he says today. 'A lot of it was anti-union stuff. They [HUAC] knocked off the heads of a lot of unions.'

This was once the unions had been infiltrated, not by Communists, but by the Mob. The head of the International Alliance of Theatrical Stage Employees which was a right-wing organisation. George Browne and his Hollywood representative, Chicago hood Willie Bioff, took vast amounts of money from studio bosses with the promise that they would limit wage demands. That was after the actor Lionel Stander exposed them and was blacklisted for his efforts. The two men were jailed for extortion – once studio executives admitted it had been a good deal for them. They had saved something like $15 million by going along with the demands.

HUAC 'knocked off' people who had seemingly done very little to subvert the state. Michael Cole put it like this: 'They had people like Jack Lawson, who was a real ideologist. But Alvah Bessie? What did he ever do to anybody? He went and fought in Spain.'

Chris Tumbo remembers a father who 'was never despairing, never an attitude he had adopted; no utility in despair, no utility: "What does it get me? How does it serve me?" Pity may be a sweet brew but afterwards it is poisonous. His attitude was constantly upbeat, almost as if it was a puzzle. It was turned into more of an adventure than it was a tragedy.'

The children were unavoidably exposed to the consequences of what was happening around them. Trumbo's children and those of John Howard Lawson and Lester Cole joined in demonstrations on their fathers' behalf – holding up picket placards proclaiming: 'Free the Hollywood Ten'. 'You knew something was going to happen, and my dad was going to jail,' Michael Cole told Barbra Paskin. Yet there was always something of a mystery about it. 'We thought he was going to Washington and he was away and then he was back. And we would stay with friends. My parents had a large circle of friends and other families who would take care of us.'

Such interruptions to normal life were rarely traumatic. Children have always gone on sleepovers at other people's houses. So there didn't seem to be anything serious in having to do that. Right from the beginning, the children were involved. Says Michael Cole: 'We had other activities we were engaged in that, retrospectively, I knew *were* serious and that we would be going some place where a lot of other people would stuff envelopes that we would send out. I didn't read the documents but they were requests for money or to petition so-and-so.' They were, he said, trying to 'garner support of the community in order to resist the House Un-American Activities Committee. I could stuff envelopes, I could lick stamps.'

As this story unfolds, it is easy to see just how hard it was for the families – to say nothing of how difficult it became to earn a living. Awaiting his impending imprisonment, Dalton Trumbo kept working, often spending whole days in his bath, writing, even if he knew he couldn't submit his work for consideration under his own name. He did something that would become a stock-in-trade of the blacklistees. As his daughter said: 'He started writing motion pictures under other people's names and selling them at extraordinarily cut-rate prices.'

This wasn't the only thing he did, however. Nikola Trumbo says that her father used the time at the ranch, building up provisions to pave the way for the time when he would be sent to jail. Not a very Communistic thing to do. Yet politics had absolutely nothing to do with personal economics. 'We had a huge porch area,' she remembers, 'a larder which he had stocked with all kinds of canned goods – and he bought 200 chickens which he raised and then butchered. He kept 100 for himself and gave 100 to the people who helped him butcher them, so that he was sure we would have enough meat and food . . . We did have a huge freezer. Yes, you could put a body in it!

'We knew it was a possibility that he would have to go to jail and we knew why he would have to go to jail. And so we believed that he was courageous and brave.'

So courageous and brave that she doesn't recall being frightened of his jailing at all. Some were not so fortunate. 'I had a friend in college,' Nikola recalls, 'and he said to me one day, "You know, if your father had been thinking about you kids, he wouldn't have done what he did."' That was, she says now, 'a kind of a stunning perspective for me to think about – and of course, it didn't make any sense to me. Because, if he had become a stool pigeon instead, what kind of role model would that have been?'

As it was, the Trumbo kids were sent to a school especially selected for its integrity. And for the kind of other children who were there. 'They were wonderful,' Nikola now remembers. 'It was quite interesting. It was a four-room schoolhouse and the principal – my parents talked to the principal before my father went to jail – really believed in the system so that nothing came back to us kids. And so we had a very trouble-free couple of years in the school.'

Dan Bessie recalls the friendships between himself and the children of John Howard Lawson and Dalton Trumbo. He went swimming at their houses. Bessie also remembered for Barbra Paskin the fact that his father talked over their mutual problems with Bertold Brecht – 'on the beach at Malibu.'

A great deal of the talking and planning about what to do once faced with the HUAC interrogation happened at social occasions, Dan Bessie remembers. He was only 12 years old, but he went along to those occasions. 'Basically, small talk about what they were doing and about their lives generally. And then I remember later on, as the Hollywood investigations came on, the mood, of course, became somewhat more sombre because they were concerned with not going to jail, or staying out of jail if possible and trying to figure out what kind of thing they could do. Trumbo was, I think, convinced they would go to jail. He saw the handwriting on the wall and he knew what was going on.'

As far as the Bessie children were concerned, a lot was done to make life normal. 'There was never any mention of any problem at all. My sister won the American Legion Award for citizenship while my father was in jail. America is a strange country.' A feeling shared by many of the Hollywood Ten families. Hilda Ornitz now says: 'As a matter of fact, my own son is very proud of his grandfather being one of the Hollywood Ten. We brag about it. We're *very* proud of it.' That is how most of the Hollywood Ten's families felt. Dan Bessie saw the hearings in a cinema. 'I felt very proud of [my father]. I was one of six people in the theatre that afternoon. This was a strange time in America.'

Dan Bessie grew up in time to see wider repercussions of the McCarthy era than merely what was happening in Hollywood. 'I think a lot of us were very concerned that there was something close to a quasi-fascist state going on. I thought that the country was on the edge of something very totalitarian.'

As he said: 'I saw police agents and what I thought were FBI men at public events like at picket lines. I was in a picket line in downtown Los Angeles during the time of the Julius and Ethel Rosenberg execution, for example, and there were police photographers and people taking notes and taking down licence plate numbers. I remember being in a rally at Madison Square Garden in New York . . . in which there were three obvious guys taking notes – they were typical kind of FBI guys, they had the men in grey flannel suits look – and one of them was being converted by the speaker and his other two friends were looking at him pretty oddly and eventually moved away from him.'

There were other occasional instances of when good things came out of the bad. Not least the generosity of friends and of people Dan had no way of knowing. As Bessie remembered: 'My father had gone into the Beverly Hills post office to mail a letter or buy some stamps and he passed a $5 bill across the counter and the man gave him the stamps and then handed him back a $20 bill for change. My father said, "You've given me too much," and the man said, "I know, but it's for the cause." That kind of thing. People who were afraid and didn't want to be known. A couple of teachers when I was in high school told me quietly when they thought I was alone how brave they thought my father was for standing up for his convictions. That kind of thing happened frequently.'

Others helped, too – some of them celebrities, such as Gene Kelly, Dorothy Parker and John Garfield. However, not everyone approached actually did offer help. Like Lee J Cobb, the original Willie Loman in the 1966 TV production of *Death of a Salesman,* who made his biggest impact in impressive screen dramas like *On The Waterfront* in 1954 and *Twelve Angry Men* in 1957 – a role that so impressed Frank Sinatra that, when Cobb was struck by a heart attack, the 'Chairman of the Board' paid for all his medical expenses and gave him a house in which to convalesce.

Dan Bessie remembered the time when Cobb, whom his father regarded as a friend, turned down his request for a loan. 'He said: "Go on being a hero to me, go on being my conscience."' It was a kind of tribute that he would never have been able to take to a bank. Cobb would later name names. Dan Bessie is kind about that. 'A lot of people [named names] because they'd achieved so much stardom or very high salaries and it was important for them to maintain that. I don't know whether their convictions weren't solid to begin with.'

Charlie Chaplin was declared a Red in the midst of the HUAC era and effectively banned from travelling out of the United States. When he finally did sail for England, the country of his birth, it was actually while on the ship that he heard that his passport would no longer be

Dalton Trumbo (left) and John Howard Lawson leave court – their appeals and their hopes denied. (© *Getty Images*)

J. Parnell Thomas, laying down the law – while his cigar and Hollywood hopes burned. Before long, he would go to the same jail as two of his victims.
(© *Getty Images*)

Arthur Miller and Marilyn Monroe. The HUAC chairman wanted to have his picture taken with the star. Both made it clear that her only companion was going to be her husband.
(© *Getty Images*)

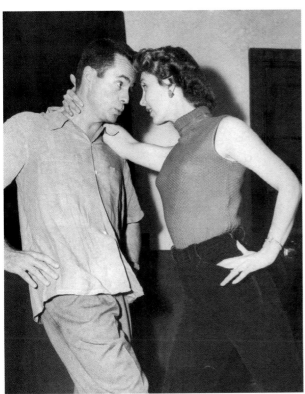

Larry Parks and Betty Garrett – dancing to a new career once HUAC had destroyed their chances of super stardom. He claimed he was made to 'crawl in the mud'. She stood by the man who was more cruelly treated than either could have imagined.

(© *Getty Images*)

Ring Lardner junior.
The public face.
(© *Getty Images*)

Elia Kazan. The director who ratted.
(© *Getty Images*)

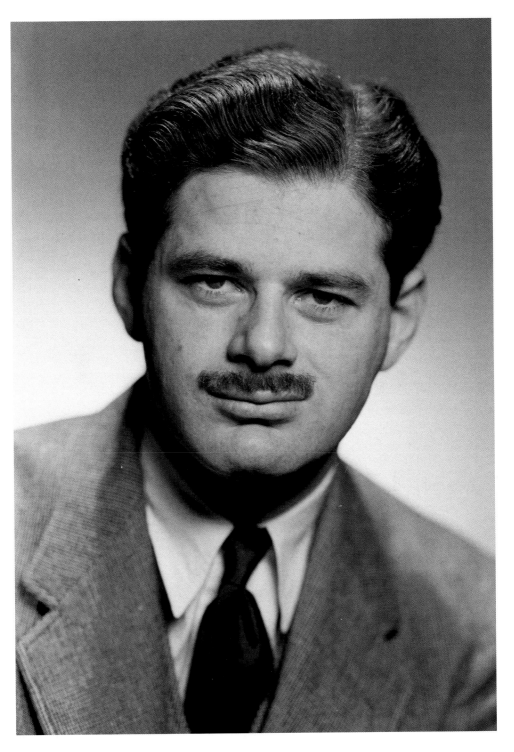

A young Norman Corwin. 'The country was in hysteria.'
(© *Getty Images*)

The beautiful people – Gene Kelly and Betsy Blair. At Cannes. She wanted to join the party. He said No.
(© *Getty Images*)

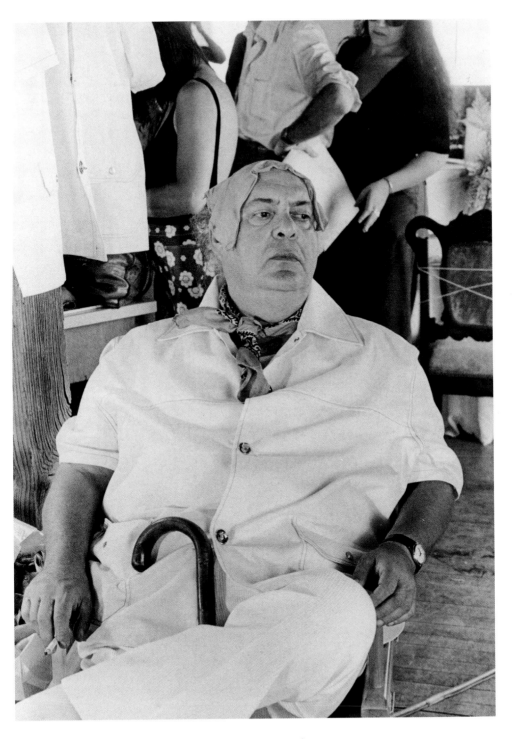

Zero Mostel. He was humiliated – but had the last word.
(© *Getty Images*)

Danny Kaye, Humphrey Bogart, June Havoc and Lauren 'Betty' Bacall. They were enthusiasts for the Committee for the First Amendment. Later, it became 'inconvenient'.
(© *Getty Images*)

recognised in the United States. This, in effect, barred him from ever returning to his American home and to the country where he had made his international fame and fortune.

Alvah Bessie had the idea of Chaplin starring as Don Quixote in a film he was writing. He went to see the great star when he was playing tennis with the former champion Bill Tilden, a man whose own career had been ruined when he was found in a compromising situation with a famous actor.

'Chaplin,' Dan Bessie remembered, 'finished his tennis game . . . took a shower and came in and sat with my father and listened with very great interest to the outline of the Don Quixote plot my father told him. Then he said he couldn't tamper with a classic . . . So he walked him up to the gate and shook his hand, then turned around and went back into the house. [Then my father saw] there was $100 in his hand.' It was a small gesture from the British actor that has stayed with Dan ever since.

There were rallies for the Hollywood Ten at the famous local Gilmore Field. Before the football game started, a list of donations was read out – including $1,000 from Charlie Chaplin.

People like Bessie would have preferred not to hold out a begging bowl. 'But,' says his son, 'he needed the money to support his family. He wasn't working at all for months and months at a time.' Politically he says he stands by what his father and the other HUAC victims themselves stood for: 'I think it was all-American.'

Chapter Eight
Larry Sings Again

The Un-American Committee – it goes back in centuries. There was an Un-Italian Committee that subpoenaed Galileo. A Committee of Un-French Activities that subpoenaed Joan of Arc and an Un-New England Committee that burned women in Salem. Out of 2,000 years of men fighting and dying, came the idea of justice in a document called the Bill of Rights.

Actor Robert Young in *Hollywood Fights Back*, 1947

Larry Parks was a young man whose whole career had been full of surprises. Parks was incredibly good-looking, but hadn't made the impact that most people expected when he was first signed up by Columbia Pictures. He was perennially assigned to B pictures like *Blondie Goes to College* in 1942 and *Reveille With Beverly* the folowing year, which also featured another youngster who had failed to excite movie audiences by the name of Frank Sinatra. Parks was a very good actor, but somehow the critics didn't notice. And then, in 1946, came a little thing called *The Jolson Story*.

It made him a superstar – at least it probably would have made him a superstar had not the real, unseen Al Jolson got a whole bundle of plaudits for the songs he recorded for the movie. Jolson had called himself the World's Greatest Entertainer – and for 30 years nobody challenged him. He had an ego that went with the size of his audiences, a man who could dismiss an entire cast in the middle of a show and cry to the audience: 'Do you want to see them, or do you want to hear me?' They always chose him. But then the singer, who made his reputation by performing songs like 'Rockabye Your Baby With A Dixie Melody' and 'Swanee' in blackface and had starred in 1927's *The Jazz Singer* (the world's first talkie), fell out of favour. As a result of *The Jolson Story*, however, he was back and bigger than ever – and so was his ego. But it wasn't all bad for Larry Parks. People at last took notice of the fellow who was now even better-looking than before, a better actor than even those who always knew he was good dared imagine.

Parks was dark-haired and with an engaging smile that was almost a style. You could recognise him beneath the blackface make-up he wore in his big film – by that smile and an engaging wink. At 32, Sam Kleusman Lawrence Parks was the perfect leading man. He could convince audiences that he was Al Jolson and still keep his own personality intact. *The Jolson Story* was a triple triumph – as a picture it was the second biggest box-office hit of 1946. It resurrected the career of an almost-forgotten star of the 1920s and 30s and catapulted him to the number-one pop music spot, which he held until his death four years later. And it gained Larry Parks the recognition he deserved. The critics were enamoured of his performance – not least by a feat that in another actor might have attracted derision: his miming of the voice and songs of a generation before his. That was no mere achievement; it was a triumph. Other actors had done it before, of course – 'straight' players who did little more than move their lips in what they hoped would be synchronisation with the songs. Parks did much more than that. He sang at the top of his own voice – while speakers blasted out Jolson's even louder; so much louder that Parks sounded like Jolson, even to himself. One critic noted 'You could even see the fur on his tongue.'

The only person who didn't rejoice in Larry Parks's achievements was 60-year-old Jolson himself, who was frightened that the younger man would take some of the glory that should have been his; besides, he thought that only Jolson could play Jolson. But Harry Cohn, the iron dictator of Columbia Pictures, loved him. The girls loved him, and the Academy of Motion Picture Arts and Sciences loved him and he was nominated for an Oscar.

The fan magazines, so important to the success of a star's career, couldn't get enough of Parks. They ran piece after piece about him. Many of those articles were devoted to the Parks' home life and his pretty actress wife, Betty Garrett, who had been a Broadway success and would make her own screen debut two years after *The Jolson Story*, in *Big City*. The whole thing was a surprise, but a welcome one. The biggest surprise came thanks to the Chairman of HUAC, J Parnell Thomas. Being called to the Caucus Room in Washington as one of the Hollywood Nineteen looked likely to end everything for Parks just as it was beginning. He went to answer charges that he was a Communist at the very time when it seemed clear that such an admission was virtually professional suicide. His Communist Party associations were well-known in the film town. He had been involved in the Mobile Theater in Hollywood. Mary Davenport, wife of the blacklisted writer Waldo Salt, said: 'We were a bunch of left-wing actors. As a collective we were making ourselves sound like the collectives in New York. Larry was under contract to Columbia and most of what we lived on was Larry's salary.'

But it hadn't seemed to have adversely affected his career. Larry wasn't called to the committee that session and Harry Cohn kept him on the payroll. Of course, he knew how bankable Parks was, that his name spelt big box office.

There were rows over contract details, and Parks made other pictures. None of them was particularly sensational. Strangely for a man who had been so popular playing a living entertainer he was put in a couple of swashbuckling epics in 1948: *The Swordsman* and *The Gallant Blade*. Then in 1949 came the sequel to the picture which had made him the big, big star – *Jolson Sings Again*. It wasn't *quite* as good as *The Jolson Story*, but it was good enough to be the most successful musical of the year and, again, his miming of Jolson's voice couldn't be bettered. He had confounded the fears of all those who believed the much put-about stories of HUAC's power to ruin Hollywood personalities. And then it happened: in 1951, the committee announced it was going back into the business of investigating Communist influence in Hollywood. And it would start where it had left off in Washington – with Larry Parks.

It would prove to be one of the cruellest moves the chairman, John S Wood, ever made. It also proved that giving the committee what it wanted would never be enough.

'We knew,' Betty Garrett told me, 'that if the committee continued, [Larry] would be called again. [J Parnell] Thomas had said, "This is only the beginning." So we never felt completely at ease.'

For the second time, a pink slip was delivered to the Parks' home. 'We were suspicious that they were taking advantage of Larry's great publicity at the time.' Suspicious and shocked. 'It's a shock to find out that someone is going to question your beliefs. It was inconceivable.' But it happened.

Betty Garrett had been a Communist at the same time as her husband. Both believed that it was the only Party dealing with the problems affecting the poor and the under-privileged. 'It was very difficult to know what to do because Larry felt that because he had been a member of the Communist Party and so had I, because we believed in the causes

they were supporting, all of those causes that we so devoutly believed in
. . . it didn't seem fair at all.' Actually, she thought she was also on
HUAC's hit-list and would be called, too. 'I think Larry found out later
that there were possible plans for calling me at the same time. But I
think they believed,' she told me, 'that summoning a nine-month
pregnant lady wouldn't look good for them.'

It was because she was so heavily pregnant that she was unable to
take the flight with her husband from Los Angeles Municipal Airport
to Washington DC. Today, Betty says she can't remember much about
the day her husband left for the nation's capital. 'I just, I guess, hugged
and kissed him goodbye and hoped for the best.'

The truth is that she remained with her mother and friends in their
home in Nichols Canyon in the Hollywood Hills while Larry prepared
to suffer the indignities enforced on him in room 226 of the Old House
Office Building on Capitol Hill. From afar, she had to experience the
hostility of the media. The press had a great time with all that was
presented to them. Said Betty: 'There were headlines two or three inches
high, bigger than the headline about MacArthur being sent home by
Truman' [General Douglas MacArthur, at the head of US Forces in
Korea, had wanted to invade China – the President, who hated the
vainglorious general, used the plan as an excuse to fire him.] In other
words, it was big, big news. And I always thought the committee knew
that it would be, because Larry was a public figure.'

They had talked about what was likely to happen. 'Oh, it broke my
heart. Larry was in agony up there . . . he believed he should say, "Yes,
I belonged to the Communist Party, but it is not illegal."'

By the time Larry appeared before the committee, Betty had given
birth to their second son, Andy. The birth only made the separation of
the couple, while knowing what was going on in Washington, all the
more painful. 'He ended up making a very eloquent speech saying he
did not want to betray friendship, that it was not an American thing
to do that. There were photographs of him when he really had tears in
his eyes.'

And tears were in Betty's eyes, too, as she heard the testimony on the
radio. 'I howled,' was how she put it to me. 'Oh yes.' The main emotion,
she said, was anger. 'I was just mad. It broke my heart. It was
heartbreaking because it was so hard for him. He broke down crying in
the middle of it. It was just too much.'

Too much of a lesson in what could happen when names are named. It
was going to be a dramatic moment, that was clear. How pressing, how

cruel HUAC's hearings could be was scarcely imaginable. Even the drama of the Hollywood Ten's proceedings had none of the sadness, the sheer wickedness, exhibited in Parks' treatment before the committee.

It began innocently enough on 21 March 1951, as Larry sat in the room with his lawyer and confidant Louis Mandel at his side. They were faced with an exercise in wheedling information to the point of gross intimidation.

The committee counsel, Frank Tavenner, set the tone at the very beginning with a seemingly polite, kind and simple question. He asked him: 'Mr Parks, what is your present occupation?' Larry answered: 'Actor.' From thereon in, it got nasty – with the ever-asked question, 'Are you now, or have you ever been, a member of the Communist Party?'

Parks: 'I am not a Communist. I was a member of the Communist Party when I was a much younger man, ten years ago.'

Tavenner: 'Do you know the names of the writers and actors in Hollywood who were members of any branch of the Communist Party?'

Parks: 'I only know the names of people who attended certain meetings that I attended . . . These were people like myself, small type people, no different than myself . . . These are people who did nothing wrong, people like myself.'

John S Wood: 'Mr Parks, in what way do you feel it would be injurious to them to divulge their identities, when you expressed the opinion that at no time did they do wrong?'

Parks: 'On the question of naming names, it is my honest opinion that the few people that I could name, these names would not be of service to the committee at all. I am sure you know who they are . . . And to be called before this committee at your request has a certain inference, a certain innuendo that you are not loyal to this country. That is not true. I am speaking for myself . . . I also feel that to be asked to name names like this is not in the way of American justice as we know it, that we as Americans have all been brought up . . . that it is a bad thing to force a man to do this. This is not American justice.'

Tavenner: 'Do you know a person by the name of Elizabeth Glenn?'
Parks: 'No.'

But he said he had met Lionel Stander, when that name was mentioned. He was virtually being given the opportunity to fall into a neatly set trap; he could have agreed to the committee members suggesting 'we understand why, without your realising it, you did some-thing "wrong".' Parks was not about to go along with the strategy. 'No,' he maintained, 'again I say that I will make no apologies for what I did.'

The Chairman Harold Velde responded: 'I don't think you are answering my question, Mr Parks.'

Tavenner would vary his approach to the actor. Later in the proceedings, a question began with the words, 'Now, Mr Parks,' as though talking to a naughty schoolboy who had joined a playground gang without realising the consequences. 'Who were the other members of the Communist Party cell to which you were assigned from 1941 on up to the time you left the party about 1945?'

Larry Parks wasn't about to answer that sort of question.

He was asked if he had been connected with the Actors Laboratory. He replied: 'I have. I was for a time honorary treasurer. I emphasise the word 'honorary'. My job was to sign a bunch of cheques. That was the extent of my knowledge of the money matters of the Lab.'

He was then asked if there were Communists in the organisation. 'There *were* Communists,' he answered.

The inquisitors liked that. It could only lead to the kind of incriminating evidence they needed. 'Were those party members trying to exert control?'

'No,' Parks emphasised. 'The Lab was a school of acting and a sort of showcase for actors.'

But what about that membership of the party? That had to be incriminating, didn't it?

'I was a member in 1941. Being a member of the party fulfilled the needs of a young man that was liberal in thought, idealistic . . . who was for the underprivileged, the underdog. I felt that it fulfilled these particular needs. I think that being a Communist in 1951 in this particular situation is an entirely different kettle of fish, when this is a great power that is trying to take over the world.'

Surely that would be enough. He was saying what they wanted to hear. Could a statement be more friendly to this committee? One which agreed that the Soviet Union was the obvious enemy. Enough? Not to HUAC it wasn't. So the actor expanded the thought: 'This is in no way an apology for what I have done, because I feel I have done nothing wrong – ever . . . In 1941, the purposes, as I knew them, fulfilled simply – at least, I thought they would fulfill, as I said before a certain idealism, a certain feeling of being for the underdog, which I am today. Which I still am at this very minute. This didn't work out. I wasn't particularly interested . . . I attended very few meetings and I petered out the same way I drifted into it. I petered out about the latter part of 1944 or 45.'

The underhand way in which the committee operated was demonstrated by 'facts' it produced. His membership number was 46944 in 1944 and the following year, 47344. Not true, said Parks. 'Because I never had a party card.'

He was recruited, he said, by a man called Davidson in California, but couldn't remember the circumstances. 'I certainly didn't seek him out.'

The committee wanted details. Were the meetings held at people's homes or in halls? In homes, he replied. Could Parks say whose homes they were? He could not – or rather, he *would* not. But why would it be injurious for him to give this information?

This was when he thought he had to come to the defence not just of himself, but of the entire movie business. It was also when he first began wearing his heart on his well-tailored sleeve. 'If you think it's easy for a man who has . . .' he said, without needing to complete the sentence. 'If you think it's easy for me to appear before this Committee and testify, you're mistaken . . . One of the reasons is that as an actor my activity is dependent a great deal on the public. To be called before this committee at your request has a certain inference, a certain innuendo that you are not loyal to this country. This is not true . . . but the inference and the innuendo are there as far as the public is concerned.'

Parks was asked if he didn't think that the public was entitled to know about the role people played in public life. 'I certainly do,' he responded. 'And I'm opening myself wide open.' His desperation was showing in the colour of the language he was using. 'It's like taking a potshot at a wounded animal – because the industry is not in as good a shape today as it has been, economically.'

He wanted no suggestions that he was disloyal to his business any more than there could be any inference of being anti-American. 'This is a great industry,' he said. This was someone who appeared so different from the man whom the public had seen singing 'Mammy' in blackface, 'Swanee' or 'Give My Regards To Broadway'. At that moment, he would have loved to have been on Broadway himself, watching a simple, non-mind-bending show. The one in which he was involved was a performance he dearly didn't want to make, a starring role he wished had gone to somebody else.

Name names?

'This is not American justice . . . It is a bad thing to force a man to do this. I am asking you not to press me on this.'

He would name the names of people who had done wrong. He would 'name instantly' a murderer if he knew one – 'because murder is against

126

the law of the land. As for Communists, being a member of the Communist Party is not against the law of the land.' He thought Communist Party members were 'guiltless.'

If they were guiltless, why would it hurt to divulge the names? He answered obliquely. 'I've worked hard in my profession . . . I've climbed the ladder . . . if you think this is easy . . .' As he said: 'The few people I knew are as loyal to this country as you are. The best you could accuse them of is lack of judgement.' And Parks went on, demonstrating how willing he was to give evidence that was worthwhile and justified. 'I have come 3,000 miles and opened myself as I have –' He wasn't allowed to finish the sentence.

Plainly, this would not be enough for the counsel or members of the committee. Francis E Walter asked him: 'Were you instructed to attempt to influence the American people through various exhibitions on the stage or on the screen?

Parks: 'I was never instructed at any time to do this. It's impossible to do this as an actor . . . A script passes through too many hands . . . They think if one man is good for jokes, they put him in for jokes. And another man, if they want a tearjerker, they will assign him to that particular portion of it. It goes to an associate producer, a producer, the heads of the studios . . . and it is my opinion, it is my personal opinion, my studied opinion, that this is an impossibility.'

The hearing was proceeding as everyone now expected. But then Parks broke off to discuss the situation quietly – or at least as quietly as was possible in this noisy room – with his lawyer. A big change was in view; the denouement in the drama. Louis Mandel took the microphone and addressed the committee: 'Mr Parks would like to say about naming names.' It was more than Congressman Wood or his fellow members could have hoped for.

Now came the most telling, the most touching, the saddest moment of the hearing, but one which made people sit up sharply. 'Mr Chairman,' Parks began, 'I chose to come and tell the truth about myself . . . So I beg of you not to force me to do this. Don't present me with the choice of either being in contempt of this committee and going to jail or forcing me to really crawl through the mud, to be an informer, for what purpose? I chose to come – to do this.'

He told Tavenner: 'This is what I have been talking about . . . that I am no longer fighting for myself because I tell you frankly that I am probably the most completely ruined man that you have ever seen. I am fighting for a principle . . . These are not people that are a danger to this country.'

Making him name names, he said, was 'more akin to what happened under Hitler, or what is happening in Russia today.' That could have been read as a criticism of Communism and in support of the committee's ethics. He also said: 'There was another choice open to me. I did not choose to use it. I chose to come and tell the truth about myself.'

His statement became more personal. 'My people have a long heritage in this country. They fought in the Revolutionary War to make this country, to create *this* government of which this committee is a part. I have two boys, one thirteen months, one two weeks. Is this the kind of heritage I must pass down to them? Is this the kind of heritage you would like to hand down to *your* children? For what purpose? I don't think I would be here today if I weren't a star because you know as well as I, even better, that I know nothing that would be of great service to this country.'

It was not 'sportsmanlike', he said. 'I don't think this is American. I don't think this is American justice for an innocent mistake in judgement . . . If it was that, with the intention behind it only of making this country a better place in which to live . . . If you do this to me, it will make it almost impossible for a person to come to you as I have done and open himself to you and tell you the truth. So I beg you not to force me to do this.'

The committee was loath to allow this golden opportunity to get away. They were going to do all the forcing they could, to press for more details, above all, for names. There was one consolation for Parks – or, at least, that was the way HUAC saw it. It would go into private session. It would take two years before details of that session were revealed. Mandel asked for the ground rules to be spelt out. 'Is it your intention,' he asked the committee, 'that unless he speaks in private, to hold him in contempt?'

'It is possible,' the chairman told him in the usual kind of bureaucratic officialese, 'that the committee may respect a citation.' In other words, probably.

Mandel responded: 'Mr Parks feels so bad,' he said. And the reason was clear. It was a matter of self respect not to give the committee what it said it needed. 'It is only saving that little bit of something that you live with. You have to see and walk in Hollywood with that. You have to meet your children, and your wife with it and your friends. It is that little bit that you want to save.'

The committee was unsympathetic. They wanted names – names which Betty told us they had already, but which they wanted to hear coming from Parks' mouth.

Tavenner asked Larry: 'If you will just answer the question, please. Who were the members of the Communist party cell to which you were assigned during the period from 1941 until 1945?'

There was quiet for a moment. 'Mr Parks, we're waiting.'

He conferred again with Louis Mandel. It was time to name names. Parks: 'Well, Morris Carnovsky, Joe –'

Tavenner: 'Will you spell that name?'

Parks: 'I couldn't possibly spell it. Carnovsky, Joe Bromberg, Sam Rossen, Anne Revere, Lee J Cobb –'

Walter: 'What was that name?'

Parks: 'Cobb, Gale Sondergaard, Dorothy Tree. Those are the principal names that I recall.'

Tavenner: 'Was Howard Da Silva a member?'

Parks: 'No. I don't believe that I ever attended a meeting with Howard Da Silva.'

Tavenner: 'Was James Cagney a member at any time?' (Later, this would be used to show how absurd the questioning was getting.)

Parks: 'Not to my knowledge. I don't recall ever attending a meeting with him.'

Tavenner: 'John Garfield?'

Parks: 'I don't recall ever being at a meeting with John Garfield.'

More names were read out. He believed that Marc Lawrence was a Communist. Karen Morley again? 'Yes, she was.'

Committee members lined up to name names that they wanted him to confirm. George Georgia Backus? Robert Rossen? Philip Loeb? Sterling Hayden? Will Geer? Andy Devine? Edward G Robinson? He didn't recall. Gregory Peck? 'I have no remembrance of ever attending a meeting with Gregory Peck.' (Certainly not a party meeting, Peck told me.) 'I don't ever recall attending a meeting with Humphrey Bogart,' he answered when Bogie's name joined the list rapped out by almost every member of the committee.

That was the point when what Parks knew was made official. Walter told him: 'I think you could get some comfort out of the fact that the people whose names have been mentioned here have already been subpoenaed, so that if they ever do appear here, it won't be as a result of anything that you have testified to.'

The absurdity of the whole affair was now spelled out. Parks was anything but mollified. 'It is no comfort whatsoever,' he replied.

Chairman Wood said: 'There can be no odium attached to persons who have made a mistake and seek to rectify it. If there were, we would give the lie to the advent of Jesus Christ in this world, who came here for the purpose of making possible forgiveness upon repentance.'

'I think that is all, Mr Chairman,' said Tavenner.

Charles E Potter concluded: 'I would like to say, Mr Chairman, that Mr Parks's testimony has certainly been refreshing in comparison with the other witnesses that we have had today.'

And looking at Parks, Chairman Wood told him: 'We appreciate your co-operation. You are excused. You do not have to remain here.'

He couldn't get away quickly enough. And that was the same with his career. His contract with Columbia was up for renewal. It was not renewed. In fact, those terrible hours before the committee ended one of the most promising careers in Hollywood. He would have been damned if he hadn't named names. Now he was damned *for* naming them. Parks had simply upset too many people on both sides – the committee for showing that he saw no crime in being a Communist, which blighted him with the studios; his colleagues for doing what many of them would not do, for naming names that the committee already knew and in doing so, he legitimised the whole HUAC operation.

He had been treated monstrously in order to give the committee legitimacy, certainly not to aid national security. But unlike some others, he refused to say that his sympathy for causes the Communist Party believed in was a mistake. Parks stood by the fact that he felt it helped the underprivileged.

Before long, it became apparent that Parks's name had been added to a blacklist – and that would go for his wife, too. But this wasn't his only concern. Betty Garret told us about the original effects of the hearing. Louis Mandel, who was his manager as well as his lawyer, took him to Florida for a few days. 'He realised how humiliated Larry was and how upset he was – and rather than come straight home . . . they went fishing and did all kinds of things like that.'

Back home, he tried to adjust to a completely new life. 'We both went on as if we were just a regular husband and wife taking care of our kids. They were in nursery school a couple of years later and Larry was like one of the mothers. He would do the carpooling and do the substitute teaching that the mothers did . . . oh, he loved all that. Larry was a very advanced husband and father. He encouraged me to work all the time and was my best and biggest supporter. He was the kind of husband who washed the dishes and bathed the kids.'

And there were Hollywood people who offered comfort and solace. There was their close friend Lloyd Bridges and the arch-conservative actor and future senator, George Murphy, who might have been thought of as a HUAC friendly. 'I must say I always loved George Murphy,' recalls Betty. 'When my husband was called, he was very kind and very lovely to me.' But, surprisingly to them both, this was not the complete story. 'Larry felt that we should all say, "Yes, we were [Communists], so what?" But people who didn't testify felt that Larry betrayed them. What happened was that a lot of people who had been our best friends shunned us in the street or in the grocery store. That broke my heart. Very often it was the wives who would come up to me and embrace me, and the guys who held it against Larry. I've seen Larry just get up and walk away. He couldn't bear to deal with it.'

There were other surprises on the way.

Betty and Larry decided to go on the road with a song and dance act. In Las Vegas, memories were recalled in a bizarre way when they came face-to-face with a man sitting at a restaurant table near them. 'We were playing at the Rancho Vegas, I believe, and the maitre d' came backstage and said that Senator McCarthy would like to buy us a drink.' Of course, Larry had had no direct association with McCarthy, but it was the heart of the McCarthyism period and the junior senator was emblematic of what had happened to him. 'Larry looked at me and said, "What do you want to do?" And I said, "I don't want to have a drink with the old sonofabitch." But Larry was a person with a great curiosity and he said, "I want to go out and talk to this man." So we went out and there he was in a big leather booth, drunk out of his skull, I'll tell you – and the first thing he did was show us his kidney scar. The funny part of this story is that the next morning Larry and I got up and my mother [who] was with us [had] taken the kids, who were then about 4 and 5, out to the swimming pool. And when we went down, there they were in the water, and there was Senator McCarthy showing them how to swim.'

Soon after Larry's appearance before HUAC, Betty told me she went to a luncheon, 'a preliminary meeting to a charity ball.' Like many film stars, and particularly those who were wives of stars, she was on the charity circuit, helping to organise functions, dinners and sales. 'All of us were there, all the MGM actresses, Debbie Reynolds, you name them. It was up at Pickfair, Mary Pickford's home. We were discussing who was to head certain tables at this big banquet. We all gave our names and a woman just ahead of me, gave her name and said, "I think I'll give my husband's name as head of the table." So when it came to me, they said "Betty Garrett." I said that it would be nice if it were Mr and Mrs Larry Parks.'

She gave it no further thought, but there were others there who had other considerations. 'Later, I met Ida Koverman, Louis B Mayer's secretary. She came up to me and said, "You idiot. What was that all about?" Next thing I get a telephone call from a woman who said that I am not invited to have a table at the banquet and it was decided that because of the testimony of my husband, I would not be a good name to be connected to this charitable event. I was at the dinner table when I got this phone call, and my husband got on the phone and just laced into this poor lady. She said it was not her idea. It was a very humiliating experience. It didn't hurt me not to be part of this charity event. It was that when this sort of thing came out in the open, I realised that there was a conservative attitude about social things. I remember bursting into tears and my husband getting so very angry. These kind of things happened quite frequently and it was devastating.'

Larry had different words for it. *Newsweek* reported; 'Parks was sick at heart and sick in bed.' But there were other words that he himself put in writing. At about the same time that the transcript of the private executive session was released, Parks wrote a letter to the then chairman of the committee Harold Velde and authorised its release for publication. The letter appeared to show that he regretted what he had said at the hearing. Not only that, he now offered HUAC his help to 'expose the methods of entrapment and deceit through which Communist conspirators have gained the adherence of American idealists and liberalists.'

The really bitter pill was in the following sentence: 'If I were to testify today, I would not testify as I did in 1951 – that to give such testimony is to "wallow in the mud" – but on the contrary, I would recognise that such co-operation would help further the cause in which many of us were sincerely interested when we were duped into joining and taking part in the Communist Party.'

It would have been only natural to think that this was an attempt at getting back to work in a film studio. But not even a climb-down of this magnitude – in an age when film makers were bending over backwards, sideways and in every other direction to show that they hated the Reds as much as they would detest someone who tried to kill their own mother, was easy to understand.

So much more was involved. Perhaps the singer Lena Horne summed it up when she said: 'Larry's taking the rap for a lot of us.'

Chapter Nine
The Second Inquisition

The only red we want is the red we've got – in the good ol' red, white and blue.

Anti-Communist rally song from the 1950s

This was war, waged incessantly by the people who claimed that their principal aim in trying to outlaw Communism was to prevent the Soviets bringing revolution and hostilities to the United States. The tactics employed by HUAC were familiar to any military strategist – start stealthily and if you succeed, march ahead. And as you do so, see your enemy crumble and proceed to the next battle.

After the Hollywood Ten and following the Larry Parks débâcle, HUAC was secure. The little mishap over Congressman J Parnell Thomas's money problems apart, it was winning all the way. In truth, they couldn't believe their luck. Nearly all the people they thought would rally against them suddenly became allies. Small men with small minds triumphed over the supposed power and the undoubted money of the studios. The producers and actors who had seemed so full of principles were putty in the hands of a committee which would prove to have done nothing for the good of the nation it constantly said it represented.

One of the first to face the big guns of HUAC after the Parks appearances was Gale Sondergaard, who went to Hollywood when she married Herbert Biberman, her second husband. That would have been enough to incriminate her in the eyes of the committee, but there was more. She was a Communist herself. As in the case of Larry Parks, the publicity value of her appearances before HUAC would be worth more than anything she could say. The tall, dark, unusually attractive actress, whose look was so sinister it had scared impressionable actors, was ideal fodder for the committee. Sondergaard had played in numerous straight movies, ranging from *Anthony Adverse* (for which in 1936 she became the first recipient of the Best Supporting Actress Oscar) and *The Life of Emile Zola* in 1937 to a string of Bob Hope comedies, all in her stereotyped sinister role. She received a subpoena, but before the scheduled hearing in October 1951, she asked the leaders of her union, SAG, to help:

Dear Board Members,

I am addressing you of the Board not only as the directors of our union but also as fellow actors. I am addressing you because I have been subpoenaed together with other members of our union before the un-American Activities Committee. I will appear next Wednesday.

I would be naïve if I did not recognise that there is a danger that by the following day I may have arrived at the end of my career as a motion-picture actress. Surely it is not necessary for me to say to this Board that I love my profession and that I have tried to bring to it honesty of feeling, clarity of thought and a real devotion. Surely, it is also unnecessary for me to state that I consider myself a deeply loyal American, with genuine concern for the welfare and peace of my own countrymen and all humanity.

Today, I read that this particular inquisition is not directed against the industry but is directed at individuals. This would seem to imply that any number of individual actors could be destroyed without injuring the industry – and that employers having been guaranteed they would not be personally involved, have given the committee *carte blanche* to attack individuals to their own purpose.

I most earnestly and fraternally ask the board to consider the implications of the forthcoming hearing. A blacklist already exists. It may now be widened. It may ultimately be extended to include any freedom-loving nonconformist or any member of a particular race or any member of a union – or anyone.

For my own security – for the security of all our members, I ask our Board to weigh this hearing carefully – to determine whether it can afford to witness its approach with passivity. I can find no reason in my conduct as an actress or as a union member why I should have to contemplate a severing of the main artery of my life: my career as a performer.

The reply from the union summed up the amazing success of HUAC. Not only was the actors' own guild not willing to help one of its members, it gave all the support to the committee that it could possibly wish. It rejected the term 'inquisition'. It disagreed with the Communist Party press for describing HUAC's activities as a 'warmongering, labor- and freedom-busting . . . witch-hunt by Congressional inquisitors.'

As the union representative put it: 'The Guild Board totally rejects this quoted typical Communist party line. We recognise its obvious purposes of attempting to smear the hearings in advance and to create disrespect for the American form of government. Like the overwhelming majority of the American people, we believe that a "clear and present danger" to our nation exists. The Guild Board believes that all participants in the international Communist Party conspiracy against our nation should be exposed for what they are – enemies of our country and of our form of government.'

For a brief moment, there was the suggestion that SAG would support its members. But the letter went on: 'The Guild as a labour union will fight against any secret blacklist created by any group of employers. On the other hand, if any actor by his own actions outside of union activities has so offended American public opinion that he has made himself unsaleable at the box office, the Guild cannot and would not want to force any employer to hire him. That is the individual actor's personal responsibility and it cannot be shifted to his union.'

Sonnergaard duly appeared – and was blacklisted.

The actions of SAG were so very different from the philosophy of the guild when it had first been established. In 1934, the second president, Eddie Cantor, said its very setting up was due to Franklin Delano Roosevelt's New Deal. It was an organisation which would work sympathetically with every other group, 'striving to attain the general betterment of working conditions through the entire field of motion-picture activity.'

To complain about the way SAG had changed was to go on a journey that led to being blacklisted yourself. The character actress Anne Revere, who specialised in playing homely motherly figures, wrote to fellow board members:

'You, the Board of the Screen Actors Guild, point with pride to your seven-year fight against the Communist conspiracy. What have you accomplished? You have sanctioned the blacklist of 23 of your fellow members because they chose to defy an unconstitutional investigation into their thoughts and beliefs. Have you given strength to the industry by depriving those artists of their art and bread? Or have you further incapacitated the industry and the art which you profess to nourish? For seven years you have purged the screen of "dangerous ideas." With what results? The world leadership, now so paralysed with fear that the screen is now inhabited solely by three-dimensional spooks and men from Mars. But there is still hope. The invalid is sick but not dead. Unlock the dungeon doors. Give him fresh air and sunshine. Take off the strait jacket and let him move about with freedom. But above all, return his conscience which you have filched from him.'

The stars remained great targets because the people who appeared daily in the newspapers were household names. But the writers remained the valuable ones as far as the committee was concerned. To see such articulate people so easily browbeaten was frightening. It showed how clever the committee was. They used the word 'unfriendly' in a way so sinister that it entered the language as a synonym for Communist. When the eminent writer Abraham Polonsky testified in April 1951, they might have guessed that they had made an enemy of a man who would figure frequently in the HUAC era. Paul Buhle, who co-wrote with Dave Wagner a biography of Polonsky, describes him as 'universally regarded as the brightest, funniest and the most lucid of everyone alive at that time.' The committee took him on with alacrity.

If those accused by the committee protested, as they did, that they were upholding freedom, rather than supporting the Communist party, they were not exactly helped by the party itself – whose description of HUAC as a 'warmongering, labor- and freedom-busting, witch-hunt by Congressional inquisitors' did them no favours at all.

As any victim of HUAC would agree, almost as bad as the hearings was the intimidation that preceded them: David Raksin experienced it all – and then, like Larry Parks – caved in.

Raksin was one of the most innovative composers in Hollywood, best known for his score of the 1944 film *Laura*, which is more highly regarded than the movie itself. Eight years earlier, he had arranged the music for Charlie Chaplin's picture *Modern Times*. The music for *The Bad and the Beautiful* and *The Secret Life of Walter Mitty* followed. And so did the pink slip delivered by the FBI.

Just before his death in August 2004, Raksin told me: 'I had once been a member of the Communist Party and I was considered, if not suspect, then people worried if I was let loose, would the country fall down or not? My view was that it would not – and acted accordingly. I had demonstrated during the war years on behalf of the Soviet Union, America's ally and also demonstrated that I was not intent on breaking up the country unless it was unavoidable. And the whole thing was a little crazy.'

Accordingly, this landed him in sufficient trouble to be on the breadline. 'I went before the Un-American Affairs Committee and I had an interesting encounter with them in one of those Star Chamber things at which they corner you with all their lawyers. They knew everything I did. I sort of embarrassed them by saying "I'm happy that you do, because if you really know anything about me, there is no way in which I could have done anything in any way questionable." I made them think a little but I went before the committee and the language of that time is still deplorable. In other words, if you were a Communist, there was no compromise on offer.'

He did what the 'Star chamber thing' wanted. He named names.

'Now, what I did was somewhat different from what most guys did. I knew I was really in very, very bad trouble.'

And like other guys in bad trouble he took legal advice – from the famous lawyer, Martin Gang. 'I knew about him because he had been the lawyer for a number of people called. He told me that I had to hold nothing back. I said "That's great!"'

'I refused to do what he said. Of course I wouldn't do that. He told me, "You're really a fool, because for every lie that you tell, you'll get one year." I said I would risk that. I wouldn't risk anything else just because [he] said I should.'

In the end, Raksin didn't take that risk. 'I went there. I was very, very careful because I had been watching the hearings. So I restricted myself to people who had already been named. I did that. But it was very hard to do and very humiliating. The funny thing is that nobody bothered to think it was legitimate for them to force me – which it was not.'

His hearings at the Federal Building in downtown Los Angeles, where every part of American government that was not the responsibility of the State of California or the city of Los Angeles was administered, were events that he said he would have given anything not to have experienced.

'I knew there was no way I could not be in trouble because I had been very open about things. I was considered too liberal. Not in the war years. But then. The whole thing was a little crazy. People like me who were liberals were betrayed by the studio people. I made up my mind I would not bad-mouth people. But I would say to some of them, "What do you mean it's not our war?" Some things like that.'

He may not have realised at the time just how bad things would be for him. Like Larry Parks, naming names didn't save him. 'Larry Parks is vilified. That makes me disgusted. The people who did this have no idea what it was like. It was terrifying. And nobody comes to your aid. Nobody.'

For a couple of years, Raksin was broke, with a wife and children to support. 'People slipped me little green stamps to buy gas' he recalled for me.

Occasionally, there were silver linings behind very grey skies which then turned even greyer. 'It really was sad. I hadn't been working for quite a long time when I was called by Fred Brisson, son of Carl Brisson.' Carl was a famous actor, his son a producer married to the star Rosalind Russell. 'He gave me a film to do. I was working for about a week when I got a very agitated call from him to go over to his house.' He didn't like what he heard when he got there. Raksin was told: 'I have been informed that if I employ you on this picture, it will not get a release.' 'I said that in that case, I'd get off the picture. I said I could accept that.' Could accept that because it seemed the decent thing to do – but he couldn't take that decency to his garage or grocery store – or to the bank.

The man who had warned the producer was the one who, just a few years before, had offered his help to the Committee for the First Amendment. As Raksin said: 'I would like to tell you who it was. It was Howard Hughes.'

Such was the climate of the time. One of the problems Raksin was facing was the question of his contract with MGM. The studio wanted him to sign a renewal, but he wondered if he were able to do this with a subpoena hanging over him. One of the rules of the game was that once handed a pink slip, it had to be confidential until the hearing took place. On the other hand, if anyone did tell all about their troubles, the studio would have sacked them anyway. He did what he thought was the honourable thing and hesitated to sign. Later, an MGM executive told him: 'Thank you for not signing because that way we don't have to fire you.' He replied: 'I know you would have done the same for me.'

Even so, just as Parks had done, David Raksin had faced the indignity of being shunned by former friends and colleagues. 'I was damned by some because they didn't know what I had been doing and why. Of course, I was on television, the movies, the radio and everything. I came to MGM – but not for long. I went to the commissary and not wishing to embarrass my colleagues in the music department, I sat by myself.' Not the easiest thing to do in a society where people in the same business gather for lunch to talk shop. 'It was uncomfortable,' he remembered for me. 'All of a sudden a guy stands up and gets up from his table at the restaurant and walks purposely to sit beside me. It was John Houseman. He wanted to make sure that people knew he approved of what I had done.' Not everybody agreed. 'One guy, for instance, told me, "You'll get yours."'

It was a familiar story among those who appeared. Houseman's act was a demonstration of real friendship. People who have been seriously ill can tell similar tales about drawing a line in a list of supposed friends; on the right are the ones who stay the same, as loyal as ever; on the left those who no longer want to know. Ellen Geer, whose father Will suffered as much as any other victim who was not actually jailed, is still bitter about what happened. 'I don't care what anybody says, you don't destroy other people's lives because you want to be safe – and to this day I have people come up to me and apologise because of turning away from Pop during that period. I don't even know who some of these people are.'

Will Geer, in those pre-Walton years, opened up a nursery in Topanga Canyon, above Malibu, where he was able to exercise his extraordinary gardening talents. 'Besides the garden nursery on the property in Topanga,' she told us, 'Pop made money because a couple of movie stars would hire him to do big landscaping jobs. But they wouldn't write a cheque to him. They'd only give him cash. They didn't want it on the record. It was a horrible period. It really was.'

For a time, before settling in to a totally new life, the Geers lived in their cars – 'sort of knowing what homelessness was before it became a fashionable word,' was how Ellen put it once. Will established his own small theatre for blacklisted artists.

He took the Fifth Amendment. Others didn't. Was Burl Ives one of the people who shopped him? 'Burl Ives was a rat,' says Ellen Geer, who suspects that he did, but doesn't know for sure. 'He named names. My mother had taught him some of his first guitar chords. He was Uncle Burl to us when we lived on the east coast.'

* * *

One of Gordon Kahn's collaborators named names but not that of Kahn himself. His son Tony Kahn won't name the namer today. 'I don't feel comfortable about it. I ended up speaking to him years later. He never thought he was doing anything wrong, because he never named my father. That's the way he rationalised it. I may have named somebody but even then I wasn't the first person to name that somebody else.'

The man's wife did name Kahn. 'She wrote my mother,' Tony Kahn now says, 'before she was asked to testify, saying, "I don't know what I'm going to do, but remember, no matter what happens, I will always love you." And my mother heard later that she had indeed testified and named my father and a number of other people as well. And that was the last communication they had. My mother refused to be in touch with her and I believe she died not too long afterwards.'

Kahn's FBI file revealed – although no one knew it at the time – that his own brother had informed on him. 'It was a brother,' Tony says, 'who was afraid that, because he was my father's brother, he might not be able to get a job and also because he was receiving copies of the *Daily Worker*. He wrote a letter to the FBI saying "I not only don't agree with my brother's politics but the *Daily Worker* was a subscription, a gift that somebody else gave me".'

The FBI file also reveals that the bureau acted on information supplied by sometimes anonymous acquaintances, neighbours and people with whom Khan worked. Some of the things said about him and his wife were often astonishing, not the sort of thing intelligent adults, as the committee members claimed to be, might be expected to take note of. They might have had reason to jot down 'Mr and Mrs Gordon Kahn belong to the Russian-American Club,' as one informant wrote. But did they need to record how 'Kahn personally remarked that he had no objection to living next door to Negroes, Japanese or any others'? That seems a somewhat less legitimate reason, but not to HUAC who took note – and acted.

It is not difficult to believe that the name of J Edgar Hoover, founder and director of the FBI, crops up again and again in the records. Not so much in relation to HUAC, but in guiding his FBI sleuths in their deliveries of the pink slips and in personally supervising a few individual cases. It is known that he was principally responsible for waiting for the right moment to strike at Charlie Chaplin.

Another of those in whom the FBI Director took a personal interest was Gordon Kahn. His son now says: 'I had no evidence it was going on until we got the FBI files under the Freedom of Information Act and I was amazed to discover that J Edgar not only followed my father's case and responded to different memos from other agents and issued orders in the text, but that he also wrote notes in the margin in his handwriting.'

It turned out that Kahn and Hoover had come together in Washington when the writer was one of the original Hollywood Nineteen called to await his appearance as a witness. 'They were in Washington having dinner in a hotel. I believe it was Harvey's, a hangout of J Edgar Hoover's, coincidentally. My father went to the bathroom during this dinner and ran into [him] coming down the stairway in the back with his live-in partner and an FBI assistant . . . He saw Hoover and Hoover saw him. They didn't say anything to each other and my father then went back to the table where his friends and fellow screenwriters were sitting and he told him: "You won't believe what I saw – J Edgar Hoover with lipstick on and he had his hair Marcelled [a Marcel wave hairstyle, intended for women but popular with gays at the time]".

'One of the people to whom he told the story at that table turned out to be an informer and he wrote a letter to J Edgar Hoover which I found in my father's FBI file, saying "Gordon Kahn just said this about you . . . and I know it's a tactic of the Communists to discredit their enemies. I want you to know that as a true patriot (I'm paraphrasing) I didn't believe a word of it. If I can be of any help to you at any time, please let me know." Hoover filed a marginal comment saying "Kahn must be thoroughly investigated."' And he was.

He was subpoenaed by the Attorney General of New Hampshire and told he had to appear in the State's capital, Concord, for questioning about his 'associations and subversive activities'. The state officials were told that the FBI had confirmed that Kahn had a heart condition. 'But they said this could be a ploy,' says Tony Kahn today. 'They said – I love this – "He may claim to have a heart condition, which would not be unlike a Communist to do something like that, but then again be careful about how you question him, because if he dies of a heart attack during questioning him, it could be very embarrassing".'

There was another letter to J Edgar Hoover: 'Dear Mr Hoover, Kahn is currently applying to bring three of his relatives to the United States from Europe. I don't know whether or not they are Communists, but I feel they'd be of the same type and there is no legitimate reason to allow any more Communists into this country. I agree with you that "now is the time for every American to stand up and be counted" and I thought you ought to know the score.'

It was a perfect weather vane to the climate of the times.

David Raksin's son Alex Raksin said that his father knew 'he would be vilified by both the extreme left and the extreme right. He was expecting a kind of ritualistic text. His way of thinking was that people who were unable to distinguish between his encounter with the committee and the victims who abased themselves were just simply ignorant.'

Alex, a Pulitzer Prize-winning journalist, told Barbra Paskin that his father was like a number of people in the arts who during the second inquisition suddenly came face to face with the results of mixing their art with politics. They saw themselves, he says, 'as pragmatists and they believed they could follow the system's rules and yet be independent at the same time. In his testimony before the committee, my father goes to great length to make the distinction and to explain why he tried to do what he did. And the more I think about it, the more I think we have to back up just a bit to understand why he came to do what he came to do.'

David Raksin had several calls, his son said, from people who said 'it would be inadvisable for him to deny his membership in the party because they had already named him.' The writer Martin Berkeley, who made a virtual profession of incriminating Hollywood personalities, thought, according to Alex Raksin, 'he was doing him a favour by saying 'don't even attempt to deny me – because I named you.' Alex added: 'I think my father felt that Berkeley who had named something like over 160 names was one of those people who was not making distinctions.'

Berkeley's is one of the weirdest stories of the age. Another writer, Allen Boretz, talked of a distraught Berkeley who had been asked to write the Laurel and Hardy film *Room Service*. It was, he knew, beyond him. The 'weakly handsome . . . Teutonic face' Berkeley wasn't a comedy writer. Boretz said he'd do it for him – 'I want to treat those lousy bastards to a little medicine of their own,' he declared. The MGM producer Bob Sisk loved his script. So did Berkeley. 'Martin Berkeley repaid me very nicely by naming me to the committee as a Communist,' he later recalled.

Such were the ethics of the age. 'It made my father think there was something of the Spanish Inquisition in McCarthyism,' said Alex Raksin. 'So he thought about the history of the Morranos, those well-known Jewish boys who, faced with the massacre of their families, chose to submit and rescind their Jewish faith and say they were Christians. Because if they had insisted they were Jews, they would have become extinct . . . that's the way my father liked to see what he was doing. (Actually the Morranos practised their Judaism in secret, lighting Sabbath candles, for instance, but hiding them in cupboards.)

'[My father] had discussions with friends like Aaron Copland who had similar strategies. So he would only name people who had already been identified and if he was asked by anyone else, he would deny that he knew them or whether or not they were members of the party.'

He always maintained that he was bored by Communist meetings. 'He said that one of his first activities was to go out and monitor ballot boxes and he felt completely incompetent and said that if someone had stolen one hundred ballots in front of him, he would never have noticed – because he was given no training.'

If, in fact, anyone from HUAC or Senator McCarthy himself had given him and his fellow members a quiz on *Das Kapital*, said Raksin, 'they'd all fail the quiz because they really had no idea.'

But what about the suggestion, as David Raksin told the committee, they were doing a service? He told the HUAC members: 'I commend you.' 'I don't know what they thought of my father saying all that. But that was my father. Did that mean he was an informant? Did he give up his principles? I think he tried to adhere to a complex set of principles – in other words, he felt that, rather than being silent, by being loquacious, he could do more . . . to enter into a dynamic with the committee.'

It was never a simple matter for him. 'I think he was confused until the day he died. He felt the guilt of those [others]. This was not very far from the Holocaust and he was Jewish. This was a lesser scale, but to those who survived the Holocaust, they're happy but they're guilty. They feel a sense of guilt. For surviving.'

The problem that David Raksin faced was not knowing what he was surviving for. It was a darker shadow hanging over him than that which affected many other victims of the committee. Here was a man of great talent, much admired by his peers, who, generations after appearing before the committee, was still haunted by it.

When the Raksin's and Parks' hearings took place in 1951, they were both significantly important to HUAC because they believed each demonstrated to the public the truth and rectitude of the committee's undertaking. Joseph McCarthy became famous for giving out numbers of the Communists he was going to investigate. HUAC members didn't need to do this. Every day, they were bringing out new fodder for their machinations. It turned out that, under John S Wood, they had 324 present and former Hollywood workers to bring before them, all of whom ended up on a blacklist.

It had an enormous effect on the film industry, especially as this coincided with the wind-down of the studio system in the wake of the advent of television. Up to the early 1950s, when each studio turned out an average of one new movie a week, the banks lined up to lend money for each project, as they were all practically guaranteed to make a profit. The studios owned the movie theatres to a considerable point, so there was rarely any uncertainty about distribution. But this was ruled out of order by competition legislation, and it worried the studios. Not as worried, however, as the people called to the Federal Building in Hollywood or to that other venue on Hollywood and Vine.

Deprived of the normal defence system, some of the accused employed their own distinctive methods of demonstrating both their individuality and their contempt for the committee. No better example of this was the appearance of Dorothy Comingore (an actress best known for her work in *Citizen Kane*) when she faced her interrogator, Donald Jackson. She was wearing a dirndl skirt and ballet slippers. As Jackson's questioning went on and on, Dorothy removed her slippers. Jackson looked at her feet and said, 'I'm glad you're making yourself comfortable'.

'It's not a matter of comfort,' she told him. 'My grandmother told me that when I was in a situation that made me angry, I should count to ten before I spoke, but I think this situation's going to require a count to twenty.'

Telling the story to Barbra Paskin, Paul Jarrico's widow Sylvia recalled: 'When she got off the stand and sat next to me, she said "Did you see that bastard with the whole deck of cards up his ass trying to shovel out the aces?"'

One thing that becomes clear when studying HUAC's activities is that there were absolutely no hard and fast rules as to why people were called before it. It was thought that Will Geer would be under suspicion because his mother-in-law, Ella Reeve Bloor, had been deeply involved in left-wing politics with which he was known to sympathise. He had also written an article in 1948, after the start of the committee's Hollywood investigations, praising Russian theatre and the cinema in the Soviet Union. That was always regarded as a dangerous thing to do.

'Pop loved Russian cinema and theatre,' his daughter Ellen now says. 'It had nothing to do with his being a Communist or not. He loved it that a government supported artists in the way Russia did at the time. It was absurd. They started following him because of Gram [his mother-in-law]. And Pop, it's like what he said in his hearing – "I didn't know Ma Bloor during that period."'

It was not unknown for HUAC victims to simply disappear. Tony Kahn, Gordon Kahn's son, told us that for a year he thought his father had died because he left home to avoid being served. 'I wasn't told why he had left. It wasn't as if I were concealing this information. I'd never been given the story, so I had nothing to tell, other than a sense that he had gone without me. I had no understanding of why.' It wasn't until the Kahn family joined the parade of blacklistees who sought new lives in Mexico that he discovered that his father was in fact alive.

His father never took the Fifth. 'I think somebody once told me that they had read some of his testimony before the attorney general and at one point the Attorney General had asked him what he did for a living. 'In a way what that was sort of saying was "Tell me where you're being published as a writer and I'll make sure that stops immediately." So my father said, "A writer." "Yes, but what kind of a writer?" "You know, a regular writer. I write whatever I can sell." "But it's like a doctor," the Attorney Generel said, "A doctor is either a surgeon or a specialist of some kind." So my father said, "Well, I'm a general practitioner." He always kept a sense of humour.' Which was not an easy thing to do when faced with the red-hunters.

Integrity was the guiding light to many of the witnesses and later victims. So was vanity. Did Tony Kahn believe that his father might secretly have wished to have been included in the much-publicised Hollywood Ten? 'It would be hard not to believe that as a human being. But he was basically very clear about what was right and what was wrong about this thing. And it was very easy for him to do the right thing. Because he couldn't have lived with himself if he'd done the wrong thing. He was one of these basic, decent people who was a little bit too unable to rationalise his behaviour. He wouldn't lie or betray a friendship.'

The hearings had a great deal in common: the bullying by the committee members and their investigators and the appeals by witnesses to be allowed to state their own case. Every time an 'unfriendly' witness appeared, he was subjected to the same treatment. As before, with the

Hollywood Ten and people like Parks and Raksin, in most cases, the witnesses could barely get their voices heard, unless, of course they were willing to 'sing'. Sometimes, microphones were mysteriously switched off in the midst of 'defence' testimony, but more frequently the unfriendlies were simply shouted down. Occasionally – and it really was occasionally – the witnesses won. But this didn't guarantee them winning their cases. Nothing they did could achieve that for them, but they didn't allow themselves to be cowed by those on the dais in front of them.

Paul Robeson wouldn't allow himself to be browbeaten when he appeared before Joseph McCarthy himself. With a bass-baritone voice like his, it would be difficult to imagine such a thing. At one stage, he said he was going to invoke the Fifth Amendment. And then added: 'I invoke the Fifth Amendment loudly.' And he managed to accuse McCarthy of wanting to keep coloured people out of normal society. He went on: 'I am not being tried for being a Communist. I am being tried for fighting for the rights of my people, who are still second-class citizens in these United States of America. My mother was born in your state . . . my ancestors baked bread for George Washington's troops as they crossed the Delaware. My father was a slave.'

He said that McCarthy's committee should go to Mississippi 'and protect my people'. And then the final rub: '*You* are the un-Americans. You should adjourn this for ever.'

Paul Robeson had encountered a lot of opposition in the movie and cultural community. José Ferrer said he condemned Robeson's acceptance of 'Stalin's so-called Peace Prize.' Ferrer was acting because he had been warned by the American Legion, the veterans' organisation, that unless he made an anti-Communist statement, they would boycott his coming movie *Moulin Rouge*. A statement the Legion made expressed 'disapproval of the distribution of *Moulin Rouge* until such time as the personnel connected with it evidences sincere co-operation with the Government. The Legion disapproves of the various [Communist] Front records of José Ferrer and John Huston [the director].'

Ferrer issued his statement and the boycott threat was withdrawn by the Legion. As far as Robeson was concerned, it was a weapon to be used against him at his HUAC appearance. With the Soviet award came another from his home country – the withdrawal of his American passport.

'Mr Robeson,' were the polite words that began his appearance before HUAC.

'Do I have the privilege of asking who is addressing me?' he broke in. 'What is your position?'

'I am Richard Arens. I am director of the staff,' his inquisitor responded.

Robeson was asked if he had filed an application for a new passport.

'I filed about 25 applications in the last few months,' he answered.

'Were you requested to submit a non-Communist affidavit?'

'Under no conditions would I think of signing any such affidavit. It is a contradiction of the rights of American citizens.'

'Are you now a member of the Communist Party?'

'Oh please, please.'

'Will you answer the question, Mr Robeson.'

'What is the Communist Party?' he countered, a question to which there was no ready answer.

'Are you now a member of the Communist party?'

'Would you like to come to the ballot box when I vote and take out the ballot and see? I invoke the Fifth Amendment – and forget it.'

Arens was now losing the cool equilibrium he had shown until then. 'You are directed to answer.'

'In the first place, wherever I have been in the world, the first to die in the struggle against fascism were the Communists and I laid many wreaths upon graves of Communists. It is not criminal . . . and the Fifth Amendment has nothing to do with criminality.'

Another who against all the odds managed to find a voice louder than anyone in the committee was the actor Lionel Stander. Perhaps it was because of its gravely nature, but he made that voice heard. There was a lot against him – he was one of the founders of the Screen Actors' Guild in the days when it really did represent the interests of its members. He was instrumental in exposing corruption in IATSE, the stagehands' union, which showed that he fought wrong-doing on both sides of the labour fence. To cap it all, he supported the Government side in the Spanish Civil War and had been a member of the Hollywood Anti-Fascist League. The cards were stacked in the wrong direction. He knew that and was going to make the most of the fact.

Stander also knew that he was a patriot – which was why he joined the Royal Canadian Air Force before the United States actually declared its own war. He then transferred to the US Army Air Corps. It was at that time that the first seeds of government antagonism were sown. Stander, who among other movies had appeared in the original *A Star*

Is Born and the 1936 *Mr Deeds Goes to Town*, was refused the opportunity to fly. Later, it was said that he was a 'premature anti-fascist'. That was a dangerous appellation because it meant that he had been fighting fascism before there was any need to do so. In other words, before Hitler had been declared an official enemy and before the Soviet Union was regarded as an ally. Norman Corwin told me: 'That was made into a term of obloquy.' In 1940, three years after *A Star Is Born*, Stander's name appeared on a Hollywood blacklist – after he had been a witness at a grand jury investigation into Communism in the film industry. Corwin explained: 'If you were accused of being a premature anti-fascist, you were in trouble. You could lose a job. If you attended a meeting, you were yourself tainted. It spread like a disease, like an epidemic.'

Lionel Stander, whose distinctive voice as the chauffeur in the *Hart to Hart* TV series made him an international star long after his time as a stock Hollywood character actor and temporary blacklist oblivion, was one of the leading personalities in the HUAC battles. In fact, he was the only actor to have the unsettling distinction of being blacklisted not once, but twice. He had been strongly liberal and earned plenty of right-wing opposition because of his work in the struggle to organise the Screen Actors Guild, of which he was one of the founders, and in many anti-fascist and civil rights causes.

Stander became a totem to many facing the onslaught of HUAC. After the first investigations into his 'loyalty' in 1940, he didn't make another film for two years, when he was finally featured in *Guadalcanal Diary*. Once the war was over, he was mostly restricted to work in B pictures.

This was the background to his 1953 appearance before HUAC. 'Nobody could shut him down. He was louder and pushier than anyone else in the room,' says his daughter Bella Stander. 'You couldn't shut him down. He talked faster and louder than anyone else.' And he was a firm believer in the ancient art of chutzpah.

He won battles no one else would dare contemplate fighting – like insisting that the cameras be turned off when he appeared. He said that he was an actor who insisted on getting paid when movie cameras were focused on him. He also said that the committee was doing it to get their faces in the papers alongside movie stars. 'He swept into the courtyard,' recalls his daughter, 'with a blonde on each arm and he took command and he yelled them down. Which nobody else did.'

He told them: 'I am shocked, shocked that you don't want to hear what I have to say. I have the names of people who desecrate Jewish cemeteries. I have the names of those who lynch Negroes or deny civil rights to Negroes. I am shocked you don't want to hear about this.'

Even stronger than words were the actions. In letters to Bella, Stander relates his pleasure at managing to 'stare down' the committee. He also said that he wouldn't join the party because it wasn't far enough to the left for him.

Stander had been subpoenaed by the first HUAC inquisition under Martin Dies, along with familiar names like Bogart, Cagney, March, Franchot Tone and over a dozen others. Dies promised clearance to all those who would co-operate. Stander was not the co-operative type.

In 1938, Columbia studio chief Harry Cohn famously called Stander 'a Red son of a bitch' and threatened a $100,000 fine against any studio that renewed his contract. He had been involved in various left-wing causes including the committee for the Scottsboro Boys, the case involving nine black youths accused of raping two white women that later inspired Harper Lee's *To Kill a Mockingbird*, and put his resonant voice to vociferous use. He spearheaded campaigns and, together with Gale Sondergaard, had his name on an ambulance sent to assist the Spanish Republican troops. But Stander always maintained that he never joined the Communist Party. 'He said he wasn't a joiner,' recalled his daughter Bella Stander for this book. As Stander himself said: 'I've always been lefter than the left.'

Yet the Communist Party did have something to offer – something that most of the other people caught up in this dreadful period seemed to recognise. Bella Stander agrees that her father was not alone in looking for that 'something'. 'I know it's been said ad-nauseam . . . most people who were Communist Party sympathisers or who joined did it because the Communist Party was standing for stuff that nobody else would. They were for equal rights and for things like social security and health insurance for both sexes and all races. Things that we take for granted now but they certainly weren't taken for granted then. It was the depth of segregation and Jim Crowe and anti-Semitism and whatever ism you want to call it, so most people who went to meetings were really for a more just and equal society and that's what the Communist Party was espousing.' However, as she added, tellingly: 'The so-called Hollywood Communists, most of them were what we'd call liberal or socialist at this point, but they certainly didn't want a Communist dictatorship – because they'd lose everything they had.'

Lionel's 1953 appearance before the committee, during the so-called second inquisition, shook those who were watching the performance of his lifetime, including his wife and, above all, the HUAC members. He had been named, he reminded the committee, in 1940, by the alleged police agent and Communist infiltrator John L Leech, and then in 1951 by an actor named Marc Lawrence, who was subsequently found to be mentally unbalanced and had fled the country. HUAC had been pressed by Stander to get Lawrence to give evidence for two years. But he also wanted to give evidence himself. 'I tried to get an immediate hearing,' Stander insisted, 'because merely receiving the subpoena . . . caused me to be . . . blacklisted.

'At the same time, I sued the witness who perjured himself before this committee, Mr Marc Lawrence in the State Supreme Court of New York, which ruled that he enjoyed congressional immunity.' Nothing said before a congressional committee, just as nothing said on the floor of the House or the Senate, could be deemed actionable. Rep Woods, the chairman, wanted to bring that point to a speedy closure. 'We are not interested in those extraneous matters,' he ruled.

Stander was exasperated. 'I don't think they are extraneous,' he interrupted. The vehemence of his objection was so strong that, unlike virtually anyone else, he was allowed to proceed; the committee plainly didn't know what had hit it.

'Extraneous when a man comes directly before the committee from the psychopathic ward under the care of two psychiatrists? I wrote this letter and informed every one of the committee, that this man, a psychopath, was used as a witness against me and under the advice of counsel . . . Then he fled to Europe and at this moment is still a refugee from this court case.' Stander was making plain that he intended to pursue his charges against Lawrence. He had his allies – like John Howard Lawson. He would say that he regarded Stander as the model of a committed Communist actor who enhanced the class struggle through his performances. In the 1938 movie *No Time to Marry*, which had been written by Paul Jarrico, Stander had whistled a few bars of the *Internationale* while waiting for a lift. Stander thought that the scene would be cut from the movie, but it remained in the picture because, he said, 'they were so apolitical in Hollywood at the time that nobody recognised the tune.' In the climate of the suspicion and calumny, the scene could have been highly incriminating.

Martin Berkeley, told HUAC that at a fundraising evening he threw at his home, Stander had introduced him to his friend, the militant labour union leader Harry Bridges. Bridges was long suspected of being a Communist. To make things worse for himself, Stander was heard calling him 'comrade'.

Despite such evidence of guilt, there were attempts at trying to reduce the political impact of the case. Stander, Berkeley said, told him: 'Get to know about Communism and you'll make out with the girls.' He wasn't the only one. It was Marc Lawrence who told the committee that Stander had recruited him into the party by telling him that 'you get to know the dames more.'

In making himself heard, Stander caused something of a sensation. He demanded that newsreel cameras be switched off, making a pitch no one else would have dared make – let alone succeed as he did. The way he asked for this was an entertainment in itself. 'I only appear on television for entertainment or philanthropic organisations,' he declared. 'And I consider this is a very serious matter that doesn't appear [to be falling into] either category.' He continued his case full of enthusiasm – although he said that wasn't how he felt at all. 'I am a professional entertainer,' he declared, 'and to come before the camera as a witness before a congressional committee, which is a very serious thing, which isn't entertainment and which certainly isn't a benefit for a charitable institution', was, he said, against all professional principles.

It wasn't easy. Stander said: 'I am not exactly calm this morning, I haven't had any sleep . . . I was unable to get a room in any hotel.'

Then he seemed to surprise his interrogators still further. He insisted he would answer questions and tell the truth: 'I took an oath and I believe in my oaths.' He was asked if he were going to answer the $64,000 question. (The term has since become an accepted turn of phrase, but at the time it was merely the title of America's most popular game show, offering the world's biggest prize.)

'I'll answer any question,' responded Stander to more shocks and surprises all round. This was an actor trying to do his job. If he didn't like his lines, normally there had to be a writer with whom to be angry. He was now his own writer – and director, and producer, too.

He was asked about his career. He was, he said, 'basically an actor. I've been a newspaper reporter, a director, produced two Broadway plays.'

'How long have you been in Hollywood?' he was asked.

'Until I was the first person who exposed the criminal records of . . . the IATSE [Union] racketeer-gangster officials, who later went to jail, two racketeers and, because I exposed them, I was blacklisted by the major studios . . . Just to have my name appear in association with this committee is like the Spanish Inquisition. You may not be burned but you can't help coming away a little singed.'

Was there any part of his career of which he was proud?

'I'm proud of everything,' he replied and continued to talk over the chairman's gavel, although it wasn't clear what he was saying.

'Would you be quiet!' the chairman overruled.

'Yes,' replied Stander. 'I'd like to hear.'

'You are here to give us information which will enable us to do the work assigned to us by the House of Representatives . . . to investigate reports regarding subversive activities in the United States.' The chairman continued, but this time he was overpowered by the voice of Lionel Stander sounding like a street-sweeping machine moving over a gravel path.

'I am more than willing to co-operate,' he announced, and then mowing down all opposition in his way, proceeded to lecture Mr Woods and his colleagues. 'Because I know of subversive activities in the entertainment industry and elsewhere in the country.' For a brief moment, the committee were stunned into the kind of silence they wished their witness would display – until he began his explanations: 'If you are interested, I can tell you right now that I have knowledge of subversive action. I know of a group of fanatics who are trying to undermine the Constitution of the United States by depriving artists and others of life, liberty and the pursuit of happiness without due process of law. I can cite instances, I can tell names. And I am one of the first victims of it. If you are interested – a group of ex-Bundists, American-Firstsers [The German American Bund and the America First organisations were among the principal fascist movements in the country up to the start of World War Two] and anti-Semites who hate everybody – Negores, minority groups, most likely, themselves.'

For an actor who was uncomfortable working without a script, he was doing quite well. Far too well for the chairman, who broke in: 'Mr Stander, unless you begin to answer questions and act like a witness in a reasonable, dignified manner, under the rules of the committee, I will be forced to have you removed from the room.'

'I want to co-operate,' Stander repeated. 'I began to tell you about them and I'm shocked by your cutting me off. I am not a dupe, a dope or a moe or a shmo and I'm not ashamed for anything I said to anyone.'

The only work left to him since he had been subpoenaed was going around the nightclub circuit. And, he added, still, 'I was not charged.'

'You are not being charged with anything,' the chairman emphasised.

'My apppearance here is enough to be blacklisted,' he added yet again.

In the end Stander was physically thrown out of the room at the courthouse in Foley Square, Lower Manhattan, amid uproar from a mixture of both left-wing supporters and anti-Communists who at times behaved as though they were at a boxing match.

So why did he want so badly to go before the committee? 'Because I was told by my agent if I appeared before the committee and if the committee was a fair committee and allowed me, that if I wanted to refute Marc Lawrence's testimony, that I would be able to get back into television and motion pictures. I had made 11 television shows in a row and one of the biggest television agencies and producers had told my agent that if I went before the committee [and told it] that I wasn't [a Communist], I would have my own TV programme, which meant $150,000 a year to me. So I had a $150,000 motive for coming before the committee.'

It was time for more threats. An interrogator interrupted: 'If you continue, I'm going to ask the chairman to turn on the cameras so that your performance can be recorded for posterity.' Stander did not protest further.

The name of Lucy Stander was mentioned. 'Your wife?' asked a committee member. 'Your wife?'

'I'm not married,' he replied.

'Or your former wife . . . Well, the name mentioned here was Lucy. Do you remember that name?'

'Yeah, I remember her vaguely.'

The audience loved that. Was he, after all that, a member of the party?

His daughter told us: 'I do know that he gave money to the party and he went to meetings, but I think from what I have read in his FBI file that he was too brash and outspoken for the party. He was a maverick. He couldn't be trusted to toe the party line. And the thing is really why should these people [have been expected to] toe the party line? It's really hilarious when you think about it. That these people who were making ten, fifty or a hundred times what the average American would make, and driving around in limousines and playing golf and tennis at the Beverly Hills Country Club, why would they possibly want to be Communists and have all that taken away from them? It's ludicrous when you think about it.'

But not too ludicrous for the FBI who, in the case of Stander, turned itself into a morals squad. They accused him of bringing a minor across the state line for immoral purposes. Actually, the woman was Bella Stander's mother, although today Bella says she cannot be certain whether they were or weren't married then. 'They pulled her into this apartment across the street and kept her for hours, asking questions. She told them that my father was a complete gentleman and never laid a finger on her.'

His appearance before HUAC was probably the most entertaining the committee experienced. It was also, bizarrely, one of the most revealing and, as history has shown, one of the most truthful and apt. Of course, the committee still pressed the Communist membership question.

'I swore in 1940 that I am not a member of the Communist party.'

'Why not do it now?' he was asked.

'Because . . . I don't want to be responsible for a whole stable of informers, stool pigeons and psychopaths, informers and ex-political heretics who come in here, beating their breasts, and saying "I am awfully sorry. I didn't know what I was doing. I want absolution. Get me back into pictures." And they will do anything. They'll name anybody.'

He was asked about the prime namedropper in his case, Martin Berkeley. Did he know him? Stander replied, true to form: 'First, he said he was not a member of the Communist Party then. When he realised you had the goods on him, he rattled off 150 names. This is an incredible witness.'

(Berkeley actually produced the names of 161 people in Hollywood he said were Communists, so many that the HUAC investigator Bill Wheeler told him: 'Don't name that number. You're just getting yourself in big, deep trouble. We don't need all this.' There was also a journalist, Leo Townsend, who named 300 people. Townsend was asked if he thought all those 300 were dangerous. 'Oh no,' he replied, years later. 'Maybe two or three of them.')

Stander was pressed: 'Do you decline to answer the question?'

'I resent the inference that anyone who invokes the Fifth, which our forefathers fought for, is guilty of anything. My name is Stander, it was adopted . . . because in feudal Spain my ancestors did not have the protection of the United States Constitution and were religious refugees. And you know that the puritans, the people that established this country, used this right.'

Stander went on: 'I decline under the First Amendment, which entitles me to freedom of belief, under the Fifth Amendment, which states that I shall not be forced to testify against myself and also under which there is no inference of guilt – it is designed to protect the innocent – and under the Ninth Amendment which gives me . . . the right to get up in the union hall, which I did and introduce a resolution condemning this Congressional committee for its abuse of powers in attempting to impose censorship upon the American theatre people.'

The committee knew when they were beaten. 'It is obvious that the witness is excited and nervous,' declared the chairman. 'You are excused.'

'May I read my statement?' Stander, having got that far, was not going to go willingly.

'No,' said the chairman again. 'You are excused.' It was a case of mutual good riddance. Stander remained on the blacklist – and would later claim to have become a successful Wall Street broker. In truth, he struggled to survive by selling junk bonds, before being able to return to acting.

All the Hollywood Communists denied they were working for the Soviet Union. In most cases they were certainly not. Even so, it is generally accepted (although no one has actually proved it) that the Communist Party of the United States was directly funded by the Soviet Union. That wouldn't have worried Norma Barzman.

'What I heard and the reason I joined the party . . . I was really put in touch. I admired it so. It seemed like the only way to do five or six things I wanted to do. They were organising the guilds and unions in Hollywood, bringing in all the Rooseveltian social justice programmes that he had initiated, really good ways of fighting fascism at home and abroad and helped the victims of fascism. They were also fighting the fascism that was rising in the United States that people weren't aware of, for there really was a rising tide of fascism in the United States. What I found so admirable in the United States progressive community was that they did try to help for civil rights.'

There were other reasons, she remembered, for joining the party: 'Creative people, I thought, gave their time for community services. You can blame the progressive community for getting teenage Latinos off for murder.'

When they heard that a group of lettuce farm workers 'were breaking their backs with short-handled agricultural tools, we helped get that changed. Maybe we were naïve. We were idealistic. We did think we were changing the world.'

And there was something else that was particularly important, it seems, for women involved in what they did persist in calling the 'progressive' movement. They were pre-feminist. This was apparent, Norma maintains, in the scripts that women writers like herself produced. Not that audiences would have noticed, perhaps. 'By the time that male screenwriters got hold of them, they were no longer feminist. But there was nothing Communistic about them either.'

The 'accused' who came before HUAC – for that was precisely what the unfriendlies were – dealt with their own individual problems in their own individual ways. Sondra Gorney remembered the day before her trip with her husband to Washington to testify. 'We took the children out to dinner. I think they were 6 and 8 at the time and Jay and I tried to explain to them that Daddy was going to be talking to this committee and that they might take away his freedom.'

That would have been particularly ironic for Gorney, who had written a song in praise of the Bill of Rights. It struck his daughter Karen – who said: 'They can't do that to you, Daddy. You sing them your Bill of Rights song.' As Sondra remembers: 'And of course, that's what he did. Out of the mouths of babes, I guess. But she guided him to do that. He'd never have thought of it.'

And nor would the committee, who were girding their loins ready for a battle royal, as well as for the sessions with the friendly witnesses who would show what decent, upright people both the HUAC members and your average Hollywood type were. Those who were not considered to be in that bracket were preparing themselves – and their families – for the worst.

Jean Porter, actress widow of the director Edward Dmytryik, was brought face-to-face with the situation without any warning. 'We were going together, doing a film together (I had replaced Shirley Temple) because Dore Schary (later head of MGM) had introduced us.' She told Barbra Paskin: 'One day he called me and said he was going to go for a drive. He said, "Do you know what this is?" "A pink piece of paper," I said. "OK, what does it mean?" He said, "I have to be in Washington. I'm being investigated. I'm accused of being a Communist." I said, "Are you?" I was a teenager without a clue. He said, "No, I used to be. They could get me for that." Nineteen of them were going. Most hardly knew each other.'

A meeting to discuss the next move was held at the home of Lewis Milestone, famous for his 1930 anti-war movie, *All Quiet on the Western Front*. 'There were three people there as I sat holding Eddie's hand. I don't know how they pulled the attorneys so fast – to find out what to do.'

Surprisingly, the air wasn't full of angst that night. 'No: fear. Puzzlement, I'd say. I don't think Eddie knew how far this was going.'

What she and the others knew was that it was a journey that was to begin in Washington DC.

Chapter Ten
One Man's Peace

The House Un-American Committee has called on the carpet some of the people who have been making your favourite movies. Did you happen to see The Best Years of Your Lives, *a picture that won seven Academy awards? Did you like it? Were you subverted by it? Did it make you un-American? Did you come out of the movie with the desire to overthrow the Government?*

Gene Kelly, *Hollywood Fights Back,* 1947

The hearings were riveting entertainment to those who could watch them from the comfort and safety of their armchairs. The writer Hal Kanter saw them on his small black-and-white screen: 'I was working with Tennessee Williams at that time on *The Rose Tattoo*. He said, "Let's not start just now. I'm watching this charlatan." "This charlatan" was Joseph McCarthy, but it was precisely how he felt about HUAC, too.

He refused to work until that was over. Kanter couldn't concentrate on anything else. After a while, I had had enough of it. Kanter admits that part of that discomfort was 'working with a man in his bathrobe drinking at 10 o'clock in the morning.' But only partly. McCarthy was far more intimidating. 'For people who had anything to hide from the House Un-American Activities Committee, it was a very nervous-making time for everyone here.'

He admits: 'HUAC absolutely fascinated everyone, just to see them in action, *and* to see the defenders of the American idea, defending the people he was accusing of being very un-American. Percentage-wise, as many people were tuning in as would later be listening to Watergate.'

As for Chairman Parnell Thomas: 'He was despicable. How he remained in office, nobody knows.' Of course, his term in office was to end somewhat abruptly.

There was a great deal of cowardice about, says Kanter. 'Always there were a lot of people who were willing to go along – in order to get along. A lot of cowards. I think I might have been a coward, too, if I were called before Parnell Thomas or McCarthy. I was in office in the Radio Writers Guild and I was asked to sign that I was not a Communist. I had nothing to hide from the House Un-American Activities Committee. Most of my friends had nothing to hide either. If I had been called up, I'd have told the truth. Fortunately, I wasn't called, so I didn't have to make that decision.'

The bestselling writer Sidney Sheldon was working in Hollywood at the time. He got very emotional, close to tears in fact, when shortly before his death, he recalled his friends who were hounded by HUAC. Sheldon told me: 'People were terrified. They were in the control of Washington. If Washington had said [a person] was a Communist, he would be fired. There was no checking if it were true or not. The fact that McCarthy or the Un-American Activities Committee said so, was enough – and many innocent lives were destroyed because they were the wrong people.'

But he added: 'I don't think this could have happened without the war. There could not have been a McCarthy without the war. But when we turned Russia into an enemy or turned themselves into an enemy, anyone in that right-wing thing thought they were trying to take on the world.'

When we met, he said that he didn't think many people joined the party. 'I think it was an innocent thing of just joining a group. A lot weren't Communist groups, they were just left-wing groups. They didn't know what they were getting themselves into. I don't think it was Communist in the real sense. I don't believe they were Communists. They were suspect with a capital S. You know what the problem was: it was an age of innocence. My friends belonged to parties that were not really Communist parties. They were very liberal. There was never any intention of overthrowing the Government. It didn't occur to them. They were just liberals with liberal ideas. They were innocents. And what happened to them shocked them because they weren't guilty of anything. But a lot of them went to prison.'

Sheldon said he was 'a Democrat. Period.' But that was enough to get himself into trouble. 'I had an experience at Metro,' he recalled for me. 'It was rather harrowing. A man named Marvin Schenck, one of the Schenck family [who controlled MGM's parent company, Loews Inc.], called me in and he said: "I have to talk to you," and he said, "You voted for X, a man who wrote a book called *The Journey of Simon McKeever*. You voted for him at the Guild meeting to be on the board of the Writers Guild." It didn't occur to me to say, "How do you know who I voted for? It's a secret ballot." He accused me of being a Communist. I said no one told me to vote for him. He said that someone must have told me to do so, "I want names!" And I got furious and I said I voted for him because he was a very good writer and we need good writers on the board.

'He said, "You went round the studio collecting money for the children of the Hollywood Ten. Why did you do that?" By now I was quite angry. I said, "You are right. I shouldn't have done that. Let the kids starve, just because their fathers are Communists." And I'm screaming and he said, "I want you to go home and tomorrow I want you to come in and give the names of the people. I had just signed a long-term contract at Metro. I couldn't sleep all night. I went in the next morning. I get angry even now when I think about it. And I said, "I quit! I want out of my contract." I was humiliated. He said, "We don't want you to quit. We talked to New York and they said if you signed a statement that you're not a member of the party and never have been, we'll forget it." I said of course I'd sign and that was the end of it.'

But was he pleased that he'd signed? 'The degradation of that stayed with me. They were accusing me of raising money for children. I was happy to sign it. All I said was I was not a Communist. That didn't bother me. But the inquisition bothered me. And the implications bothered me. It was degrading, but that was the attitude of the town. I could never have thought it could happen. But then the country never thought it could happen.'

There were those who considered themselves lucky to have escaped. Like Gloria Stuart, a star of the 1930s, who had a late new blossoming in 1997 playing the narrator in *Titanic*. She told me: 'My husband and I had wanted to get into the war. I had founded the Hollywood Anti-Nazi League and with Dorothy Parker, the Committee to aid Spanish orphans. We worked very hard to get us into the war and to help what later became our allies. We gave parties, we raised money, we wrote letters, had petitions, all we could do to organise political protest. At that time, the studio heads were supportive of the Anti-Nazi League; they gave money to organisations like that. Our trouble was that we were liberals – and they are not liked by the extreme left or the right.'

What many like Larry Parks and then Sterling Hayden, the screen tough-guy who had made his name in films like *The Asphalt Jungle* in

161

1950, couldn't countenance was the naming of names. Hayden's proved to be one of the most famous testimonies, for he later recanted, calling himself 'a rat, a stoolie'. He admitted he had joined the party in 1946 'in a moment of emotional disturbance.' He was presented with a list of names and asked to confirm that they were party members. Among other things, he said: 'I wouldn't hesitate to name Karen Morley . . . we had meetings at her house and some at the home of Morris Carnovsky.'

Hayden's attorney sent a letter to J Edgar Hoover. It said that Hayden had joined in June 1946. 'In November, he decided he made a mistake and terminated his membership. He is concerned that his brief membership of the Communist party might prevent the use of his services. He is married and has young children . . . the purpose of this is that people can ask the FBI and the FBI can notify a prospective employer that there is no reason not to employ our client.'

Hayden was at least honest about his statement. His reason was purely economic. He was frightened of losing his job. This was no attempt at saying that all he wanted to do was to say how much he loved pure, Republican America and how much he detested the Soviet Union.

Another who recanted his party membership was Abe Burrows, writer of *Guys and Dolls*, one of the most outstanding Broadway musicals of the 1950s. He told HUAC: 'I wanted to get this thing cleared up. My Americanism being under suspicion is very painful to me. I have no recollection of ever applying for membership.'

He was asked if he ever attended party meetings. For a minute it seemed he was standing in the shoes of Harry the Horse or Big Julie. 'I used to attend more parties than anyone. They got a little out of hand. People would say, "Come to the party." I never turned down an invitation.' There may have been smiles all round. If so, it was a rare moment of levity. And he was appearing to be on the committee's side.

'There was no word of Communism at meetings,' he said. 'I went to study groups. Because of my work, my satire, I wasn't really trusted.' That was precisely what HUAC wanted to be able to record in its minutes. Was he ever requested to pay dues to the Communist party? 'Not to my knowledge,' he replied.

He was told: 'You were pretty naïve.'

Burrows: 'I would say I was stupid. I want to fight Communism. They can't take it. I read somewhere they don't like jokes.'

He was asked: 'Are you a member of the party?'

He replied: 'No, sir.'

'Have you ever been?'

His answer: 'I was considered a Communist and that's why I've come here. Not in my own heart I didn't. I committed enough acts to be considered one.'

He was asked again if he attended party meetings, despite all he had previously said about identifying where meetings were held. His answer was suitably vague: 'I attended meetings at which Communists were present.'

As a result of the hearing, Paramount dropped the $75,000 option they had taken on *Guys and Dolls*. Samuel Goldwyn, by far the least co-operative mogul as far as HUAC was concerned, took it up. It became an exceedingly successful 1954 film, starring Frank Sinatra, Marlon Brando and Jean Simmons.

One of the most impressive appearances was by Lillian Hellman, famous for her performance in the 1961 movie starring Audrey Hepburn, *The Children's Hour*. In a letter she sent to the Committee two days before her hearing she wrote the now famous line: 'I cannot and will not cut my conscience to fit this year's fashions,' declaring that if she gave names, others would do so a lot more easily. 'I am not willing now or in the future to bring bad trouble to people who, in my past association with them, were completely innocent of any talk or any action that was disloyal or subversive. I do not like subversion or disloyalty in any form and if I had ever seen any I would have considered it my duty to report it to the proper authorities.'

Hellman took what became known as the Diminished Fifth, admitting what she did herself but refusing to compromise others, but she explained herself: 'I was raised in an old American tradition – to try to tell the truth, not to bear false witness, not to harm my neighbour, to be loyal to my country. It is my belief that you will agree with these simple rules of human decency and will not expect me to violate the good American tradition from which they spring. I am prepared to waive the privilege against self-incrimination and tell you everything you wish to know about my views or actions if your Committeee will agree to refrain from asking me to name other people.'

HUAC did not require her to do anything of the kind. They wanted names – and her decision to take the Fifth Amendment stood.

When Arthur Miller was finally called in 1956, reporters from all over the world came to hear his protestations, with pencils and notebooks poised. Like Paul Robeson, he had been denied a passport, which he needed because he wanted to go to London for the opening of his play *A View From The Bridge*. It was about an informer.

He was asked the $64,000 question.

He said he had had associations with Communist writers. But 'I broke with [them] for personal reasons.'

'Who were they?' he was pressed.

'I understand your philosophy behind this question and I want you to understand mine. I am not protecting the Communists or the Communist Party. I am protecting myself. I could not use the name of another person and bring trouble upon him. I ask you not to ask me that question.'

Congressman Scherer responded, 'We do not accept the reasons you gave for refusing to answer the question, and it is the opinion of the Committee that, if you do not answer the question, you are placing yourself in contempt.'

To which Miller replied: 'All I can say, sir, is that my conscience will not permit me to use the name of another person.'

Miller told HUAC: 'I have been to hell and back and seen the devil.'

Behind the scenes, Chairman Francis Walter (who, ironically at the end of the hearing, admitted that he had participated in some activities himself and had made a sizeable contribution to an anti-Fascist Committee) offered Miller the big deal: 'He made an offer to my lawyer. If a photograph could be taken of him with Marilyn Monroe, he would cancel my appearing. That's how dangerous he really thought I was. When I said "No," he then got back on his horse. He acted as though I were really a danger to the country.'

The matter went to the floor of the House – where he was found guilty of contempt by 373 votes to nine. Later, however, the decision was revoked. Miller did not go to jail. Of the whole affair, he said: 'I felt distaste for those who grovelled before this tawdry tribune of moralistic vote-snatchers, but I had as much pity as anger toward them.'

*   *   *

Five years before his triumph as choreographer of *West Side Story*, and immediately after choreographing *The King and I*, Jerome Robbins made an appearance before HUAC in 1953. He told the committee that he had joined the Communist party in 1944. 'I belonged to a group known as the Theatrical Transient Group [which was] well named because they shifted from place to place.'

He was asked what 'brought about your termination?'

Robbins replied that at the last meeting which he attended in 1947, 'a fight broke out with everybody arguing and yelling about parliamentary procedure and I realised I was in the midst of chaos, of an unorganised, frantic group. It was too much. I didn't know what I was doing there or what I was accomplishing by being present and I had no more interest in continuing to participate.'

He said that Madeleine Lee, wife of the actor Jack Gilford, asked him 'what dialectical material' could be inserted in the Leonard Bernstein ballet *Fancy Free*, which Robbins was choreographing. Lee certainly would not accept Robbins' memory of this incident. *Fancy Free*, with music by Leonard Bernstein, had already been written and successfully performed before Robbins joined the Communist Party. After one of his early meetings, Madeline says she asked him how dialectical materialism had influenced the production of *Fancy Free* and asked if he'd lecture about it. Robbins told Tavenner, 'I found the question a little ridiculous and a little outrageous,' and he had no qualms about naming her. Among several others, Robbins also named an actor called Elliott Sullivan and the writer brothers Jerome and Edward Chodorov.

Kearney said: 'I would like to express my own thanks to the witness for his very rank and honest testimony before the committee this afternoon. I will say it was a bit unusual.'

One member of the committee commented: 'I am going to see *The King and I* tonight and I will appreciate it much more.'

Doyle: 'I want to join in heartily complimenting you on doing what you have done. You realise no doubt that when you volunteered the names of other Communists whom you knew to be Communists that you would, by those people at least, be put in the class [of stool pigeons and informers]?'

Robbins: 'Yes sir.'

Doyle: 'In other words you did it with your eyes open?'

Robbins replied: 'I did it according to my conscience. I've examined myself.

Congressman Doyle told him: 'I think I made a great mistake in entering the Communist party. I think I am doing the right thing as an American.'

Doyle: 'Again, I want to compliment you. You are in a wonderful place, through your art, your music, your talent which God has blessed you with, to perhaps be very vigorous and positive in promoting Americanism in contrast to Communism.'

Chairman Harold Velde added his own praise: 'You have performed patriotic service to the committee and I am sure all Congress and the American people are very thankful to you for it.'

The American people, apart from Elliott Sullivan, Madeleine Lee and the brothers Chodorov, that is. Madeleine Lee has particular reason to feel angry, even today.

She told Barbra Paskin: 'I was at a union party and I had been looking for Jerome Robbins, who was an Equity member. A young, cute man came up to me when I was dancing and he said he was Jerome Robbins. He said, "I'm doing a ballet called *Fancy Free*. I want some street dancers. Would you teach me the Lindy Hop?" We became very close friends, we dated and I took him to see a play about lesbianism.'

He offered her a part in *Fancy Free* but then they lost touch.

However, their names were to be linked again in 1952, just after the Hollywood investigations began again when the blacklist was beginning to take hold. She was by then the wife of Jack Gilford and they had a son and a daughter.

'I was being followed for *Red Channels*,' Lee recalled. She was angry about *Red Channels*, in which she and her husband were listed along with Lena Horne, Harry Belafonte and Eleanor Roosevelt. Jerome Robbins was salt in her wounds.

Madeleine had been standing on the slippery slope of supporting left-wing causes and it would have been strange if difficulties were not arising. 'Friends rang and said, "Turn on your radio or television. Jerry Robbins has just named you on television."' There were other names listed on that broadcast like the Chodorovs and Lloyd Gough. 'Jerry Robbins had this hit show *Wonderful Town*, written by Jerome Chodorov. We were the kind of activists they wanted to knock off.'

Lee maintains that Robbins was subjected to wire taps, as a result of which he was accused of soliciting an under-age boy. He had been told that unless he cleared his name of charges of being a Communist, he would never make a film or work on TV again. He chose to do so by incriminating his friends. But not his family, although there was no sympathy for him from much of its members.

It was around the same time as when the Rosenbergs were facing the prospect of going to the electric chair. 'I went to Washington,' Madeleine recalls. On this trip, a strange woman approached her. 'I was sitting in front of the White House. She said, "I'm Sonia, Jerry Robbins' sister. I will never speak to him again. You could have been the Rosenbergs."' There would be a nice coda to this story, which comes later in the book.

Edward Chodorov said in a publication produced by the Writers Guild that he associated with Communists because he became 'angry at my studio [MGM] and at all the studios who kept insisting that business as usual must go on in Europe and that it was none of our business. It was unthinkable to me that Louis B Mayer, who was a Jew, knew what was happening in Germany with the Jews – especially after *Kristalnacht*, after that terrible night that signalled the smashing of all Jewish shops and so forth throughout Germany. And the concentration camps. Unthinkable to me that he would still insist everything was OK. Well, I and many other people just looked around for things. I joined the Anti-Nazi League, the Spanish Refugee Committee, everything that held out some promise of action.'

But the Communist party? Edward said he didn't know. 'Because later on, when I went to get my passport back after it was taken away, the man said to me: "Do you deny being a member of the Communist party?"' The man listed all sorts of organisations to which Chodorov replied: 'Well, I guess I'm a member of the Communist Party,' but was quick to clarify that there were very few 'diehard Communists' in Hollywood.

It was easy to find who was and who was not a member of the Communist Party. For most parts of the local party, there were lists. Nikki Trumbo recalled one young girl who managed to beat the system. 'I had a friend who was the secretary of the local branch of the Communist Party . . . and she was called before a committee when she was 16 years old. And she ate the mailing list. And then promptly forgot every single name and address on it and never was able to remember them after that.'

Other Communist officials gloried in their ability to make HUAC sit up and think – and be grateful for the 'horse's mouth' information with which they were presented. One of the most important testimonies to the committee was that William Ward Kimple. He was a find, but because his testimony didn't come before June 1955, its impact has been lost in the mountain of documentation that makes up the HUAC story.

Kimple had been a member of the intelligence unit of the Los Angeles Police Department for the 20 years from 1924 to 1944. However, he lived a double life. Under the name of William Wallace, from 1928 to 1939 he was a member of the Communist Party. He was a literary agent working for the party and was also a 'unit educational director' and then assistant membership director. He was, in fact, a spy – supplying the police department with information about the party.

Why it took all those years before he was called has never been properly explained, unless HUAC felt they still needed him under cover.

He told Tavenner that he and the dues secretary of the Los Angeles branch worked as a team. 'She was the LA County dues secretary for the Hollywood subsection. She was also secretary of the Los Angeles County disciplinary committee of the Communist party. And working together, we kept the police department pretty well informed.'

Kimple said: 'I furnished [my police superior] copies of the Communist Party membership records and, where possible, I furnished him copies of the Communist Party membership registration and, where possible, I turned in to him . . . the Communist membership books.'

This was a veritable goldmine. Congressman Donald Jackson summed up the value he presented to the committee. 'It is by virtue of informed testimony such as this that it has been possible to piece together across the years the nature and the extent and the objectives of the Communist party of the United States. Of course, anyone who serves on this Committee is automatically a heel in the eyes of the comrades.' Knowing it was good to show that he had adopted the vernacular of his enemies, he added, 'Your future will be that of a stool pigeon.'

Kimple was ready for that one: 'I've been so labelled many times.'

Jackson wanted to assure him: 'I feel that that will reflect a very small, vocal minority viewpoint and that by and large the people of the city of Los Angeles, California in general, and of the nation, owe to you and other people who have been willing to take on assignments of this kind in the line of official duty, separating yourself in large part, as I know you must have, from family associations, social things you would very much have preferred to do, a debt of gratitude.'

Kimple then said he could 'positively identify the Communist Party membership of close to a thousand people.' It was information, he said, that he had handed over to the committee. It was also in addition to that given to HUAC by Max Silver, the organisational secretary for the Southern California Communist Party from 1938 to 1945. He had 4,000 names to give. There was one other spy, Roy Erwin, an FBI informer who had worked in radio in Hollywood.

It has to be admitted that refusing to name names was never an easy option. Joanna Rapf, daughter of Maurice Rapf, said: 'It took tremendous courage not to. Tremendous courage.'

*

Like Larry Parks and David Raksin, Budd Schulberg, who achieved fame with his Hollywood novel *What Makes Sammy Run* (which was seen as anticipating the blacklist) and later the classic movie *On The Waterfront*, named names – but ones which the committee already had in front of them. It earned him the opprobrium of most of the unfriendlies. That, of course, wasn't difficult.

The position of Edward G Robinson, one of the outstanding performers of the pre-war era who first made a huge impact in the title role in *Little Caesar* in 1931, may not have been unique, but it was unusual. He had been seen as the iconic Warner Bros gangster, although his range was much bigger than that. His role as the father in Arthur Miller's *All My Sons* in 1948 would be one of the most significant of his career. In *Key Largo* that same year, he gave Humphrey Bogart a run for his money. But when it came to HUAC, it was the man everyone in Hollywood knew as Eddie who did the running – from the accusations that he was a Communist. The danger point came when he sent a cheque for over $2,000 to Dalton Trumbo whom he claimed wrote to him asking for financial support. It was a generous move on his part, for Robinson soon had to sell his world-famous art collection, partly to cover a divorce settlement. The Trumbo cheque was a big black mark against Robinson. Even worse for the man who had in fact been born Emmanuel Goldenberg in Romania was his membership of the American Committee for the Foreign Born, which was inevitably dubbed a Communist front, despite the fact that people who choose to become citizens are usually the most patriotic in the land.

So Edward G Robinson chose to put himself in the guise of Emmanuel Goldenberg, immigrant. Like many who came to a new country, he adopted it as much as it adopted him. 'It was very painful for him,' his granddaughter, Francesca Robinson Sanchez, now says. 'He came to this country, loved this country. To be accused of destroying it was a terrible, terrible thing.'

Eddie denied he was a Communist in three appeals to HUAC.

An article in a publication by the Catholic Information Society, entitled RED STAR OVER HOLLYWOOD, written by Oliver Carlson claimed: 'Names like Edward G Robinson – to take a notorious example of an actor who has sponsored literally dozens of Red undertakings and organisations – gain . . . an audience a hundred thousand times greater than any avowed Communist can muster. And such names have been standard on all pro-Soviet and Red-dominated lists.' To say nothing, of course, of the value they offered to HUAC.

It was standard practice among the opposition to Hollywood's Reds to plant articles, some of them unsigned, in a series of spurious magazines. One of them was entitled: CONQUEST OF HOLLYWOOD DESIGNED IN MOSCOW. The article claimed: 'As we now know, the Communists have had America marked down for conquest since as far back as 1917. But they knew that they could not hope for success unless they could first break down on defences and resistive power from within. Their first was to capture and enslave Hollywood and the radio.' The anonymous writer added: 'This enslavement was decided upon and designed in Moscow in 1920 when the Cinema Bureau of the International Union of the Revolutionary Theatre was organised.'

Nobody accused Edward G Robinson of belonging to that organisation. But they got close to it and he had to defend himself. He said that he had prepared a list of every organisation to which he ever belonged and sent it to J Edgar Hoover personally. He received merely a perfunctory reply. What makes Robinson's case so unusual is that he didn't respond to a subpoena, but actually asked to appear before the committee. They said that no accusations had been made against him – apart, that is, in the Catholic Information Society article and the inevitable inclusion of his name in *Red Channels*. It was enough. Enough, as it turned out to make him, in a phrase he used in his autobiography *All My Yesterdays*, a pariah. Robinson first appeared in 1947, thanks to the then mayor of Los Angeles who thought it right that he be given a chance to explain himself.

Robinson became emotional at this hearing. 'I think I have not only been a good citizen,' he told the committee. 'I think I have been an *extraordinarily good* citizen and I value this above everything else. I think I may have taken money under false pretences in my own business and I may not have been good as a husband or father or friend as I should have been, but I know my Americanism is unblemished and fine and wonderful and I am proud of it and I don't feel it is conceit on my part to say this and I stand on my record or fall on it.'

As he later wrote, he fell. He couldn't get a film part, doing only a little radio and a stage play. In 1950 he appeared again before HUAC. Robinson said that he believed the committee wanted him to say he was 'a dupe, a sucker, a fool, an idiot, that I'd been double-crossed and everything I believed in was negated by the clubs to which I belonged – that I was a tool, an unsuspecting agent of the

Communist conspiracy. I didn't say it,' he wrote in his book, 'because I didn't believe it.'

Two years later, Eddie Robinson was again hauled before HUAC. The Chairman told him: 'This committee has never had any evidence presented to indicate that you were anything more than a very choice sucker. I think you are the number one on the sucker list in the country.' It was rude and did the star no good at all. Until his appearance in *The Ten Commandments* in 1956, his film output for various studios was listed under the letter B, an ignominy almost as severe as being called a sucker. It was a situation that affects his family to this day. His granddaughter Francesca wants to put the record straight about the consequences of his involvement with HUAC. 'There are people who say he was not blacklisted. But he was. His passport was taken away from him. He was in *Red Channels*. Suddenly, a man who was in top pictures was doing B pictures. And after that B picture period, he was not able to get any work at all because no one would hire him. As one friend told us: 'He gave $100,000 to the USO [the United Services Organisation which organised troop concerts in the war]. He not only gave money, he gave of himself.'

It had a terrible effect on his wife, Francesca says. 'She was heartbroken. She cried about it.' She says it destroyed their marriage and ultimately was responsible for their divorce.

They tried to keep their grief to themselves. 'Nobody saw it, but the family did. There was just a quietness about the house.' As she said, people decided there was no smoke without fire. Could he be a Communist? 'He was for people, he wanted to help people. He was so grateful he was able to earn a living without tyranny. He would do anything to help someone else.' And to try to clear his name.

When it no longer mattered, when only Robinson still thought about it, the pain remained. 'I feel that Eddie never got over it,' said his granddaughter. 'It was like a sword in the heart.'

Perhaps one of the principal swords that the Red-baiters had at their disposal was the ability to access the hearts of their victims rather than the hearts of the perceived problem. Robinson tormented himself about being a HUAC victim. Others were able to make it seem like water off a duck's back.

Not everyone immediately knew that they had been put on what was still considered by many to be a mythical blacklist. The writer Walter Bernstein was working on a TV film called *Danger*. His producer at

CBS, a man called Charles Russell, 'came to me one day and said, "I can't use you any more. I'm not supposed to tell you, I'm supposed to tell you you're going in a new direction. Your name is on some kind of list; you are unemployable." It was the first time I knew about it.'

The composer Aaron Copland appeared before McCarthy himself in May 1953. Was he a Communist sympathiser? 'I am not sure I would be able to say what you mean by the word "sympathiser,"' he responded.

'Did he attend Communist meetings?'

'I am afraid I don't know how you define a Communist meeting.'

'What was his view of the Hitler-Stalin pact?'

'I don't remember any specific view of it.'

Others, of course, remembered every moment and every incident in which they were implicated.

Shortly before his death, I asked Larry Adler if people tried to persuade him to co-operate when he appeared before McCarthy. 'Oh yes,' he told me, 'even my own brother did. He said, "Why put yourself in such a spot?" There was one argument I found hard to resist. And that argument was, "Larry, your principles are very fine, but you have a wife and three children to support." And my answer was, "What the hell kind of father or husband can I be if I've sold out, if I betrayed other people?" That for me was the unforgivable sin – if I had betrayed someone else.'

Roy Cohn, McCarthy's number-one aide, made his pitch about fighting City Hall when he offered Adler a deal. 'Roy Cohn said, "I am only seeing you because of a mutual friend, Ben Sonenberg. We made a special deal in your case. No one is going to know about it. We know you don't want to give names." I said, "Really?" He said, "I'm going to give you a list of names that has been given to us by others. In other words, we have these names, so by just reading out this list, Larry, you're not hurting anyone. We already know these names."'

I asked him if he ever regretted his decision. 'Oh, no. I'd feel the same today. I know I would.'

One can't be sure if John Garfield, the soulful toughie who had had two Academy Award nominations – for best supporting actor in *Four Daughters* in 1938 and best actor in *Body and Soul* in 1947 – regretted what he had done. He appeared before HUAC when he refused to name names particularly that of his wife, who had been a party member up to the death of their elder daughter. He never admitted to being a Communist himself and was due to appear again only to die of a heart attack shortly beforehand. There were rumours that he was about to recant and provide the committee with what they wanted.

By that time, Garfield had been blacklisted by the big studios. Rumours persisted that this was not the main reason for his name appearing on that list. Rather, it was because he tried to beat the big boys at their own game: Garfield set up his own production company called Enterprise. It made three movies – *Body and Soul, Force of Evil* in 1948 and *He Ran All the Way* in 1951. It was a rare thing to do in those days, even rarer than naming names. None of the films made any money and one of the partners ran off with much of the takings, but they were still considered a threat by mainstream Hollywood.

Garfield was born the son of an immigrant Russian-Jewish tailor on New York's Lower East Side, where he attended a school for problem children. Paul Buhle says of him: 'It's very much like the plot of [a] boxing film where the boxer agrees to take a fall and then at the last minute recants and knocks out the opponent. Garfield was not an intellectual, a cerebral kind of individual, but at the same time he represented something in Hollywood.'

Walter Bernstein, who became one of the most significant blacklist figures, says he is sure that HUAC wanted Garfield to be a friendly witness, hence the feeling that he might have been about to name names. But Bernstein isn't so sure. 'He wasn't a Communist himself but his friends were. His sympathies were on the left and he was torn between being John Garfield, an actor and being Julie Garfinkle, who was on the streets where the worst thing is to be a snitch. They [the committee] wanted him to testify. He testified to this by dying.'

The truth of the matter is that there were very few people in Hollywood who were as popular, and that is despite the rumours about Garfield's intentions before the committee. 'He was a lovely guy,' remembers Joan Scott. 'I think [he was] a very principled man.' So very principled that he showed up to speak at a Shrine meeting on the day (or the day after, she isn't sure) that his elder daughter had died from an asthma attack. 'One of my assignments was to keep him in sight, to make sure he was OK and didn't wander off alone because he was in very bad shape, emotionally. He was devastated and in a state of shock. It was a matter of having someone there with him to see that he made it and I think it was amazing that he kept his commitment to appear.' Such was the mood at the time.

Scott concurs with Bernstein about Garfield refusing to be a snitch. 'I personally never believed Garfield would name names. I thought he was gutsy and the time that I spent with him, I felt he was a gutsy person, a trustworthy person and although you couldn't always know a person's breaking points, I felt confident in him.'

Not surprisingly, that is how he is seen by his daughter, the actress Julie Garfield – and this despite the fact that he allegedly died in the process of having intercourse with a woman who was not his wife. Julie was just 6 years old at the time; old enough to know that she was in love with him. 'I knew that I was in love with him. He was like a god to me. He was so handsome and wonderful. But he wasn't around that much.' His presence was, however. Two days after he died, the FBI, with their usual demeanour and in their usual uniforms, rang the doorbell while Julie, her brother and her mother were having dinner. Her mother went to the door 'and she got very angry. She told them: "He's dead; you got what you wanted. Go away! These are my children. My husband's dead . . . now get out of here."' And, she remembers, 'they went away. I remember they said something like "We want to look around." She said: "You're not".'

Julie suspects her father was chosen by HUAC, along with Edward G Robinson, because they knew he was very liberal and 'probably very interested in Marxism' . . . They picked Julie because 'the studios said, "Take him; you can have him."' That was, she believes, because he had bucked the system and formed that independent production company.

To HUAC, setting up alone was just the sort of nasty, underhand thing a guy like Garfield would do. Julie admits he had been involved in a street gang as a kid, 'a little wild and a little rough round the edges there,' and even spent a day in jail. There were other claims against him, too – like being a member of the Group Theater and being a friend of Clifford Odets, who had written the boxing drama *Golden Boy* for him. (Odets testified before the committee and named names.) Whether being instrumental in getting the Hollywood Canteen (a place where servicemen about to be shipped to the front would be entertained by film stars who acted, sang and, more importantly, served doughnuts and coffee and then danced with them), going had anything to do with his subpoenas is a matter for speculation. He wanted to do his bit and a heart condition had ruled out his serving in the forces himself. The fact is that even his most patriotic gestures were readily construed as un-American.

The extent to which Garfield was hounded left scars on his family. Julie recalls that FBI men followed him when he went to see the dying actor Canada Lee, with whom had starred in *Body and Soul*. 'There was one of these FBI guys lurking on the corner and Daddy goes up to him and says, "Hey, I see you there. I'm John Garfield. How you doing? I'm coming here to see my friend Canada Lee and he's dying." And this guy apparently looked very sheepish and was embarrassed. But he was trailing him.'

Of course, it didn't end there. 'One of these guys calls my father up and summons him down to FBI headquarters during this whole last year of his life when he's trying to clear his name.'

It wasn't just a matter of more questions. The FBI was eager to bring his wife into the affair, too – and not very subtly. 'The guy puts before him my mother's cancelled cheque to some kind of what they called a Communist cause. I think it was a contribution to the war in Spain and to the refugees – and the other was [an] expired, twelve or fifteen years expired, Communist card.

'And this guy says, "Look, all you have to do is sign this affidavit, saying you knew your wife was a member of the Communist party and we'll let you go." To most people that would have been a red rag to a bull. To a former street gang member, that invited a left hook – and not the kind he was writing about. He almost lost his cool. 'Daddy said, "Screw you!" and he walked off.'

So did CBS. He was invited on to a big TV variety show to perform a scene from *Golden Boy*. The scene was recorded but then pulled by the network because he was already blacklisted.

When he appeared before HUAC, he took the Diminished Fifth. He told the committee: 'Ask me anything you want about anything, but don't ask me to talk about my wife and don't ask me to talk about my friends. I will not talk about my wife and I will not talk about my friends.' Lillian Hellman would later say much the same. The committee heeded only part of his request, still asking about his wife. 'They made him testify for I think it was like twelve hours and they wouldn't let him go to the bathroom. They treated him horribly.'

Julie describes the scene: 'There was this long table with all these senators (sic) firing questions at him. And you have to remember that John was different from a lot of them. He was not an intellectual. He didn't know how to talk his way out of a situation. Like how brilliant Larry Parks was on the stand. My father had had no education, he'd been kicked out of school right and left . . . and I think he was scared shitless, frankly – and hadn't the slightest idea how to testify. I think he didn't know how to conduct himself in a courtroom. He accidentally perjured himself. He said that he did not attend some kind of demonstration for one of the anti-war rallies. Apparently he did attend it – it wasn't intentional; he'd forgotten about it. And they picked up on it and they decided he had perjured himself.'

Despite the haranguing he received when he actually did appear, when it was all over, the committee members, many of them far from home, hung around – even going to the same restaurant in Washington that evening – so that they could be photographed with Hollywood star John Garfield. It was as though they were big-game hunters or anglers wanting to show off their catch of the day. Garfield looked terrible in pictures that were taken during the hearing itself. 'He looked a mess. Huge bags under his eyes, he was completely tormented.'

The committee's answer to the perjury charge was to tell him to come back again. Garfield wanted to clear his name. His lawyer came up with the idea of his writing an article for *Life* magazine protesting his innocence. Julie Garfield remembers: 'That's when he and my mother got into a big fight about this. She said, "You don't have to clear your name. You didn't do anything. Why should you have to clear your name? What are you clearing your name of? What did you do?" And he's saying, "Well, I'll never work again and I want to work. And acting is my passion."'

His wife suggested that they go to Europe where he could work 'and we'll come back and it'll all be over.' But that was not the way Julie Garfinkle street fighter operated. He had to clear his name. He started working on the article which he thought should be called, I WAS A SUCKER FOR A LEFT HOOK. In it he claimed that he was a Roosevelt Democrat and had been hoodwinked by Communists into signing various documents. The article was never published, but it could form the basis for the charge that he was about to confess to the committee.

Julie Garfield says John was undoubtedly going to co-operate with HUAC. 'But some people translated that into meaning he was going to name names. That isn't true. He never had any intention of naming names. He was simply prepared to appear before the committee again and to him that's what was meant by co-operating.'

It all hit his wife harder than anyone could have imagined. Her daughter recalls her mother escaping into the bathroom and turning on all the taps fully – so that the children wouldn't hear her crying.

The fights between the Garfields intensified when it became clear John intended to publish his piece. 'They separated. He moved out and had visitation rights to come and see us. In fact, the day he died he was supposed to see me. We had a date and I looked forward to these dates we had. He'd come and take me out somewhere, take me to the park and we'd go rowing or something. These were my special times with him. And the day he died, he didn't show. Because he died in Iris Whitney's apartment. She was a woman he'd had an affair with.'

And all the time the FBI had been following him – in California and in New York, too. Soon after his death, it emerged that HUAC were going to leave things as they were. 'The saddest thing about the whole thing,' says his daughter today, 'was that right after he died, [his wife] found out that they were going to clear him anyway. They had decided to clear him but he had already died and it was too late.'

And too late to help his reputation. His daughter denies the charge that John died during sex with the other woman. 'That was not true. The night that he died, he was absolutely tormented. He hadn't slept in about a week. He was trying to clear his name and suddenly movie stardom [was] taken away from him. He was separated from his wife. Of course, he'd had an affair with this woman, but the night in question when they said he died in the sack, he actually had been working all night with this guy, Forster. Arnold Forster, a leading member of B'nai B'rith, who was helping him write that article I WAS A SUCKER FOR A LEFT HOOK, and then he'd gone to eat dinner at Luchow's. He was depressed, binged on food and drink, and smoked too much and he hadn't slept in days and went back to her house. They were supposed to go and visit a friend in Gramercy Square also and Daddy said, "I don't feel well." He went back to her apartment and she put him to bed in the living room. And when she woke up, she went in there and she found him dead. That's how it happened. And then everybody made up this horrible thing that he'd died in the sack.'

Joan Scott would also appear before the committee. She had joined the party at 16 and was expelled from it three years later – because she was in psychoanalysis 'and the party wouldn't have that.'

She worked for a firm of lawyers brought in to defend some of the Ten – which is how she met her husband, Adrian. She didn't last long at work, though, because the fight to beat HUAC took on a very personal aspect. Her boss, Morris Cohn 'had a thing for me and in those days when you were chased around the desk . . . you didn't say "Fuck off!" and most cases you didn't sleep with the boss either. You just ran around the desk. You'd drive up to Ventura for a steak dinner and sit in the car and get fondled and run around the desk. That seemed to work reasonably well until in my case Morris Cohn became one of the lawyers for the Ten and Adrian came by to pick up some of the legal papers and called me the next day and we started dating. And I got fired.'

The second batch of hearings lasted from 1951 to 1953. But in some cases it appeared that a lot of the HUAC's enthusiasm for lambasting Hollywood figures was fading. Bernard Gordon was one of the last to be called – except that in the end, he didn't take what served as the witness stand. 'They'd got to the bottom of the barrel when they got to me because this was after most people had been called. As I explained, because I hadn't been a member of the Writers' Guild, I wasn't known [to be] the stool pigeon like [Martin] Berkeley. There were a few people who knew me and did become stool pigeons, but if they weren't asked directly, they didn't say anything. They didn't want to be voluntary stool pigeons.'

Gordon was blacklisted just the same. Not being called to actually face the committee and answer the $64,000 question didn't mean that he was not subpoenaed – because, once it was obvious that it wasn't enough to depend on a little girl being told that FBI men were actually magazine salesmen, the time came for him when a pink slip found its destination.

Gordon's summons stated he was to appear 'before the Committee on Un-American Activities or a duly authorised subcommittee thereof of the House of Representatives of the United States of which the Hon. John S Wood is Chairman in their chamber in the city of Los Angeles, California, on September 5 1952 at the Federal Building at the hour of 10am there to testify touching matters of inquiry committed to said committee and he is not to depart without leave of the said committee.'

So Gordon appeared. He recalled for me: 'It was a fairly large room, it held about one hundred people, fitted up with a large table up on a dais in front, and folding chairs.' The committee, 'about eight or nine [of them], together with a lawyer or two', who posed many of the questions, were on the dais. 'A man would be called and they asked him questions.'

That man wasn't Gordon, however. 'There were very few writers left to be subpoenaed. Now at this time, they were subpoenaed doctors and lawyers.

'The doctors and the lawyers were among the last people who were subpoenaed and forced to testify. They were the ones who put up the best fight against the committee. They were very articulate and they had a lot to say and, they knew what to say – they knew their rights and refused to be silenced by the banging gavel. I was there in the room, waiting for my turn to be called. I didn't have to wait outside. They wanted an audience – and this was all being broadcast on radio.'

He was in the room when a doctor who had been awarded bravery medals in World War Two flung them down in disgust at how he saw the cause for which he had been fighting so woefully exploited. Thus the doctors and lawyers shielded him from the committee onslaught. As Gordon said: 'They argued so much and so well, they ran out of time.'

He had had rehearsals with his own lawyers. 'Of course, I was very articulate and did most of the talking and lawyers liked to cross-examine me because I was enjoying myself at that point. There was nothing to be afraid of. We were all working together. And I suppose I was hogging the microphone.'

There were appeals for money 'because we have to pay the lawyers, maybe a nominal sum. Even though they themselves were in some cases people who'd been subpoenaed.'

The generosity of some people was remarkable. 'I had a couple of interesting responses. One was from Bill Alland who had borrowed a book from me and now he was returning it. But he didn't want to be seen having anything to do with me, so he put a $20 or $50 bill, I don't remember, in the leaf of the book and left it by my front door. He was giving me the money, but secretly, see?'

There was another man who gave him $50, but said it had to be a secret because he didn't want his wife to know about it. Gordon gave him back the money because he didn't want to create marital discord.

As he said: 'I was ready to be called, with my statement in my hand. I had to consider myself still under the subpoena. So I didn't have the glory of being known as a blacklisted writer.' For the time at least. That would change. He was sent a telegram demanding his appearance instead on 2 October 1952. That was cancelled, too. Not, however, his status on the blacklist. Just to have been called was enough for it to remain there indefinitely.

So what purpose did the blacklist serve? Certainly not to gain information. The fact that the named names were essentially known to the committee and probably contained not a single surprise shows that there was an ulterior motive – or motives. HUAC wanted to demonstrate its power for its own self-aggrandisement.

What's more, by persuading supposedly decent Americans to recant, they were consciously weakening Communist influence. They did so to a degree they could never have imagined. The blacklist was a product of the studios, but the collection of names called before HUAC served the same purpose – the destruction of the careers and of innocent people.

Chapter Eleven
The List is Black

Whenever an investigator in this country challenges a man's right to challenge his own thoughts, he is discrediting every fighting veteran of World War Two – for, among other things, that war was fought to get rid of fear and intimidation.

Norman Corwin, 1947

Directors didn't come more exalted or more popular than Vincent Sherman, at least as far as the studios were concerned. The man who had become Bette Davis's By-Appointment director, with films like the 1943 *Old Acquaintance* and *Mr Skeffington* the year later under his belt, he was, to use the Hollywood vernacular, 'bankable'. That was until the day after he had moved from Warner Bros to MGM, when he got out of the elevator and walked towards his office.

The sight in the distance could not be ignored – there was a workman standing outside his office with a screwdriver in his hand. What he was doing was removing Sherman's nameplate from his office door. Why? This man only knew that he had instructions, and the man who did know, of course, was Dore Schary. Sherman stormed into Schary's room. 'What's going on?' he demanded.

'Oh, Vince,' the studio head of production, responded, 'I'm so sorry, but you saw the trades today?'

'No,' said the director, picking up the *Hollywood Reporter*. In one line was the answer to the question: 'What's this about Vincent Sherman being a Red?' Sherman demanded to know more. 'There's no allegation,' he pointed out. 'There's no accusation.'

The production chief was embarrassed. 'I know Vince,' he replied. 'But we've got to deal with the banks and they're just so sensitive about anybody being associated with Communists.' Then, he went on: 'You know, Vince, there's a way you can prove your loyalty. Tell us whom you know who is a Communist.'

180

Thus, the backlist took root. HUAC didn't set up that list. It was entirely the work of the producers and studio bosses who were running scared.

Sherman had to deal with the studios' blacklist at the same time as his wife had to cope with his various admitted infidelities. She had learned not to protest. According to their son, he told his wife, Hedda: 'I'm not going to be physically faithful. You are a free person, you take it or leave it.' But the studio was not going to be so accommodating.

'Here's how poor my mother was. Her family owned a Jewish delicatessen in Brooklyn. They were so poor, they couldn't eat their own food, so they would starve and be serving food to others all day. She considered it and said OK. Consequently my father would come home every night after his dalliances and say, "Hedda, guess who I slept with tonight?" and she'd say, "Who?" and he'd say, "Bette Davis," and my mother would say, "Gee, I hear she can be kind of vicious. Watch your step," and she'd roll over and go to sleep.' A man who slept with Bette Davis while his wife was in bed at home was likely to be an easy target for HUAC.

The Hollywood trades like *Daily Variety* and the *Hollywood Reporter* kept quiet about his affairs, but loved the rows between studio bosses and Sherman. He had frequently sided with employees whom the studio wanted to sack when he considered them important to a particular project. 'However,' recalls his son, 'the real thing used against him was a 1932 picture directed by William Wyler called *Counsellor at Law*, where my dad played a Communist. This was used as ultimate proof of his sympathy to the Communist Party.'

By that reckoning, any actor who ever played a Nazi, including the dozens of Germans who came to America as refugees from Hitler – could have been branded a sympathiser, but they weren't. HUAC never worried that much about Nazis.

Sherman didn't work from 1952 to 1956, in fact until Harry Cohn eventually took those first steps to break the blacklist. 'My mother said, "Vincent, go in there and threaten them. Tell them you're going to expose the whole rotten game." And my dad said, "Hedda, I don't want to rock the boat."'

But boats were already being rocked. The trouble was that the whole HUAC *raison d'être* was rocking boats. The unions continued to play to the committee's tunes. When HUAC demanded that the Screen Writers Guild hand over all their records to them, they did just that.

It caused huge bitterness, right from the time of the Hollywood Ten. Michael Cole recalled how his father, Lester, one of the Ten, regarded SWG. 'He was bitter about the way he was treated by his own union. It wasn't like he was being driven crazy or that he was in that sense being hounded. It was the inability to work. And, sure, it was the government's fault. But it wasn't just the government's fault, it was also his colleagues who went along with the blacklist. They, after all, were not required to do this. There was no law that they had to keep these guys from writing. Jack Warner and these other people went along with the blacklist because of their own ideological reasons and, of course, it was profitable for them to do that. They were out to make money and they didn't approve of what my father believed in. They sure as hell didn't approve of the unions, they fought the unions as long as they could.' But now the unions were playing the employers' game. It was more than HUAC could have hoped for.

It took 50 years for SWG to apologise. In 1998 Richard Asur, the president, issued a statement: 'It is impossible for any of us to fully understand the pressures that were brought to bear on the Board members of 50 years ago, what caused them to make the choices they did. We are in no position to judge our predecessors. However, with all the clarity of historical perspective, we must accept responsibility for the actions which they took. When Guild members were being threatened with the loss of their professional lives simply because they held political beliefs which were unpopular at the time, SWG, under pressure from the United States government, collaborated with those who sought to "purge subversives from the film community", ending or severely damaging the careers of many of our members.'

As we have seen, there were no more than 400 people on that list, including not just stars, directors and writers, but grips, gaffers and electricians, to say nothing of continuity girls and secretaries. For years, there were still Hollywood executives who would deny that such a list existed. But it was there, in the drawers and the filing cabinets of producers and others with the power to hire and fire. Sixty years later, at the dawn of a new millennium and at a time when Hollywood had changed radically, the *M-A-S-H* writer Larry Gelbart told me: 'I was a young man talking to a producer in his office when the telephone rang. I heard the conversation clearly. The producer was being asked about employing somebody for a film. "Wait a minute," he said, opening his drawer, from which he produced a list. "Sorry," he said. "We couldn't use him". The man's name was on that list. And so his career was imperilled.'

If HUAC had the FBI behind it, the studios had their own detectives, just like the policeman who importuned David Raksin in the toilet for immoral purposes (the purposes of extracting incriminating evidence, that is). And others who might have done better, writing fiction.

Eric Sherman said that Schary – 'a spineless asehole' is how he describes him – 'produced from his desk, a dossier . . . 18 pages, legal-size paper, single-spaced typed with a list of donations my father had made to the Communist Party. Item after item. Communist cell meetings my father had attended. And my father scanned through this and he said, "Dore, it's all fabricated."'

It wasn't a unique situation. As the younger Sherman remembered: 'There was this famous detective agency that fabricated dossiers and they would use that to get people to say, "No, that's not right. The person who's really in the party is so-and-so".'

Director and studio then parted company. And Sherman never made *Lone Star*, written by Borden Chase of the Ward Bond-John Wayne set – whom he suspected of planting the *Hollywood Reporter* story. Sherman was luckier than many for he had money behind him. But, recalls his son, 'My father was at the height of his career, producing and directing major stars. He was earning probably $5,000 a week, so, given inflation, that would be $200- to $300,000 a week. And my father was out of work for five years thereafter – until the blacklist was finally broken.'

The relationship between bosses and employees was nearly always fraught. Mel Shavelson recalls meeting Harry Cohn – one of the first studio chiefs to break the blacklist – when the Columbia boss was in a conciliatory mood. 'I don't join anything,' Shavelson told me. 'I was called up by Harry, who wanted to know if I were a Communist. I told him our job was to write jokes. He said OK. But later we had a fight. Later, he said, "Why should we fight? We're in the same business – of trying to screw the government". That was his basic philosophy.'

The employees were mainly in the business of trying to screw the blacklist, but at first their efforts had appallingly little effect.

While it was true that it *was* virtually impossible to insert propaganda into movies, there were occasions when the timing was all wrong. Like Abraham Polonsky's 1951 film *I Can Get It for You Wholesale*, based on the garment industry and the empowerment of women. It opened in Los Angeles in 1950, in the week that Polonsky was called on to testify before HUAC. 'So,' Paul Buhle notes, 'the chance of making a very strong statement was eradicated at a stroke.'

Thirty years after HUAC's worst days, Walter Bernstein, himself a blacklistee, wrote a film starring mostly other blacklisted actors, with much of the production staff and technicians also blacklisted. The one exception was the star of *The Front*, Woody Allen. Two incidents in the movie, both featuring the actor Zero Mostel, give a sad illustration of the effect of having your name on one of the dreaded lists. Zero was an angry man in many ways, a big explosive man. He would try to get nightclub work. There was a scene in *The Front* when he goes to one of the Catskill mountain resorts. 'That actually happened. I took him up to The Concord, where he had been used to getting $2,000 a night. He got $500. His rate was cut even more. There were 2,000 people there. They loved it. He cursed them in Yiddish – and the more he cursed them, the more they liked it. In his rage, he went through half a bottle of whisky. We drove back next day. I wanted him to play it in the film, but at first he didn't want to. It was still too raw.'

Mostel testified before the committee and as a result his space on the blacklist was confirmed. In another scene in that movie, Mostel, totally distraught now at what was happening to his career, books into an hotel, orders champagne from room service, tips the waiter generously – then opens a window, and jumps to his death.

This actually happened to the actor Philip Loeb, who for years had starred as Jake in one of America's principal radio soap operas, *The Goldbergs*. The TV version was produced by his co-star and screen-wife, Molly Berg, but he was dropped from it after his name appeared in *Red Channels*. He fell to his death from a Manhattan window.

Less dramatic perhaps but equally sad was the death of the American actor J Edward Bromberg, who died in London during the run of a West End play in which he starred. It was 1954 and every evening he would play chess with Theodore Bikel, the actor who bucked the trend of regular exodus of left-wingers from the United States to Europe. Bikel went to return to America, where he still lives and performs. That evening, he had a phone call from the stage manager to say that Bromberg had failed to turn up at the theatre. Together, they went to his flat. Bromberg didn't answer the doorbell. They broke in and found him inside, dead. He had had a heart attack or, as we have seen, Bikel put it to me: 'He died of a broken heart.'

It was the death of Bromberg that got the actress (and later director) Lee Grant on to the blacklist. She was speaking at a memorial gathering for the man whom she admired very greatly. 'I said that HUAC had killed Bromberg. He was made to be in a state of terror. It was the day that I was in *Red Channels* and realised that I couldn't work any more.'

As she said: 'My heart fell to my stomach. I couldn't believe that that could happen to me.' Looking back now, more than half a century later, she thinks she was probably used by people to speak at the meeting, people who realised what it could mean for her. 'Someone must have known I wouldn't survive that and should have advised me at that point that if I got up to speak, then I might never work again.' Grant knows that, since then, she has actually done the same to other people – and regrets it. 'I realised later that the cause was more important to me than getting other actors into trouble – I would never do that again.'

The blacklist had her name on it from then on. 'I was blacklisted right from the beginning. I had done *Detective Story* with Kirk Douglas and it was my first job after my play. I was nominated for an Academy Award for it and received the Cannes Festival Award for best actress of the year.' But that wasn't enough to protect Grant. 'By the time I got to our apartment, I couldn't work anywhere – in television or film.'

She says that she devoted 12 years to fighting to get the blacklist outlawed and collecting signatures for petitions to that end. 'But to put a name on that paper was a very dangerous situation for all of us. That was what *Red Channels* said about me.'

How to get off the blacklist? How to get *Red Channels* to rub her name from their own list? 'A lawyer from the William Morris agency said that I could get off the blacklist if I testified against my husband. It was like a death sentence. It would have been like committing suicide. I said I don't care if I never work again.' Actually, she cared very much, but the price offered was too high, much too high.

It is easy to be bitter. She now says she understands the fear of other people 'and why other actors crossed the street when they saw me coming. They wanted to keep on working.'

For all those years, however, Grant harboured a sense of revenge. 'I knew what was fair and what was not fair. My obsession was getting back at the people who had been my friends. It became all encompassing for me for the 12 years I was blacklisted. Such a period of growth and excitement in terms of what I had learned to do and was important in life. A couple of times people called from television stations and said "I think you're off the blacklist".' But she wasn't. 'It developed a fight in me. The fight was thrilling and the air was so clear and was so black and white.'

Eleven years after it all began, she consulted a well-connected lawyer who took on her case without fee. He went to the committee, which, though on its last legs, was still in existence. 'They said no – unless she testifies against her husband. 'Now, Arnie had been named. He had been named by another writer. He hadn't been called before the committee.' The lawyer said, "Why don't you let her go? Enough! It's eleven years." They said, "not unless she testifies against her husband." He made the point that a wife couldn't testify against her husband in law [the committee always maintained, of course, that it wasn't a court of law]. I said to my lawyer, "You might as well commit me". I would spend the rest of my life in an insane asylum. My message was "Screw you".'

Grant's name appeared in *Red Channels* for as long as it was published. Anyone who had ever signed a petition against fascism was likely to be featured. They were still after the 'premature anti-fascists'. As Theodore Bikel said: 'Premature anti-fascist, a wonderful phrase because it meant that it was all right to be anti-fascist once war broke out. Premature anti-fascists were those who fought fascism in the 30s.'

Walter Bernstein put it like this: 'My feeling is that there are certain people who are bitter and some who are not. I never felt bitter. I felt angry, angry a great deal of the time. I had friends, particularly among actors, who felt bitter. But, thinking about them, they were bitter already. I might have been an envious person, a jealous person, but not a bitter person.'

Marsha Hunt didn't find herself entirely without work, but almost so. 'I think I made perhaps three films in all the 1950s. But I was asked continually to take out ads [stating] my non-Communism in order to fend off threats of picketing the film if I remained on it.'

*　　*　　*

For a time it seemed that Betsy Blair would be free of the problems her fellow actresses had experienced. Significantly, she had a famous and successful husband. 'I may have been protected by Gene. He did treat me like the little girl whom he loved.' What he was protecting her from was the news that a planned loan-out from MGM to Columbia had been scrapped. 'It was easy to say that Metro wouldn't lend me to Columbia. He was protecting me. He didn't want to say that Harry Cohn didn't want me because of my left-wing activities. True, I would have felt bad. I was never personally frightened – partly because I had never suffered. We didn't have to go to Europe. We didn't have to flee as many people did.'

Their relatively undisturbed life was nevertheless punctuated by a series of ominous warnings. 'A journalist called me on a Saturday morning. Could I see him tomorrow? I said, not on Sunday. Sunday's when everybody's home, playing volleyball. He said, "It's not an interview, it's *for* you". There was something in the way he said it. He came at 11 o'clock on Sunday morning on the bridle path on Rodeo Drive. He said that on the Monday, in the *Hollywood Reporter*, there would be an editorial about the ground-breaking ceremonies for the Actors Lab Theater. The Actors Lab was the theatre I worked in. I had the first copy of *Red Channels* hot off the presses and . . . it was going to say we are all Reds and a disgrace to the community.' She told the reporter that 'they are all very good actors and I'm very proud to be named with them.'

Unfortunately, that wasn't the only news in the paper. When Betsy looked at the back page she discovered that an English actress was going to appear in a film called *Kind Lady*. Until that moment, she had believed that part was hers.

'I was very upset. When I complained about being on a blacklist, I was told there was no blacklist.'

She told Gene, and she told her agent that very Sunday afternoon, which was also an unusual occurrence. 'I said, "I'm not taking this. I'm going to the newspapers. I've been learning an English accent. My portrait has been painted. There's no reason for this."'

The next call had to be to the studio boss, Louis B Mayer himself. 'I was all dressed up in a blue suit and little white gloves. He said, "Sit down, sit down. I want to talk to you. I don't know what's wrong with you people. I had to talk to Spence and Kate [Spencer Tracy and Katharine Hepburn], too. Don't you appreciate what you have? You live in the greatest country in the world that God loves. How can you be making all this trouble and complaining about things?"

'I said, "Yes, Mr Mayer, I do appreciate this country. It's about democratic principles about the American constitution", and he went on about you having a husband who loves you, a beautiful child. And, "I understand you're not some Betty Grable. They tell me you're a great actress." I thought, "Oh, Betty Grable!" He went on and on and told me about his former wife Ida. He said, "It's true that I had to divorce Ida . . .".' But switched to talking about Betsy herself.

'"I know you're the kind of girl who would talk to your mother." At that moment, I thought I might as well give up, so I just sort of listened. Then the secretary came in. Gene, who had been shooting on the lot, thought an hour was enough. He came in and [Mayer] marched us out. He put his arm around my shoulder, with his other arm around Gene's shoulder and he said, "Well, Gene, she's a lovely girl – as American as you and me".'

Did that mean Betsy was off the blacklist, thanks to the word of the immigrant studio head? Gene looked at her and said: 'You must have given an Academy Award performance in there.'

It was a performance good enough to get her part back in the Edwardian melodrama *Kind Lady* (1951). It wasn't much of a movie, but enough to slam down any suggestion of her being on a blacklist. At least she and Gene Kelly thought so. 'We thought we had won. Then I *was* blacklisted – and for years, there wasn't another part.'

Mayer had 'obviously decided we are not going to make a fuss about this B movie and the actress who has a third role in this B movie – because she is married to our big star and she's going to make a big fuss in the papers. We'll just quietly blacklist her.'

Blair told me about the effects this episode had on the wider Hollywood community. 'Certainly, the pall was completely evident and shocking and awful because of the mistrust and the fact that you wouldn't know for sure . . . your friends, could they be trusted? When someone testified and [had] been a rat or a fink, as we used to say, it was clear you didn't invite them for dinner, hated it if you met them in a restaurant, didn't want to see them. It changed everything, it changed the fun. It think it changed the movies, the whole industry changed and there wasn't the same confidence there that had been before because the joy went out of the studio. For instance, you wouldn't know for sure that the Arthur Freed unit [where the musicals like the ones made by Kelly were produced] was the same. Bill Grady, whom we know for sure – he was the casting director at Metro – said that Kelly should get rid of that Commie wife of his. The atmosphere was not nice any more.'

Gene finally got the blacklist lifted. 'He went to see the head of Metro, who by now was Dore Schary, a much more civilised, educated, liberal man. Gene said, "You know her. You know she's not going to overthrow the country. Do something, or I'll tell you, I'm going to walk off the movie [*It's Always Fair Weather*]". I'm going to overthrow the country, do something.' So Dore, who I think sympathised with me, called the American Legion and they cleared me.' (The American Legion was more than just a gathering of ex-war veterans. They could provide the stamp of death to films and film actors. It was their magazine *The Legion* which listed Charlie Chaplin, John Garfield, Burt

Lancaster and Judy Holliday as Communists and demanded a boycott of their films. Studio heads courted the Legion and offered tasty titbits to its members, like introducing them to stars and taking them on trips round the soundstages.)

But their clearance didn't help Blair's personal or professional life. 'We were getting a divorce, so I went to France. It was just a different life.' Later in 1951, she made the film that should have guaranteed a great career – *Marty*, the story of a 30-something couple (she and Ernest Borgnine), each of whom think they will never find love. It won her an Oscar nomination, but not a lot of work.

She told me: 'After *Marty*, which was a big success, and I was nominated for an Academy Award, I made two big movies in Europe. But I hadn't had a single offer in California.'

Betsy went to see Lew Wasserman, head of the MCA agency. 'He said, "I've got lots of writers who say they have parts for you. I'll check it out". Later that afternoon, he phoned and said, "I've checked it out. You're going to have to speak to somebody and make some kind of statement or write a letter, which means you have to name names. You're still blacklisted". Well, I didn't.'

A few years later and living in Paris, Blair had a message to go to the George V Hotel, where the concierge had a screenplay waiting for her. 'So I trotted over the Champs Elysées with a note from Lew Wasserman, saying I should do that because Ward Bond was in this movie and if you're in a movie with Ward Bond, Hollywood will think you've been cleared. So I was in that movie [It was the 1957 *The Halliday Brand*]. It was again slightly right-wing and was the only time I ever worked in Hollywood.'

She made a number of European films, notably *Calle Mayor*, in Spain in 1956 and the Italian *Il Grido*, the following year.

Betsy was so tied to Gene, not just as a doting wife but as a woman who regarded her husband as her political mentor as well as her lover, that it has always seemed strange that Kelly wasn't blacklisted or in some way implicated alongside her. Or was he? 'He was probably protected by Metro. He was probably a very big investment for them, a very important money-maker for them, whereas I was not. I was a little actress who occasionally got a part.'

The point about Kelly being an important investment for MGM is apposite. The blacklist years were also the years of *An American in Paris* in 1951 and, much more importantly, *Singin' in the Rain* the following year, regarded by many as the finest musical to come out of the Makers of Great Musicals studio. On the other hand, it is possible that MGM thought it wise to get him out of the way until perhaps the troubles died down – which with hindsight looks like wishful thinking. 'There's a story,' says Betsy Blair, 'that Metro was happy to send him to Europe for eighteen months. As far as I know, the story of those eighteen months we spent in Europe, just at the heart of the McCarthy era, was that Standard Oil had arranged it so that if you stayed out of the United States for eighteen months, you didn't have to pay any income tax. And so Gene said, since the big capitalist companies have gotten this law for their benefit, why shouldn't showbiz people take advantage of it? Whether Metro was colluding in this or happy to have him go, I have no idea, whether it was part of their protection or not, I don't know.'

Equally beneficial to the advantage of Metro was the possibility that Frank Sinatra benefited from Gene Kelly's position on the margins of this greylist (had Kelly actually featured on the greylist he would have had no work at all; the problem for those who *were* was that it was sometimes difficult for them to know if they were barred employment for political reasons or simply because of the uncertainties of the industry).

Sinatra starred in the movie *Pal Joey* in 1957, not by any means his greatest role. The eponymous hero in the original Broadway show had brought the name Gene Kelly to national attention and quickly to Hollywood for the first time in 1941. Many critics believe Kelly would have made a better job of the film than the Chairman of the Board, still revelling in Oscar triumph of *From Here to Eternity* four years earlier. He was also selling hugely successful albums like *Songs for Swinging Lovers*. In most other cases that would have been reason enough to give him the *Pal Joey* film role, but Kelly did have *Singin' in the Rain, It's Always Fair Weather* and all the other classic musical roles behind him – and recently behind him at that.

'I did have a theory about his being excluded from the role for political reasons,' his former wife told me. 'I know he was very disappointed and angry. It would have been a much better movie with him. He had been sensational in it on stage on Broadway.'

The wife of Larry Parks, Betty Garrett, was not as lucky as Kelly. Soon after her name appeared on the list she was fired from MGM, 'who were building me very well there. They had offered me *Annie Get Your Gun* [which later was offered to Judy Garland and then when she was fired, it went to Betty Hutton].' The stigma, as Betty put it, did not remain for her the way it did for Larry. She did several TV shows. But

Parks was out. 'If it hadn't have happened, I think there would have been another Jolson film

[Actually, that might not have happened. Jolson had signed to make a film himself about troop entertaining, *The Stars and Stripes Forever*, just a few weeks before he died. His widow, Erle Krasner told me: 'He was getting worried about Larry's Red associations, so I am not sure that he would have wanted to continue the series.'.] He would have gone on to be a very big star. As he got older, he got better looking. He could do anything. I imagine he would have had a wonderful, long, beautiful career and that breaks my heart.'

Even if he *had* been blacklisted, Gene Kelly had made enough money to survive – and survive more than merely comfortably – and, like his wife, would have worked freely in Europe, like when he made *Invitation to the Dance* in London in 1956. Others were not so lucky. David Raksin was broke and suffering for it. Just occasionally, he still got the odd job. 'I was orchestrating something in the middle of the night – someone else had been unable to finish the work. The next afternoon, an elderly gentleman told me that he was being kicked out of his apartment because he couldn't pay the rent. I gave him half of my fee. My wife wasn't offended by that. She was great.'

It was one rather different way that a family could be affected by the blacklist. There were strange implications for many of those on that piece of paper. Like the writer Oliver Crawford, who was among the few who fled to New York to work in television. He worked at home, which surprised his 5-year-old daughter Joanne. 'I didn't know what my dad did,' she told me, 'because he didn't go out like other fathers did. One day at school, the teacher asked us all to say what our fathers did. When it came to my turn, I didn't know what to say, so I just blurted out, "He's a bank robber" – and ran out of the room crying.'

That, of course, was how the blacklistees regarded the people who named names – as bank robbers who had taken away livelihoods, not to mention dignity. Those who did the naming were the stool pigeons of the day. One of them was a Stool Pidgeon – Walter Pidgeon, then President of SAG, and always one of the most respected and elegant actors on the American screen, who was Mr Miniver personified when he played opposite Greer Garson in *Mrs Miniver* the 1942 blockbuster, MGM's rose-cottage tribute to the brave British fighting the Hun alone.

When a group of Hollywood exiles made a film about striking Mexican-American zinc-miners in New Mexico, Pidgeon reported the fact to the FBI. There had already been trouble over the strike. The mine owners got an injunction banning the miners from picketing, which they said was contrary to the terms of their employment. But there was nothing to prevent their wives from picketing instead, which they did. They were attacked by police and arrested by the dozen. It became a *cause célèbre* which the movie's writer, Paul Jarrico, thought a wonderful opportunity to make a movie that matched the blacklistees' own philosophies. Money was collected to make the film privately because it was clear no studio would have anything to do with it.

Then Pidgeon stepped in. 'He thought it was his patriotic duty,' said Sylvia Jarrico, whose husband wrote the film, *Salt of the Earth*. Paul once said of Pidgeon's action: 'The FBI swung into action and the movie industry swung into action and we found ourselves barred from laboratories, barred from sound studios, barred from any of the normal facilities available to film makers and we found ourselves hounded by all kinds of demonstrations on the floor of Congress.' Newspaper columnists claimed that the film had been made on behalf of the Russians. The fact that the film was being shot in New Mexico – where the atomic bomb tests had been held – didn't help, 'because where you find atom bombs, you find Communists.'

The publishers of *Red Channels* believed you also found them within their pages. *Red Channels* was a sore point. The Motion Picture Industry Council (MPIC) set itself the aim of helping people escape from *Channels*. Hardly surprisingly, when you analyse what was behind it, this idea came from SAG president, Ronald Reagan. It would 'place on record his own statement of facts applying to himself, which he believes will clarify his position against Communism and explain relationships with organisations linked to Communism.'

Reagan's plan was more subtle than most of the things for which he is given credit. He would root out the people named in the journal – and allow them the chance to clear themselves. The Council (MIP) whose true colours were soon revealed – yet another Red-baiting Hollywood group – said it would direct those statements, acting like an agent, to a studio or producer, but wouldn't evaluate their value. 'Its evaluation will rest with anyone to whom the statement shall be furnished.'

Reagan said the 'voluntary statement of affirmation' would include an oath of allegiance to the United States and support the United Nations war in Korea. (The oath stood in place until 1967 when it became optional. It was abandoned altogether in 1974.) It left a terrible taste in the mouths of the actors. Marsha Hunt said: 'I had to declare my undying opposition to Communism. I didn't know or care about

Communism. I was terribly worried about what we were doing to democracy.' She was never called to testify and neither was her husband, but she was blacklisted just the same.

Hunt was told that if she named Adrian Scott in particular as a Communist, she would be all right. This she manifestly refused to do. 'Adrian was probably the main reason I flew to Washington. I didn't know the other people who were in that Hollywood 19, but I knew Adrian very well and was very fond of him. He married my best friend, Anne Shirley. And I knew Adrian to be one of the finest people I'd ever known.' She told this, she said for this book, to the executive director of the Screen Actors Guild, John Dales. Marsha told him that she was never a Communist. 'You mean you're not?' he asked her. 'You mean you're not a Communist? I was so sure you were.'

'I said, "No, Jack, whatever gave you that idea?" He called two meetings, one was with a man who came with a briefcase of background on people.' This was the man, named Costigan, who asked her to name Adrian Scott. 'I said, "Mr Costigan, I don't know you, I've never seen you before today. But I do know Adrian Scott, and he's as fine a man as I've ever known, beside his talent as a writer and producer and the landmark films he's already made. But no, I wouldn't dream of signing that. And I would never believe that Adrian Scott would harbour a disloyal thought about this country. I'm sure he loves it quite as much as I do".'

There were no other names she was asked to give. 'What I was required to say and swear to in order to work again, the statement said that that flight to Washington had in fact been masterminded by Communists and that we were dupes. Innocent dupes at the time, but in fact our whole trip to Washington had helped the Communist cause and I deeply regretted this. Now that I understood the Communists had been behind it all, I would try and atone in any way I could by fighting Communism. Any way I was able for the rest of my days. And I was to sign that, have it notarised, swear to it and I could work. I couldn't do that. He said, "Nobody will see this. It'll be locked away in the back of a drawer." But I would know.'

So that was the end of a career which Marsha now says 'was about to go into full blossom.' As she told me: 'I realised that things were out of my hands. There was nothing I could do. I was what they called unemployable. To keep sane and to keep earning something and also to keep doing my chosen work, I did plays wherever I could find them. I don't know how many of the fifty states I went to, doing plays, one week's rehearsal, one week performing and one week home, a lot of work. To memorise the principal role in one week, that's all you have, you rehearse one week and then you play it and just as you're beginning to feel your way in it, you close – and you go home with your modest paycheque. But I was acting, I was functioning, and that kept me sane.'

Things had hitherto been a lot easier and more impressive. At the start of the new year of 1948, three months after the First Amendment Committee trip to Washington, Hunt was starring on Broadway. 'What a way to break in! Broadway was nothing but delightful and helpful. Every player laid down their cloak in the mud and said, "Walk on it." They couldn't have been more gallant to this newcomer.' She was appearing on radio and TV, on guest talk shows with people like George Kaufmann and Abe Burrows. But everything changed when *Red Channels* published her name in June 1950. 'I had just finished *The Devil's Disciple*, which put me on the solo cover of *Life* magazine in March 1950.' Everything in her garden looked as lovely as she was.

'We went off to my first trip to Europe. We ran across Eleanor Roosevelt in Paris with her son, Elliott, who was among three producers of TV shows which were wooing me to star in my own show, *The Marsha Hunt Show*. And I hadn't decided among the three that were being offered . . . so I said I would decide when I got back from Europe.

'It was Elliott Roosevelt who said, "Haven't you heard?" I said, "Heard what?" He said, "*Red Channels*." I said, "What's that?"'

Elliot told her she was listed, not as a Communist – because that could be libellous, alongside other Hollywood names, with the organisations to which they belonged or with whom they had been associated in some way.

'I had about six activities, I think, all of which were true and consistent with my beliefs and none of them remotely Communist.' But it spelt the end of stardom.

Red Channels had a wide brief. As Norman Corwin told me: '[It] was a compilation of names of people who had been active in social movements. If they were for rent control, if they were for human rights, if they resisted racial discrimination, they were suspect immediately.'

The legend was that *Red Channels* was restricted to the broadcasting industry. This was not so. Dozens of theatre people, actors, directors and producers were listed, even though there was never any blacklist for the stage. Sam Jaffe, an honoured character actor, who played the lama in *Lost Horizon* in 1937 and the title role in *Gunga Din* two years later, was nominated for an Oscar for his role as the criminal brains in *The*

Asphalt Jungle and later became known for playing Dr Zorba in the *Ben Casey* TV series. When he was blacklisted, he became a maths teacher and lived with his sisters. He would say: 'There were signs in the casting rooms that anybody who was on any of the lists need not apply. In movies, agents were told not to present your name if you were on a list.'

Joseph Losey suffered, too. 'Joe was negative from the day I knew him,' Marsha Hunt now remembers. 'He was never content, never really joyous. Except one trip to New York when he heard I was in town, he tracked me down. I was in New York by myself and he took me to lunch and told me about his new marriage and how much it meant to him, and how for the first time in his life, he was content. And that's the only time I ever saw Joe happy. He was chronically unhappy, angry, a bitter man if things were not going his way. [He believed] there were plots against him.'

Jules Dasin reacted differently, working in France and marrying the Greek actress Melina Mercouri. Hunt says, 'Julie, I loved from the time we did two pictures at MGM and my first play on Broadway, which he directed. That's how I found the courage to do it. We were so close.'

The music business was almost, but not quite, as much a target as the film industry. Pete Seeger was constantly under HUAC and McCarthy attack. He appeared at concerts with Paul Robeson – the first of which was called off before they could start because of the uproar from the anti-Communist audiences. 'They wouldn't let him [Robeson] sing,' recalled Sondra Gorney. 'They were stoned by rednecks. The concert hadn't begun but people were sitting down and they had to cancel it. And afterwards, about a week later, they did give the concert. They were determined to do it. It was for a union cause. The second time it was given in another place.'

The roughnecks at the first concert, Gorney recalled, 'were threatening the audience . . . they tried to rough them up. And the second concert, when people were coming away, these roughnecks were up on a cliff throwing stones down at them. A lot of people were hurt. One man lost an eye because the stone went through the glass of his windscreen and caught his eye.'

Sondra's husband Jay was another music man who became a Blacklist victim. The fact he had written 'Brother Can You Spare A Dime?' probably hadn't helped. He was fired from CBS, where he was a TV producer and writer as well as a composer. Sondra said: 'He was teaching a course at Hunter College of how to write for musical theatre and he was fired from that. He was fired from practically everything and couldn't get work at all. He started to teach at the American Theater Wing and the theatre was always a little bit more liberal and broader and they didn't have a blacklist as such like they did in television and film. He got a big kick out of that, but very little money. He got very depressed. He did continue to write with Henry Myers – they wrote several beautiful shows, but they could not sell them – they couldn't get producers because the theatre producers said the only way that a musical theatre production could recoup its cost is to sell it to movies – but because they were blacklisted, they could never sell it to movies. He kept writing and teaching. But he got more and more depressed and it was sad to see this really congenial man who had such social ability to work with people grow more and more into his shell. And then he became ill and went downhill from there. But I think the blacklist started him downhill, that whole struggle.'

It was never difficult for HUAC or the FBI to track down Communists. Some of their methods could be filed under 'farcical'. One of the provisions of the McCarren Act was that members of the Communist party were required to register. Booths were set up all over the country with the result that practically nobody did. One report said that only six people had turned up to give their names. That was gratifying to all those who thought it reminiscent of the Nazis' demands for Jewish registration in Germany and occupied Europe.

The truth was that HUAC didn't need registration or any other 'real' evidence of Communist attachments. Eileen Ryan Penn, widow of the writer Leo Penn, told us: 'Leo wasn't a card-carrying Communist. He was just interested in what was going on and he just went to a meeting of, I guess, mostly Communists. And the people who were supposed to speak didn't arrive and they asked him to speak instead – and he was photographed at the meeting. That's how it happened.'

The charge that being either current or former members of the Communist party meant devotion to the Soviet Union was crushed by the fact that Paul Jarrico was virtually blacklisted twice – in America and in the Warsaw Pact countries. He had been in Eastern Europe in 1948 and made statements critical of the Communist regimes. As a result, he was, according to Sylvia Jarrico, 'not as warmly greeted as he might have been otherwise. That's what he meant by saying he had been challenged on both sides of the Iron Curtain. I don't know that he was actually blacklisted there, though.'

Sometimes, the studios weren't sure who they were blacklisting either – or why. Jeff Corey couldn't act any more, so he taught acting. 'He just wanted a job,' his wife, Hope Corey told me. 'He was a teacher so he worked the whole time, but acting was his main love. The studios liked having him teach so much, they kept him teaching. Even when they were giving him jobs as an actor later, after 12 years. The studios that had put him on the blacklist were sending him actors to teach even when he was on the list.'

The people they would like to have trained were the writers. The actress Karen Morley, named by several HUAC witnesses, who had made films in the 1930s like *Scarface* in 1932 and *Dinner at Eight* a year later told a Screen Actors Guild publication that the quality of film-making got worse as a result of the blacklist. 'The stories had always been fairly violent, in the old days writers had tried to show *why* people were violent – because they had a cruel father or they were poor. Violence became an art, a cult and with that came the passive women. The beautiful, strong women went and they were replaced by other beautiful ladies, but ladies chosen more for their figures and their faces than for their characters. The passivity is what I found distressing. Soon, not only was there passivity but there was cruelty towards women, brutality, ugliness and rape. The treatment of minorities simply disappeared.'

And so did a great deal of integrity. Albert Maltz was much admired by Frank Sinatra, who made helping along talent part of his *raison d'être*. Sinatra hired him to write the screenplay of a picture he was desperate to film, *The Execution of Private Slovik*, about the only American soldier to be shot for desertion on the battlefield. The film town went into virtual apoplexy when the news was first revealed. It seemed to be one battle that HUAC's supporters could not possibly win – and if they didn't win it, the whole pack of cards could fall to the ground. Sinatra was not one to cross. He may not actually have been a member of the Mafia, but saying no to him could represent a death sentence to the unwary.

When he heard the criticisms of his hiring Maltz, he went into action with all guns blazing. 'No one is going to tell me who to hire,' he told his lawyers truculently. 'Maltz is the best one I can hire.' Then, he put his sentiments into print by taking a full-page advertisement in *Daily Variety* and the *Hollywood Reporter*: 'This statement is made by me so that the public will have all the facts before passing judgement in regard to my hiring of Albert Maltz to write the screenplay of *The Execution of Private Slovik*. I bought the William Bradford Huie book which tells the true story of the only execution of a soldier by the United States

Army since the Civil War. Since I will produce and direct the picture, I am concerned that the screenplay reflects the true pro-American values of the story. This means that the picture must be an affirmative declaration in the best American tradition. I spoke to many screenwriters but it was not until I talked to Albert Maltz that I found a writer who saw the screenplay in exactly the terms I wanted.'

In this unprecedented step, Sinatra made two unexpected statements: nobody would believe that he would go out on a limb for anyone but the little man (as he had in *From Here To Eternity*) and also that of all the people to prove his point, he chose a man who was not only on the blacklist, but had gone to jail as one of the Hollywood Ten.

The statement continued: 'Under our Bill of Rights, I was taught that no one may prescribe what should be orthodox in politics, religion or other matters of opinion. I am in complete accord with the statement made earlier this week by J D Nicola of the Catholic Legion of Decency, who said: 'The Legion evaluates films on the basis of art, not the artist.' As the producer of the film, I and I alone will be responsible for it. I accept that responsibility. I ask only that judgement be deferred until the picture is seen.

'I would also like to comment on the attacks from certain quarters on Senator John Kennedy by connecting him with my decision on employing a screenwriter. This type of partisan politics is hitting below the belt . . . I make movies. I do not ask the advice of Senator Kennedy on whom I should hire. Senator Kennedy does not ask me how he should vote in the Senate.'

Sinatra concluded by saying he was standing on his principles and awaited the verdict of the box-office patrons.

But Kennedy didn't like the association with the name of one of the Hollywood Ten. He would soon run for President and he was worried that it could harm him. At the same time, Sinatra saw himself as one of the future President's blue-eyed boys, if not yet Ol' Blue Eyes. And he had almost come to blows with John Wayne in a parking lot. The actor called him a 'Commie'. So almost as quickly as it would take him to sing a chorus of 'My Way' (had it yet been written) he called a meeting of reporters. The result: the *Los Angeles Examiner* headlined a story: SINATRA OUSTS MALTZ AS WRITER. The Hearst newspapers all carried the same headline: SINATRA FIRES MALTZ.

Another paid-for advertisement soon appeared in the papers: 'In view of the reaction of my family, friends and the American public I've instructed my lawyers to make a settlement with Albert Maltz. I had thought that the major consideration was whether or not the script would be in the best interests of the United States. My conversations with Maltz indicate that he has an affirmative, pro-American approach to the story, but the American public has indicated it feels that the morality of hiring Maltz is the more crucial matter and I will accept this majority opinion.'

A big-screen film was never made although there was a television version starring Martin Sheen in 1974, and the blacklist stayed intact. Just before his death in 1985, Albert Maltz was quoted as saying: 'Sinatra threw down the gauntlet against the blacklist. He was prepared to fight. Something had come from behind that caused him to change his position.'

Meanwhile, neighbours came up from behind blacklistees and their families to express the fact that friendships could easily be forgotten. Waldo Salt's wife Mary Davenport told Barbra Paskin: 'I was fearful. I couldn't discuss anything with my grocer. When I wanted to buy meat, I had to buy the meat and get out. With my children's paediatrician, I cried and ran out. I noticed that my neighbours' houses across the street were occupied by FBI with their cameras. Any cars that came, their number plates were taken.'

Waldo Salt answered his subpoena – and was immediately fired from his job of writing what was to be Burt Lancaster's 1952 film *The Crimson Pirate*. Mary's mother got divorced at that time. The Judge told her that if she got any money, she would give it to her Communist son-in-law. So there was no settlement.

The actors, of course, couldn't use fronts like the writers – which is why those who were lucky to get stage work in New York, which paid a lot less handsomely than a job for one of the studio bosses, had to be grateful. Theodore Bikel, a former head of Actors Equity, told me: 'We were very proud of our stand, which, in effect, said no to HUAC and McCarthyism.'

The actor John Ranolph totally agreed. He was quoted as saying: 'Equity fully supported their members but you have to remember that censorship is a dirty word around the stage and any pressure by anybody to limit creative expression has historically been met with strong resistance by stage performers. The strength Equity displayed at that time came from the clear unity of rank-and-file members.'

The actors weren't going to get it all their own way – or, at least, that was how it seemed. One of the nastiest groups was Brooklyn Against Communism, which picketed plays featuring blacklisted artists. The

League of New York Theaters decided to fight the group from across the river. They inserted flyers into theatre programmes stating that nobody had the right to tell anyone else what they should or should not see on the stage.

* * *

There were always those who said that the blacklist never existed. Ronald Reagan made at least two speeches denying its existence either officially or as a general theory. There are also those who to this day think that the blacklist was all about money. Historian Larry Ceplair told Barbra Paskin: 'Nothing is all about anything. But I think that was the basic factor in the decisions to institute a blacklist. The Committee on Un-American Activities wanted a blacklist but that was for a different reason. They wanted a blacklist because they wanted to censor politicial thinking and cultural imagination in the United States for the purpose of the Cold War. But *they* couldn't have created a blacklist. They could have demanded it, they could have threatened, they could have intimidated, but the only way a blacklist can work is if the people in the business agree not to hire people and they do that, I think, out of financial concerns.'

Dalton Trumbo told the SWG: 'The blacklist was a time of evil. No one on either side who survived it came through untouched by evil.' What people now remember are his parting words: 'It will do no good to search for villains or heroes or saints or devils because there were none. There were only victims.' Which is quite an extraordinary statement from the man who was seen as the banner waver of the Hollywood Ten. But all victims? 'Because almost without exception, each of us felt compelled to say things he did not want to say, to do things he did not want to do, to deliver and receive wounds he truly did not want to exchange.'

That got him into trouble with Albert Maltz. 'There is currently in vogue,' Maltz responded, 'a thesis pronounced first by Dalton Trumbo, which declares that everyone during the years of blacklist was equally a "victim." This is factual nonsense and represents a bewildering moral position.'

Do we accept that this was the blackest period in Hollywood history? The blacklist blackened the name of all America.

Chapter Twelve
Cowardly Oscar

You've heard Article One of your Bill of Justice . . . a heritage that
gives you a right to speak your will without fear, a heritage that
gives a man a right to answer his accusers, a right to be protected
from slander and misstatements of fact. In no court in this land is
action taken on the basis of hearsay or personal opinion.

Actor Van Heflin in *Hollywood Fights Back*

Two of the Ten Commandments have particular relevance to the HUAC
years. They were both broken somewhat spectacularly in two distinct
cases by the Academy of Motion Picture Arts and Sciences, the
institution familiarly known among the Hollywood élite simply as
the Academy. It was, naturally enough, aided and abetted by two
studios, one American, the other British, who happily set the balls
rolling. The broken commandments were 'Thou shalt not steal' and
'Thou shalt not bear false witness'. The Academy stole and bore
witnesses so false that it is almost incredible to believe, especially since
it was all carried out first in broad daylight, and then later in the evening
in front of ladies in glamorous gowns and men in full evening dress and,
more significantly, before the microphones and cameras that carried the
facts of the case to a world unaware of what was going on.

The GFD company in Britain had come to the aid of the jobless and
newly exiled Larry Adler, who more than paid them back with the magical
mouth organ solo that served as the score for their charming 1953 movie
based around the London-Brighton vintage car run, *Genevieve*. It was a
short process between agreeing to do the film music and the final
attempted ignominy.

'First of all, United Artists, who were going to distribute *Genevieve* in
America, tried to get me fired from the picture, Adler told me. 'If I did the
music, they said they wouldn't give it an American release because I was
blacklisted. My agent managed to get my contract upheld, even though it

wasn't signed yet. I did make the picture and my name was on the picture. But six weeks before it opened in the United States, the exhibitors asked for a print with my name removed. And when the picture opened, there was no composer [listed]. Dimitri Tiomkin won the Oscar that year for the score of *The High and the Mighty*.' As we have seen, Adler said he was grateful there was no Academy Award – which would have gone to the musical director Muir Mathieson, the man who was nominated as the composer (instead of Larry) but who hadn't written a note.

The second case was in some ways even more important – because *The Bridge on the River Kwai* was a more important, more expensive, more prestigious movie. The screenplay of *Bridge* had been written by Carl Foreman and Michael Wilson on the understanding that when work began in Europe, there would be no writer credit. Wilson's daughter told us: 'He was grateful for the work because he knew he was one of the fortunate few who managed to get hired and keep writing during this blacklist period. And I think it was a tremendous relief for him and for my mother to be out of that terrible oppressive environment which we all experienced in Los Angeles.'

By the time Columbia Pictures had put up the film for Academy nomination, the name on the writer credits at the start of the film was that of Frenchman Pierre Boulle, author of the original novel. That alone would have been galling enough, but there was an additional factor which was more exasperating still. Not only had Boulle not written the much-changed story, he could not speak, let alone write, English. Yet Kim Novak accepted the award on his behalf – with his blessing and showed no sign of purloining something that was not rightfully his. There were no protests from the other Oscar winners, the director David Lean, the star Alec Guinness, the cameraman Jack Hildyard and Malcolm Arnold, the composer.

At first, Carl Foreman's son Jonathan Foreman told me that Columbia prepared to take a gamble and use blacklisted writers for a picture which they accepted couldn't be a simple British movie – much against the wishes of David Lean who was particularly unhappy having to have an American, William Holden, as one of the principal stars.

'It is a gamble,' he said, 'having a named blacklisted writer. He writes the screenplay and Michael works on it, too. He had also been blacklisted, but then they, Columbia, lost their nerve.'

The producer, Sam Jaffe, and David Lean were the principal nerve losers, he maintains. 'And the film comes out without the names of the writers of the screenplays. They worry, "Oh, we'll get boycotted, get into trouble." The irony is that the screenplay wins the best screenplay award. Who is it supposed to go to? And the film amazingly actually has a lie on it. It says screenplay by Pierre Boulle.

'The man actually had the nerve to accept an Oscar for something he hadn't written. It was such an appalling thing not to get it. [My father] had built his career and is told, "You can work but you still can't get credit for things you did".'

Michael Wilson's daughter, Rosanna Wilson-Farrow, told Barbra Paskin: 'That really pissed my father off, by the way. He was really mad about that. He understood about the blacklist and he understood he wouldn't get a screen credit. But what made him really furious was that Pierre Boulle had the audacity to accept the award.'

Lean, in fact, always refused to recognise the injustice of what happened and either of the two writers having anything to do with it.

It took nearly a quarter of a century for the Academy to right that wrong. As Jonathan Foreman said: 'It took a while, for the Academy hated admitting its mistakes and this was such an obvious one, giving the screenplay credit to people who hadn't written it. The Screen Writers Guild's very purpose is to establish things like this. This was an extraordinary lie – and they wouldn't answer the telephone.'

If anything justified the criticisms of the actions of the Hollywood guilds during this sordid period, it was their action over *The Bridge on the River Kwai*.

Rosanna Wilson-Farrow says it was an experience her father had known before. In 1953 the Academy actually decided that no one who was being called before HUAC as an unfriendly witness could receive an Academy Award. In 1951, Wilson – called, named and condemned by the committee – was nominated and actually awarded an Oscar for the screenplay he had written with Harry Brown of *A Place in the Sun*, the Elizabeth Taylor and Montgomery Clift vehicle based on Theodore Dreiser's *An American Tragedy*. The award came four months after his appearance before the committee. Much to his wife's regret, he didn't go to the ceremony to collect the award 'because,' says his daughter, 'Mike was too pissed off at Hollywood, understandably, because of the blacklist.'

The brazenness of Boulle's acceptance was what struck the Foreman family most. As Jonathan Foreman says: 'We grew up with this very strong sense that you have to do things that are right. There are certain kinds of injustice that involve groups of people who are behaving badly to individuals. They are unacceptable forms of behaviour.'

Michael Wilson wrote a letter to Boulle, saying: 'Dear Pierre. Hello there. How are you? We are fine and hope you are the same. Say, by the way, do you think you might send us our Oscar, COD, and we will work out the custody for same between us. Thanking you in advance, yours truly, Mike and Carl.'

Michael Wilson was experiencing constant *déjà vu*, and not merely due to *A Place in the Sun*. There had been similar rows with David Lean over *Lawrence of Arabia* in 1962, most of which Wilson wrote, although the picture was credited to Robert Bolt. There was a contract stating Wilson was the writer, but it took the end of the blacklist and action by the SWG before his name could be added to the credits.

'He went through hell on *Lawrence*, for example,' says his daughter today, 'as he felt he'd been so wronged.'

And then there was a film about the simple life of Quakers that was not at all simple for him. Lean had written most of the screenplay of the 1956 film, *Friendly Persuasion*, but the author of the short stories on which the script was based, Jessamyn West, together with Robert Wyler, brother of the director William Wyler, tried to take full credit, knowing the strength of the blacklist. Wilson took the matter to the Screenwriters Guild and for once they were helpful. Through their efforts, a compromise was reached – no writer's credit at all. It was a minor victory and the first time it had happened.

There's a lovely irony to this particular episode. In 1988, President Ronald Reagan went to Moscow and took with him a copy of President Gorbachev's favourite movie – *Friendly Persuasion*. The former head of SAG, who had proudly aided the blacklist all the way, was without his knowledge aiding and abetting the work of a blacklist writer. In his speech, he said, 'Allow me to raise a glass to the work that has been done, to the work that remains to be done and let us also toast the art of friendly persuasion, the hope of peace with freedom, the hope of holding out for a better way of settling things.'

Lean's daughter says: 'Our dad would joke about this, saying that *Friendly Persuasion* was the first, perhaps only, time a Hollywood film was released that wasn't written by anyone.'

In 1956, Wilson sued the two Wylers, Jessamyn West, Allied Artists, Paramount and Liberty Films and won a settlement out of court. But his credit wasn't listed until 1996, 20 years after his death.

Students of the HUAC period, or at least the ones who sympathise with the unfriendly witnesses, would probably list Gary Cooper as among those who were 'unacceptable'. As we have seen, he said he didn't like what he knew about Marxism, which implied that he was with the committee and probably the studios in opposing Communist members. His attitude to Carl Foreman was in total contrast to the image that has been created around him.

It was during the filming of *High Noon*, frequently regarded as the greatest of all Westerns, that it seemed inevitable that the writer whom everyone knew as 'Uncle Carl' was destined for the blacklist. His star, Cooper, wasn't going to have any of it. 'Gary Cooper is not very sophisticated,' says Foreman. 'He goes before the committee and says he is against Communism. But when the push comes to shove, he won't allow himself to be part of it, whereas many people who were on the Left, friends of my father's, [crossed] the street, wouldn't answer telephone calls. My father tells a story about that: he was on the set and had to tell the people, "I'm going before the committee, we don't know what will happen." People were very supportive.

'He was walking back to his car afterwards and suddenly he hears this noise. He turns round and suddenly there is Gary Cooper loafing after him. The big, very tall Gary Cooper calling, "Uncle Carl, Uncle Carl."' And he gave him a big hug and said, "You do what you think is right, but don't let them put you in jail. I'm behind you all the way". And it was *the* most moving thing. It was true. He sort of kept his word completely. He is blasted as an un-co-operative witness and my father thinks his career is over. And then Cooper, who was essential to the making of the film, came to his aid.'

The star was the link with another Foreman supporter. The man, a Californian lettuce farmer, was Cooper's close friend and had put up the money for a movie now seen itself as an indictment of the HUAC process. He offered his unqualified support. The two men, 'Republicans both of them, stood up to the head of the production company, Stanley Kramer, who wanted to get rid of my father: "Just get him off the set, ban him from the set." He was so terrified and Cooper said, "No. This is how we're going to play it."'

How 'Coop' decided to play it was to set up a joint production committee. 'And as soon as the film was over, *Variety* had this big announcement: Cooper and Foreman had set up this new company. It was all Cooper's idea. He was just a stand-up guy. My father used to say he was a real American, compared with all these people. It was an extraordinary, heart-warming story – and Cooper was forced to suspend that company under tremendous pressure. My father felt tremendous loyalty to him. For the rest of his life, he always loved him.'

The way Jonathan Foreman puts it, 'public pressure forced it to be abandoned.'

The story of *High Noon* was in a way a precursor to what would happen with *Bridge on the River Kwai*. Foreman wasn't merely the writer of the movie, he was also the producer, while Stanley Kramer 'was off doing something else at the time.' But there was no producer credit on the movie.

Meanwhile, as the picture was being shot, the pink slip arrived, subpoenaing him to appear before HUAC. 'He knew it was coming. He had been named several times – in perjurous testimony.' In fact, he was one of the 161 names named by Martin Berkeley, whom Foreman knew. 'But he had never been to any meeting with him.'

Carl Foreman had been a Communist. 'He had left the party several years by then . . . he knew it was coming. He testified. He didn't know what to do: should he not co-operate and go to prison? In the end, his lawyer persuaded him to take the Diminished Fifth.'

It was not a particularly satisfactory course of action. Foreman wouldn't be saved from the imputation of guilt and, at the same time, 'infuriated the committee because they were not getting what they wanted. They wanted people to go along with the ritual. It didn't matter that [people] had been named many times. My father wouldn't go along with the ritual and that meant he would be very quickly unemployable. They had deemed him unco-operative. But it was the studios who blacklisted. You became this pariah thing and people wouldn't want to be associated with you.'

It summed up the attitude of the film town to crises of any kind. As Jonathan Foreman said: 'Hollywood has never been noted as a place for courage. That is true now and it was certainly true then. And great friends of his suddenly abandoned him. People crossed the street just to get away. Of course, other people turned out to be loyal.' Cooper was one of those. 'When people like Stanley Kramer said, "Look at this. You have got to leave, it will destroy this film," Cooper said, "If he goes, I go".'

Foreman's son Jonathan said: 'So my father came back to the set. He finished the film, finished the editing. And my father, when he had been named, he knew he would have to leave.' So began Carl Foreman's exile, briefly to New York and then to England, from where *Bridge on the River Kwai* was made.

It took a great deal of time to discover the extent of HUAC's fight against Foreman. 'Years later, we got my father's FBI files under the Freedom of Information Act. It's quite extraordinary what they revealed. Names and addresses were always wrong . . . "Followed subject home, he went back to his wife . . . nothing to report". There was never anything to report. The only things against him were from unnamed individuals. There was amazing stupidity.'

His conclusion now is clear: 'It was very odd. My father had very strong feelings about anything that smacked of witch-hunts, of betrayal. He was very selective about the people he was angry with.'

Here we see a difference between the witness and HUAC itself. It was not selective at all.

Chapter Thirteen
The Moguls

There is not a court in America which would admit questions or put words in the mouths of witnesses to get exactly what answers are wanted, yet this Un-American Committee has repeatedly done this with the examination of witnesses. Time after time, they have put questions which begin, 'Is this what you mean to say?' or, 'Does this sum up your feelings?' or, 'In other words, would you say this?' In spite of this technique of putting words into the mouths of witnesses, no one has been able to point to any character, any scene or any line from any picture which can be understood to advocate the overthrow of our government.

Paulette Goddard, *Hollywood Fights Back*, 1947

Ever since they first discovered that by projecting shadows onto a screen, they could make a fortune, the moguls of Hollywood had been unassailable. They dictated what people all over the English-speaking world did for entertainment. More importantly, they headed the most important communications medium of the twentieth century. At the same time, they created an art form which has influenced virtually every human being outside a nunnery, monastery or yeshiva.

The moguls were emperors with their own realms. They were dictators, called the big shots and could influence the smallest detail. You didn't argue with the likes of Louis B Mayer, Sam Goldwyn, the Warner brothers or Harry Cohn. Not if you wanted to keep your job, that is.

Some accounts have called them ignorant money-grabbers. That is totally unfair. Or at least in large measure unfair. Harry Warner may have declared that he didn't want his studio's films to be good, he wanted them Tuesday. As he also said, messages should be left to Western Union. On the other hand, the moguls still cared for the artistic integrity their studios represented. Goldwyn, in particular, searched for quality and accuracy above all – which is why he ordered the filming of girls dancing round a fountain of peppermint ice cream to stop. He had put a finger in the fountain and discovered that the ice cream was pistachio.

Mayer, whose studio's motto was 'More stars than there are in heaven,' regarded himself as the benevolent father of a school of sometimes naughty children – which is why he was not above knocking an errant star to the ground with a left hook if he thought the man deserved it or, as happened when Clark Gable ran over a woman and her child, ordering an underling to go to jail in place of the star.

When Harry Cohn died, 2,000 people went to the funeral. 'Just shows you,' joked the comedian Red Skelton, 'give the people what they want and they'll show up for it.' The result, no doubt, of Cohn walking through the lot with a baseball bat to prevent shirking by any employee stupid enough to be caught resting under a tree. Or perhaps the result of bugging the dressing rooms of his stars, as he did when he suspected Glenn Ford was having an affair with Rita Hayworth.

There was no nay-saying of these hugely powerful people. You wanted them on your side, which is why President Franklin D Roosevelt so often needed their help.

On the other hand, the moguls wanted to prove that they were totally independent and that they went along with public taste. As Mel Shavelson told me: 'You give an audience what an audience wants. Occasionally motion pictures try to lead – but that's a good way to lose money.'

If anyone's word was law it was theirs. Except when they got scared. Which is why, until America entered World War Two, there were virtually no anti-Nazi movies. Chaplin's *The Great Dictator* in 1940 was an honourable exception, but then he partly owned his own studio. MGM's *The Mortal Storm* in the same year dealt with the sacking of a beloved professor because he wasn't Aryan. Nobody used the word 'Jew' – Mayer, like his fellow moguls, was afraid of compromising his Americanism by letting anyone think he was fighting for his fellow Jews.

But when HUAC set up shop seriously, the moguls caved in like a pack of cards blown over by one of Walt Disney's three little pigs. At first, it seemed that they would side with their stars and writers. Pious words were spoken at the start. As long as these people did their jobs as well as they always had, it wasn't for the studios to interfere in their private lives. After all, the unspoken word was that the studios needed them. They were responsible for all the money that poured into the box offices and their own bank accounts.

But once J Parnell Thomas banged his gavel, they grovelled. The moguls didn't want anyone to think that Hollywood wasn't the most patriotic place in all America. Only Sam Goldwyn spoke out against the blacklist, but once it had been drawn up, he too had to give way. The clinching factor was a meeting of studio heads at the Waldorf Astoria Hotel in New York – note, *not* in Hollywood – on 24 and 25 November 1947. One reason was that they were scared of the reaction of people in their own home town where they feared being lynched. Another, and probably more salient factor, was that New York was the centre of the business part of the studio operation. Wall Street was flexing its muscles and the men with the books, who cared only for the financial results and not one jot for the artistic merits of what Hollywood produced, dictated full, unconditional surrender.

It remains a matter for speculation on what could have happened had the studio bosses not got out their black ink and decided who would survive and who would fall. It also seems hardly likely that if they had all stood up for justice for their employees, HUAC could have done anything but give way. There is abundant evidence pointing to the fact that the committee got far more than they ever could have originally imagined from their meeting with the moguls in New York.

It is also true that before the groups met at the hotel, there were no plans for anything approaching a blacklist. Eric Johnston, the president of the Motion Picture Producers Association (MPPA), couldn't have been more firm in denying there was any such plan.

'As long as I live,' he stated, 'I will never be a party to anything as un-American as a blacklist.'

The Waldorf meeting was held in the shadow of the Hollywood Ten's appearances before HUAC in Washington. All the big studio bosses were there – with the New York business brains looking over their shoulders. They attended under the guise of the Association of Motion Picture Producers, the Motion Picture Association of America (MPAA) and the Society of Independent Motion Picture Producers (SIMPP).

At the conclusion of their closed-door deliberations amid the gilt and crystal of Manhattan's most prestigious hotel, they issued a statement that right from its first sentence left people (particularly the members of HUAC) in no doubt where they stood. Just a month after his previous anti-blacklist comments, Eric Johnston read a statement that lambasted the Hollywood Ten. The statement read: 'Members of the Association of Motion Picture Producers deplore the action of the ten Hollywood men who have been cited for contempt by the House of Representatives. We do not desire to prejudge their legal rights, but their actions have been a disservice to their employers and have impaired their usefulness to the industry.'

From this start, it was evident that they were concerned more than anything for their own businesses. The threat – and the reality – came in the next paragraph, with no room for equivocation. 'We will forthwith discharge or suspend without compensation those in our employ and we will not re-employ any of the Ten until such time as he is acquitted or has purged himself of contempt and declares under oath that he is not a Communist.'

Without a 'desire to prejudge their legal rights', the moguls were prejudging the Ten. And introducing a new factor – the demand for a loyalty oath, whether the one given to the committee or to themselves was not specified. The threats continued: 'On the broader issue of alleged subversive and disloyal elements in Hollywood, our members are likewise prepared to take positive action.'

The 'positive action' was spelt out very clearly: 'We will not knowingly employ a Communist or a member of any party or group which advocates the overthrow of the government of the United States by force or by any illegal or unconstitutional methods. In pursuing this policy, we are not going to be swayed by hysteria or intimidation from any source.'

The framers of this declaration were aware of the consequences – which they decided to face head on. 'We are frank to recognise that such a policy involves dangers and risks. There is the danger of hurting innocent people. There is the risk of creating an atmosphere of fear. Creative work at its best cannot be carried on in an atmosphere of fear. We will guard against this danger, this risk, this fear. To this end, we will invite the Hollywood talent guilds to work with us to eliminate any subversives, to protect the innocent and to safeguard free speech and a free screen wherever threatened.'

It was this statement and the subsequent studio actions that resulted in the crumbling of the Committee for the First Amendment. No sooner did the moguls get back to their offices with the thick-pile carpets and bespoke furniture, they ordered all the major talent agents to come for talks – which amounted to a final decision that any statements made by their clients that were 'detrimental to the industry' would not be tolerated. It was war with an immediate, if premature, announcement of victory and no tolerance of anything which would give a contrary impression. People living under Hitler, Mussolini and Stalin would have recognised the situation.

One of the producers who at first opposed the action was Dore Schary, who later took over from Louis B Mayer as head of MGM. His daughter 'Jill Robinson Shaw' told me that one of his objections was the participation in the action of people like Adolphe Menjou. As for the Waldorf Declaration, she said he was 'furious'.

She says that the first she remembered of the blacklist were discussions Schary had with stars and writers advising them to keep their heads down. Before long, he was following the studio party line. 'He had fights with people and they never talked to each other again. My father was a liberal but he was very anti-Communist. He warned people to stay away from the Communist Party. The committee called him but he wouldn't give names and wouldn't testify. He was just smothered somewhere in the middle. He was in a dreadful position. He had no money and was working on a job and liked that job and needed to keep that job.'

The cost, she says, was high. He made enemies. 'He thought Larry Parks was an asshole and had told both him and his wife to stay away from the party.'

Plainly these were subjective judgements about a good man who was badly treated and tormented by circumstances. Sidney Sheldon told me: 'Schary was totally dishonest. He called a meeting and announced, "I will not fire anybody because he was accused of being a Communist". He took over at Metro and fired someone accused of being a member. The Writers Guild were so outraged, they called a meeting. Dore came to the meeting. He said, "I want to tell you why I'm not resigning because I could protect all of you" – and he was booed out of the room.'

As Sheldon said: 'The mood in this town was so cowardly. They were terrified. The studios were all in that bag. They were under the control of Washington. If Washington said that Joe Dokes is a Communist, he was fired.'

To Norman Corwin, it was all part of HUAC's publicity campaign, 'for their witch-hunting. The repression was sweeping.'

Paul Buhle says it was a matter of 'a terror that swept through Hollywood that great fortunes would be lost. Films made ten years earlier were being re-released because there wasn't sufficient confidence in the new batch of films.'

The moguls probably had no intention of banning all Communists in 1947. That came later. There were a few who were instantly picked out

– but not, officially – for their political leanings. The writer Waldo Salt, one of the Hollywood Ten, was fired at MGM right after the hearings, although Dore Schary maintained the reason was simply because he didn't think he was up to the job.

Schary emphasised that there was no intention of instituting a blacklist after the Waldorf Declaration. Those who were dismissed, including the Hollywood Ten, were not fired 'because they were believed to be Communists, but because it was believed that they have impaired their usefulness to the industry by their actions.'

Louis B Mayer didn't plan to pull wool over anyone's eyes. The producer's first duty, he said, was to protect the film industry 'and draw the greatest possible number of people into the theatre.' On the other hand, Nicholas Schenck, head of the MGM parent company, Loew's Inc, said that although he was against Communism, he was not in the business of taking any action against its followers 'until it hurts the industry.'

It was a unique situation. Jill Robinson Shaw speculates about what could have happened if the studio bosses had not acted. 'There would have been enormous taxes on making films; making it impossible for the industry to survive. There would have been additional censoring. I can't tell you how often films had to be reshot because of censors. The Legion of Decency could make your picture a near disaster. It should also be noted that movie receipts were by then down 25 per cent on the previous year.'

Of course, there are dissenting views about explaining the studios' attitudes. Hal Kanter summed up a common feeling of the period: 'The studio heads seemed to have no guts at all. They were scared to death what would happen to them. Very little heroism came from the studios. If you could get all the studio heads together and all speak with the same voice, that would be a miracle.' Except in this case, because, as he says: 'They were all out to protect their own asses and a lot of asses were working for them to protect theirs.'

Chapter Fourteen
HUAC the Anti-Semite

A good many citizens of Hollywood have been called Communists, to the evident delight of Mr Thomas and his witnesses. There are, without doubt, circumstances under which such an investigation as this one would be proper. If the moving pictures were undermining the American form of government and menacing it by their content, it might become the duty of Congress to ferret out the responsible persons. But clearly this is not the case – not even the committee's own witnesses are willing to make so fantastic a charge. And since so much danger exists, the beliefs of men and women who write for the screen are, like the beliefs of any ordinary men and women, nobody's business but their own, as the Bill of Rights mentions. Neither Mr Thomas nor the Congress in which he sits is empowered to dictate what Americans shall think.

New York Herald Tribune **Editorial, 22 October 1967**

One fact is often overlooked when assessing the history of HUAC and its relationship with Hollywood. There is a strong argument to show that it was as much an anti-Semitic conspiracy as an attempt at rooting out Communists. A quick glance down the list of blacklistees shows just how many of them were Jewish. Most of the Hollywood Ten – to say nothing of stars like John Garfield and Edward G Robinson – and, with a few exceptions, most of the writers who followed the Ten, were Jewish.

It was one reason, of course, why the moguls were so scared; they would let nothing like the small detail of their religion threaten their existence or power. The fact that they allowed their compatriots to be thrown to the wolves with the millstone 'Un-American' hung around their necks gives an idea of how afraid the Moguls were. The committee, on the other hand, who could find no reason to condemn the moguls, grabbed the opportunity of not only arraigning unfriendly witnesses who happened to be Jews, but made reference to their Jewishness at every available opportunity.

Neither were their thoughts confined to interviews or private conversations. Congressman John Rankin of Mississippi took his beliefs to the very floor of the House of Representatives. He took advantage of a question asked by a member who intended to ridicule what HUAC was doing. Congresswoman Helen Gahagan Douglas asked which films members of the committee really believed were helping the Communist party. Rankin took this as the perfect opportunity to raise the petition which had been submitted by the Committee for the First Amendment. He decided to read some of the names on the petition: 'One is Danny Kaye,' he began. 'We found his real name was David Daniel Kaminsky. Then there was Eddie Cantor. His real name was Edward Iskowitz. Edward G Robinson, his name is Emmanuel Goldenberg.' Rankin then added, enjoying meting out each grain of salt he was pouring into what he hoped were deep wounds, 'There's another one here who calls himself Melvyn Douglas, whose real name is Melvyn Hesselberg.' Melvyn Douglas just happened to be Helen Gahagen Douglas's husband.

The young Congressman and HUAC member Richard M Nixon decided this was a perfect moment to condemn his colleague – using the sort of unparliamentary language that is still stunning in its vulgarity. 'Helen Gahagan Douglas is pink,' he declared, 'right down to her underwear.' The congressmen loved that statement, even though it would have been ruled out of order in a school debating society. At least the committee found it amusing, laughing uproariously at their man's joke. Not many, however, laughed at the letters they were sent by Rankin. Larry Adler told me: 'I saw some of these letters – addressed, "Dear Kike" and "Dear Nigger".'

There are people who think that the anti-Semitism wasn't simply a matter of Jew versus Gentile. Hilda Ornitz said: 'It was Semite against Semite because the people who had influence could have stopped it, but did not.' She felt their behaviour was akin to that of the Jews who chose which of their fellow concentration camp inmates went to the gas chambers, which is going perhaps more than a little too far. On the other hand – the theory still persists in some people's minds that emphasising the number of implicated Jews was not good for the Jewish people, with the Jewish studio bosses wanting it hushed up. Paul Buhle believes this. 'Jewish agencies such as the Anti-Defamation League [of B'nai B'rith] and their branches ferociously favoured the blacklist – and saw it as an opportunity to get rid of left-wing Jews whom they'd always regarded as competition to their leadership.' That, too, seems a harsh judgement.

Buhle's view seems like a very harsh judgement, also things were more straightforward. The writer Walter Bernstein told me: 'HUAC was very anti-Semitic.' As for himself, 'I don't think anything could make me feel more Jewish than I am. Almost all I knew were secular Jews. And it really wasn't persecution like that that was going on in Germany.'

Germany was an important country for Hollywood, whose films had a significant share of the market – a strange state of affairs when one thinks of Jewish books being burned in the streets, and the existence of the labour and concentration camps. As long as the studios didn't go too far and directly criticise the Nazis, American films were given the green light – perhaps not least because Hitler himself loved them. This tacit co-operation between Hollywood's Jewish leaders and the Nazis went deeper than most at the time imagined. The idea that the studios could imperil this goldmine must have sent shivers from Burbank to Culver City.

Nazi officials were allowed to vet movies before their release, while some moguls even suppressed certain projects lest they harm the studios' finances too drastically. Universal Studio boss Carl Laemmle had a meeting with the German propaganda minister, Josef Goebbels, about films that could have been regarded as suspect in case something offensive to Nazi tastes found itself in the final cut. 20th Century Fox, MGM and Paramount subsequently fired any Jewish workers in their offices in Nazi-held territory.

If anyone's word was law at this time, it was that of the moguls. Except when they got scared. Until America entered the war, there were virtually no anti-Nazi movies. Chaplin's *The Great Dictator* in 1940 was an honourable exception.

HUAC and the moguls were not the only ones in Los Angeles who demonstrated degrees of anti-Semitism. The actress Carol Eve Rossen, daughter of the writer-producer-director Robert Rossen, who was blacklisted and then partially given the all-clear after a second round of testimony, told me she had a 'wonderful family existence' living in the WestSide of Los Angeles, not the kind of area used to people like the Rossens. She left the University High School because of anti-Semitism. At the age of 12 she was told that she was not welcome at the school and so transferred to the famous and more friendly Beverly High. It was much better than the other school where she had been taunted by being called 'the kid of a Commie; your father's a pinko.'

Carol remembers when Senator McCarren, in particular, 'considered Commies and Kykes one and the same. Yes, of course Hollywood was mostly Jewish at that time. They were of the new breed. They were not looking for the Messiah in Orthodoxy. They were looking for something to believe in. They found it in the activism of the party. When it was anti-fascist and when my father stayed with the party, he was not taking the party line. He stuck with the likelihood that the Russians were better for the Jews than the Nazis.'

What is undeniable is that HUAC took advantage of the 1918 Sedition Act to attack Jews. The Act allowed the government to declare that anyone who was foreign-born, even if subsequently naturalised, could be declared a non-citizen. A number of the blacklisted writers and some of the actors had sought refuge in America from Nazism, and some of the older ones from Tsarist pogroms in Russia. Martin Dies himself had spoken of invoking the Act because he said there were too many Jews in Hollywood.

Much of HUAC's support, as far as the Hollywood investigations were concerned, came from the Roman Catholic Church, some members of whom had been stressing that help for the Republican cause in the Spanish Civil War was Jewish-inspired and an opportunity to attack what some called President Roosevelt's 'Jew Deal'.

Ed Asner told me that he thought it was a case of 'the lynch mentality out in full force. So it was America's version of the Doctor's Plot – a wake-up call to the Jews.' He went on: 'It was all very clear that in the history of the freeing of the South, the Communist party and the Jews were always very pertinent to the pursuit of civil rights for blacks.'

Actress Norma Barzman agrees: 'Many members of the committee were anti-Semitic. It's no accident that of the people in Hollywood who were fighting for labour rights, so many were Jewish. There is certainly something within Jewish culture about this. There were just a bunch of American playwrights who were Jewish and brought with them a cultural interest in justice.' Not at all the kind of thing that HUAC liked to hear.

To Theodore Bikel there was no doubt about the whole matter. 'Scratch a fascist and you'll find an anti-Semite,' he said – and the members of HUAC *were* fascists.

Chapter Fifteen
Ratting in Hollywood

In all my Congressional experience of 32 years, I know of no committee so broadly condemned because of its conduct by people of all stages of life and from all parts of the nation.
Representative Adolph Sabbath, Chairman of the House of Rules Committee

Winston Churchill had a word for what he did when he left the Conservative Party to join the Liberals. He said he 'ratted'. Then, he 'double-ratted' when he reversed himself and went back to the Tories.

The Blacklist story is replete with the names of people ratting. Some of them were hailed as HUAC heroes and thus ostracised by former friends as a result. Others have had more sympathetic reactions from fellow victims of the list. The first post-Hollywood Ten unfriendly witness, Larry Parks, is looked on a lot more kindly now than he was at the time. History has shown that, notwithstanding his later pleading, he was subjected to unbearable pressures before, to use his phrase, he 'crawled in the mud'.

Many people still think of Edward Dmytryk in similar terms. He was the one member of the Ten to change his mind and 'rat'. But strangely, he gave up his fight only *after* doing his time in jail. That gave him a certain credibility – and even understanding – when he said that he had reconsidered his position and was now willing to give names – but only those which were already known and presented by HUAC. After Parks, Dmytryk was perhaps the most famous case of a blacklistee going against his own principles, although by his very actions he could convince that his principles were still intact. Except that they were not the same principles.

The case of Elia Kazan has few redeeming features – apart from the fact that in extreme old age the Academy decided to award him a special Oscar. The decision was backed by the so-called Ad Hoc Committee for Naming Facts (a nice twist on the naming of names, which was intended as a triumphal thumbs-down to the anti-blacklist lobby, but looked more ridiculous than simply showing how bright one could be with tongues firmly placed in cheeks), formed by the Ayn Rand Institute, named in honour of one of the most vociferous anti-Communist witnesses to HUAC. It was a time for the right-wing organisations to come out of their burrows and, as they saw it, to finally counter all the bad publicity HUAC and its Hollywood supporters had had for half a century.

A statement issued by the ad-hoc committee stated: 'During the HUAC hearings in 1952, it was Mr Kazan who was supportive of the principle of industrial rights and his Communist opponents who were its enemies. Mr Kazan showed great moral courage in testifying about the influence in the American film and theatre industry of those who wished to replace freedom with totalitarianism.'

The Ad-Hoc Committee decided to hold a demonstration in favour of Kazan outside the Dorothy Chandler Pavilion at Los Angeles Music Center. The group was determined to open old wounds; it was not ready to surrender just yet. The Committee announced it would name facts, including 'the people named by Mr Kazan were Communists, a fact they have not denied. The mission of the party, financed and directed by the Soviet Union, was the violent overthrow of the US Government and the imposition of a Soviet-style dictatorship in America. The Hollywood Communists were ideological enemies of human rights – including the right of free speech that they brazenly claim was being denied *them*.'

The announcement went on: 'The US Government has the right to investigate an organisation that declares its intent to overthrow a free society on behalf of a foreign dictatorship. It was not the Communists' ideas, but their threatened actions which were the legitimate targets of inquiry.' And then came the real rub: 'Private film studios have every right to blacklist, i.e. to refuse to hire and give platforms to people whose views they found repugnant. Americans deserve the truth. The Hollywood Communists were the villains, not the victims. The real defenders of rights were not the Hollywood Reds, but the brave men and women who acted to oppose them.'

People in the audience that night of 21 March 1999 gave Kazan a standing ovation. Others walked out or, like the actor Warren Beatty, surprised their fellow members staying for the proceedings, joining the standing ovation and clapping. Beatty, an ardent fighter against everything that people like Kazan represented, thought that the time had come to simply pay tribute to his professional talent. Stephen Spielberg did not join the standing ovation, but he did applaud from his seat.

David Geffen, his partner at Dreamworks, stayed silent in his seat. The boss of Paramount Sherry Lansing sat emotionless. Nick Nolte did, too. So did Ed Harris, but Meryl Streep, who has a reputation for supporting left-wing causes, stood and cheered. Others wanted more active protests. Bernard Gordon led a fruitless campaign to prevent the presentation of the Life Achievement award. He demanded that the Academy apologise for having 'aided and abetted' the blacklist. The Academy refused.

Abe Polonsky was among the nay-sayers. 'He's got two Oscars for directing, why give him another for honouring his life?' he asked of the Elia Kazan love-in. Eric Sherman remembers having a discussion about this with his father, Vincent, who welcomed the veteran's award. 'I, who didn't know Kazan but watched the effects that his squealing had, said, "Come on, Dad, how can you be like this?" He said, "Well, son, if you were in that position, maybe you'd think differently."'

The man who had directed some of the most important plays and films of the twentieth century wanted to continue working. If that meant saying he hated the Communist party of which he had been a member and naming those who had been his loyal friends and colleagues, then so be it. Elia Kazan, known in the business as Gadge, continued to work and directed many more films and plays.

Hardly surprisingly, the mention of the name Elia Kazan provokes little short of hatred in the dwindling blacklist community. But it was not so much Hollywood that proved to be his principal victim. The Turkish-born son of Greek parents had joined the Group Theater in 1932 and it was there that he learned his skills as a director. It was also where he met Communists and joined the party himself. In 1952, the names he gave were essentially those of people he had known while at the Group and then of the Actors Studio which he had helped found. By that time, Kazan had discovered Marlon Brando and cast him in the original Broadway 1947 production of *A Streetcar Named Desire*. When it came to filming *Streetcar* in 1951, Kazan directed Brando in the story once more. By that time, his stage directing had included *The Skin of our Teeth*, *One Touch of Venus* and *All My Sons*.

In Hollywood, Kazan had directed *A Tree Grows In Brooklyn* in 1945, *Gentlemen's Agreement* in 1947, *Panic in the Streets* (1950) and in the year he listed names, Brando again in *Viva Zapata!* It was in 1954 that he added *On the Waterfront* to his roster of iconic movies. It was said by some that this was a way of atoning for going to HUAC with his list of names that he was naming. When I met Kazan in the 1960s, he denied this accusation, but of course at the time the blacklist was still unofficially still in force. 'I thought it was a wonderful story about the anger of people forced to go against what they believed was decently right, the violence,' he told me. He did not mention the fact that it also dealt with informers. He had appeared before HUAC twice. Before any pink slip came his way, Kazan said he would not talk about his 19 months in the Communist Party. 'I'll tell them to screw themselves.'

But subpoenaed he was. On the first occasion Kazan appeared before HUAC in January 1952, he said in a private executive session that he had no names to name. 'While I would tell the whole truth about myself, I would refuse to name any of my old friends,' he declared, piously. He was asked about the writer Clifford Odets. Kazan said he would give all the co-operation he could 'about myself but would not discuss others.' He was told he would have to come back again and reconsider his stand.

For months, as Kazan wrote in his memoirs, he wrestled with the problem, felt ill, decided to give up film making and would concentrate on live theatre. The second appearance was different. It was held in public and he named the 17 names. He took the same comfort as others had when told they had been named before. Kazan said that his membership of the party had given him 'first-hand experience of dictatorship and thought control. It left me with an abiding hatred of Communist philosophy and methods and the conviction that these must be resisted always.'

The names came fast. 'For 19 months of my membership [of the Communist Party] I was assigned to a unit composed of members of the Group Theater . . . Louis Leverett, J Edward Bromberg, Phoebe Brand [later Mrs Morris Karnovsky] Phoebe Miller [later Mrs. Lee Strasberg] . . . Clifford Odets.'

He earned a treat deal of something close to hatred for this – even inside his own office.

His secretary left him after he had taken an advertisement in the *New York Times* advising others to co-operate with the investigations. Other friends and contacts followed suit – a reversal of the situation faced by many Hollywood people. Lillian Hellman was among the chorus of disgusted readers of the ad, which had been written by Kazan's wife, Molly. Hellman described it as 'hard to believe for its pious shit.'

Kazan explained: 'I did what I did because it was the more tolerable of two alternatives that were, either way, painful, even disastrous, and either way wrong for me . . . that's what a difficult decision means. Either way you go, you lose.'

Kazan wrote: 'I'd turned violently anti-Communist. But the yearning for meaning, for dignity, for security in life, stirred me . . . The Communists got their influence and their power by speaking up for these desires. It seemed that I hadn't changed. They had.'

Ring Lardner's daughter said that her father found Kazan 'particularly disturbing. He could work in the theatre [without a blacklist]. My father was more sympathetic to those who couldn't get work.'

Jeff Lawson said that his father, John Howard Lawson, wouldn't talk to Kazan 'who was a man who was made by the Group Theater, which gave him his opportunity and all that and then, to save himself, turned on his friends. And some of those people were not even Communists that he turned on. Most of the people that I know felt it was a terrible betrayal, but people look out for their own financial interests.'

There were more arguments with Lillian Hellman, in particular. 'I laid everything on the table,' Kazan wrote in his autobiography, 'I told her I wouldn't be able to work in films if I didn't testify to everything I knew. Then I told her that while it would be a blow, I'd be prepared for it and could get along OK without film work.' He said that Hellman was 'silent as a coiled snake. I didn't realise until later how threatened she felt in the same emergency. She said nothing to turn me away from where I seemed to be moving.' Hellman interpreted the meeting somewhat differently. She said she had no interest in talking any further and that the director had told her: 'It's OK for you to do what you want, I guess. You've probably spent whatever you've earned'. Which was an example of the bitterness the situation created.

Hellman said Kazan told her that he had made $400,000 the previous year from the live stage, but Spyros Skouras, the head of 20th Century Fox, told him that if he did not co-operate with the committee, he would never make another movie. She said that Kazan told her that he and Skouras had met J Edgar Hoover in Washington and they both told him to name names. He agreed because what he called 'Communist activities' amounted to 'a dangerous and alien conspiracy.'

It took until 1988 before Kazan would show public remorse. In his autobiography he referred to a dream he had about one of the people he named, Tony Kraber. 'I thought what a terrible thing I'd done. Not the political aspect of it . . . but the human side of the thing. I said to myself: "You hurt another human being, a friend of yours and his family, and no political aspect matters two shits." What good deeds were stimulated by what I'd done? What villains exposed? How is the world better for what I did? It had just been a game of power and influence and I'd been taken in and twisted from my true self.'

Eric Sherman, reflecting on his father's attitude at the time, said this of the director: 'Kazan was an absolute rat who would turn anyone in for a nickel. And did. Abe Polonsky . . . hated Kazan . . . it's fascinating what Abe told me about Kazan. Kazan was a nasty man who would betray, and did betray, every woman he was involved with, many of his business partners and most of his colleagues. Abe Polonsky told me that when Kazan did his famous newspaper column where he said he'd never really been much of a Communist, Abe said he saw him at Communist cell meetings two weeks before he wrote that article. So he was a liar.'

Polonsky himself said of Kazan's testimony, 'It was not a moral, ethical or political question at all. It was a practical question – but people don't like to see it that way because it makes their character less worthy.'

Polonsky was a man who wrestled with the problem, not like Kazan of naming names which would always have been beyond the pale, but of giving enough to HUAC to keep himself out of jail. He took the Fifth.

Arthur Miller was divided between his personal affection for Kazan, the director who had helped him bring *Death of a Salesman* to the world, and his hatred for what the man had done. He wrote about the 'anger rising against the committee more than against Kazan '"whom I loved like a brother."' But he added: 'Had I have been of his generation, he would have had to sacrifice me as well. And finally that was all I could think of. I could still be up for sacrifice if Kazan knew I had attended meetings of party writers years ago . . . it was sadness, purely mournful, deadening.'

As for America, what sort of country was it that could promote a committee like HUAC? Kazan's answer: 'I was experiencing a bitterness with the country that I had never even imagined before, a hatred of its stupidity and its throwing away of its freedom.'

Kazan actually asked Clifford Odets if he would name him. Odets said yes – probably because he was about to name names himself. However, he said that the writer needed to have 'people respect him as their hero – something I could, as I finally had to, get along without.'

The real effect of Kazan's second testimony was probably best demonstrated by the Committee chairman's reaction to all he had said: 'Mr Kazan, it is only through people such as you that we have been able to bring to the attention of the American people the Communist conspiracy of world domination. Thank you, Mr Kazan, we are very grateful.'

As is now obvious, Hellman and Dalton Trumbo didn't see eye to eye during the blacklist period. Hellman said about Trumbo's 'We're all victims" philosophy: 'Forgiveness is God's job, not mine.' To which Trumbo replied: 'Well, so is vengeance, you know.' But it took a great deal of self-assurance, to say nothing of courage, to forgive *or* forget. Some were able to forgive. None could forget.

One of the most strident books about the atmosphere surrounding the blacklist was Budd Schulberg's epic novel, *What Makes Sammy Run?* It focused a lens on a Hollywood that had blacklists, where Red-baiting was a way of life and where the studios were concerned only with what would, a couple of generations later, be called the bottom line. It was an onslaught on the film town's philosophies and HUAC wouldn't have liked it. But 10 years after the novel was first published, Schulberg appeared before the committee and it liked what he said very much indeed. He was listed under the heading 'friendly'. Schulberg had written *On the Waterfront,* which was directed by Kazan. This was after they had both had their experiences with HUAC.

Joanna Rapf, daughter of Maurice Rapf, Schulberg's best friend, says the film was a reflection on the blacklist. Kazan himself always saw it that way. 'There's no question about that. I went through the Kazan papers and there are whole notes on the script, about the shooting . . . he really identified with Terry Molloy in that movie [the Brando role of the young boxer forced to do the will of the union bosses]. And it was about the blacklist. But it was not for Budd. And I believe Budd. My father never believed Budd on that, but I do. Because he'd worked on the waterfront crime issues for so many years before the movie and I think it really was about the labour struggle for Budd. He'd been much more involved in that kind of thing than Kazan had.'

Schulberg's was one of the names originally listed by Richard Collins. Once named himself, he sent a telegram to HUAC. He said he was willing to help in any way he could. He gave very personal views on why he had left a party of which he had become a member as a result of a youthful indiscretion. The party, he said, had called his work 'decadent', which since Stalin first decided to be the arbiter of artistic taste, was as serious an allegation as could be made.

To this day, Schulberg has attacked other former Communists, but has not recanted on his 'friendly' evidence. He, too, crossed swords with people like Lillian Hellman, of whom he said: 'They question our talking. I question their silence. There were premature anti-fascists. But there were also premature anti-Stalinists.'

Joanna Rapf, says that when Schulberg named names it 'was really shattering because they were like brothers. They grew up together. They had been best friends since they were 6 years old, one of those long, deep friendships – and so when Budd named names and he was close friends with my dad's friends, too, that was devastating. He couldn't speak to Budd. It broke their friendship. And he didn't speak to Budd until 1964, for 10 years.'

It was Rapf's wife who said, after those 10 years, that 'enough is enough. Let bygones be bygones, shake hands and be friends together.' They shook hands and the HUAC naming never came up again – until he spoke at Maurice's funeral. Meanwhile, their sons had become close friends, too.

Schulberg had brought Ring Lardner Jr into the party. His daughter now says: 'My dad said he would be interested in having conversations with Budd Schulberg. He was as a person, as a reporter, very interested in what happened with Schulberg.'

They eventually met at the Rapfs' golden wedding party. All the people still around who had known them when they were first married were invited. 'It was the first time that [the two and other blacklistees] had been in the same room and they had to speak [to Budd] and be civil. And they were. But it was the first time in all those years. It was a very poignant occasion . . . There was a lot of tension in the room. There really was. It was real tension, but it was a happy occasion.'

The recanting by Sterling Hayden – perhaps his ratting and then reratting – wasn't a happy occasion at all. Hayden, a former sea captain, who went into films after a modelling career and was dubbed the Most Beautiful Man In The Movies joined the Communist party, influenced by what he had seen as a member of OSS (roughly, the predecessor of the CIA) in Greece and Yugoslavia during World War Two. The man who was a party member for just 6 months was there, but long enough to name names in the 1951 sweep of Hollywood and to be commended by Congressman Walter for 'speaking out as an intensely loyal citizen.' Hayden himself said 'there is a service to be offered out there to people who are in a similar position to mine. The suggestion made by the chairman of this committee that people come forward is fine.'

Hayden didn't name *all* the names he could have. Bernard Gordon, who worked on Hayden's 1954 film *Crime Wave,* is forever grateful that the star couldn't remember his name when he presented his list – beginning with 'I wouldn't hesitate to name Karen Morley' – and then said there was 'Bernie somebody.' It's a shame that Hayden's memory lapse wasn't enough to save Gordon from the blacklist. Hayden said that meetings had been held at Morley's house and some at the home of Morris Karnovsky.

The actor's lawyer wrote a letter to J Edgar Hoover, in which he talked about Hayden's journey to Communism. 'In June 1946, in a moment of emotional disturbance, a young man became a member of the Communist Party. He is concerned that his brief membership of the Communist Party might prevent the use of his services. He is married and has young children. If his services are not needed by the United States . . . our client can of course answer honestly and frankly that he is not a member of the party . . . the purpose of this [letter] is to permit our client, if the compound question is asked of him, to say in answer to the question "Please inquire of the Federal Bureau of Investigation." The FBI could then notify the prospective employer that there was no reason for not employing our client.'

It didn't save Hayden from his psychiatrist's bills. Ernest Philip Cohen, one of HUAC's informers, recommended that he would feel better if he gave all the names at his disposal. Unlike many of the others who named names, he showed what appears to be genuine remorse for his actions. The recanting and apologies came 12 years later, when Hayden discovered his psychiatrist was unqualified. Furious, he lambasted: 'If it hadn't been for you, I would never have been a stoolie for J Edgar Hoover. I don't think you have the foggiest notion of the contempt I had for myself for doing that thing. I was a rat. The names that I listed, some of them close friends, were blacklisted and they were deprived of their livelihood.'

Dmytryk put his disillusion with the way things were going down to the original hearings and what happened after the flight to Washington by the Committee for the First Amendment (CFI). 'I was so happy with the support of the CFA and the others,' he said, years later. But he thought their efforts fruitless. The result was that in May 1951 Dmytryk went before the committee – and gave 26 names. He explained that he no longer believed in Communism and couldn't bear not being able to work.

Dmytryk made his first statement about being out of sync with the other Hollywood Ten prisoners while still in jail. It was in April 1951, soon after being released, that he testified in front of the committee. The following month he wrote a lengthy column in the *Saturday Evening Post*, headed WHAT MAKES A HOLLYWOOD COMMUNIST. In it, he explained: 'I had long been convinced that the fight of the Ten was political . . . I believed that I was being forced to sacrifice my family and my career in defence of the Communist party, from which I had long been separated, and which I had grown to dislike and distrust.'

It was not an instant decision or change of mind on his part – Dmytryk and Larry Parks had discussed the situation at length. While in jail, he had also been quietly working on a statement with his lawyer Bartley Crum, in which he stated he needed to make it perfectly clear that he was no longer a member of the party and that he owed his allegiance to the US.

He appeared before HUAC and said that he now believed there were people who would refuse to fight for America against Soviet Russia. 'I now believe that there were.' Asked what he felt was the real object of the Communist Party in Hollywood, Dmytryk replied without hesitation (probably because he anticipated the question): 'They had three purposes: to get money, to get prestige and to control the content of pictures. The only way they could control pictures was through the guilds and unions.'

'What guilds?'

'They were successful a time in controlling the Screen Writers Guild. They were not successful at all in controlling the Screen Directors Guild.' There were about 225–230 members in the directors' organisation.

'Any Communists?' he was asked.

He replied insouciantly, 'Frank Tuttle, Herb Biberman, Jack Berry – he's the Berry who lives on Kings Road – Jules Dassin, Bernard Voorhaus and myself.'

Dmytryk made the decision in the face of what he knew he would have to do. 'I would have to name names and I knew the problems this would cause. My decision was made easier by the fact that . . . I couldn't name anybody who hadn't already been identified as a party member. Weighing everything – pro and con – I knew I had to testify.'

If that was stinging, the real poison was in the tail of his statement. 'I did not want to remain a martyr to something that I absolutely believed was immoral and wrong.'

One result was what he was hoping for. The blacklist now had one name missing and Dmytryk was once more a film director. The other result was eagerly anticipated. As the only member of the Ten to renege, he was immediately beyond the pale to the other 9, although Ring Lardner Jr said that he wasn't going to impose a blacklist of his own. Lardner's daughter Kate said her father – actually her adopted father; he had married his late brother's wife and taken her children as his own –

said: 'He was very disturbed about Dmytryk and his statement in prison. This was very upsetting to Ring. He was very sympathetic to Parks, because it was so painful to him.'

Newsweek magazine saw it all in a particularly cynical stance. It declared 'Hollywood's show . . . was almost good enough to bring back vaudeville.'

Michael Cole said his father Lester regarded Dmytryk as 'a total shit. He could never abide people who turned. You did not do that.'

Historian Larry Ceplair now thinks that there were real personal reasons for Dmytryk's turncoat action. 'Dmytryk, I think, went back and informed because his wife was on the verge of a nervous breakdown, thinking he wouldn't work again.'

Norma Barzman saw it all at first hand. 'Eddie Dmytryk said it was not fair. Later, in London, in 1949 he was ready to direct Ben Barzman's story *Christ in Concrete* (later called *Give Us This Day* in Britain; *Salt To the Devil*, in America). The story, about Italian immigrants in New York, was not the greatest production he'd been involved with. 'Dmytryk persuaded J Arthur Rank to make the film. Rank then asked him a question. He thought it was going to be about the blacklist. Eddie said he was scared to death. But here was the question: Rank said, "Mr Dmytryk, do you believe in God?"' He must have satisfied the man, who was probably the British Methodist Church's principal benefactor, for he made the film.

Lee Grant says that she doesn't 'put him in the same camp as Kazan. I am sure that Dmytryk found a *raison d'être* for what his actions are. He wasn't one of the Ten any more.'

Perhaps he didn't work hard enough on his former colleagues. Joan la Court, soon to marry Adrian Scott, disliked him thoroughly. 'I met him with all the Ten when we mounted appearances. They all seemed decent men, but I took an instant dislike to Edward Dmytryk. One of my jobs was lining up the Ten alphabetically backstage and Dmytryk was, to me, very unappealing. He would always sit on the table when the photographers came through so that his shortness would not show.' This was the tip of the iceberg for Joan. 'He was kind of a snooty, egotistical little man. And also his former wife and his son were very involved with Adrian, so I got to see all the personal unpleasantness [when] Dmytryk's son and Adrian's son went to the same boarding school and all the pain and sadness that these two little boys endure. Adrian was dating Dmytryk's ex-wife. When Dmytryk informed, the two little boys were ripped apart by the situation.'

Madeline Dmytryk, the ex-wife, died after an accidental drug over-dose. The newspapers headlined their story: MYSTERY DEATH IN RED NEST.

The Ten all contributed to-camera pieces to a documentary called *The Hollywood Ten* – which in turn presented problems to Dmytryk's colleagues and to himself when he recanted. Through his lawyers, he asked for his contribution to be removed from the picture – which wasn't easily done without re-cutting the whole project, but most of his part in the film was eventually removed.

If there is sympathy to be found for the 'ratters', there ought perhaps to be most for Robert Rossen, writer, producer and director, with films like the 1947 *Johnny O'Clock* and *Body and Soul* behind him. His film *All the King's Men*, won an Oscar for best film in 1949. He had been one of the Hollywood Nineteen, but during the suspension of HUAC hearings, Rossen worked normally, not appearing before HUAC until 1951. His was a familiar story – son of Russian-Jewish immigrants, living on the Lower East Side. He was involved in gang fights before briefly becoming a professional boxer – a career he quickly abandoned when, very young, he became a writer and director, first off-Broadway and then on Broadway itself. In 1936 at the age of 28 he went to Hollywood, where he soon joined a Communist party cell.

Before the committee, he took the Diminished Fifth, refusing to name names. Like John Garfield, it was against his street-cred code to be a snitch. But then two years later, he contacted the committee and agreed to name names. His daughter, the actress Carol Eve Rossen, is still scarred by the experiences of the father she loved. She had known injustice before. She insisted to me that she was not 'a Red-diaper baby' – in other words, one that had been brought up surrounded by Communism. Looking back on it all now, she says: 'The important thing is that it is not properly understood how these guys wound up being in the position they were in . . . They were Depression people. My father said he wanted to attach himself to history . . . into the intellectual élite of this country.'

Like many others, Carol blames John Howard Lawson for trying to subvert her father's position. 'He was called in by Lawson and they did a whole number on his head.' What leading members of the Hollywood party resented was *All the King's Men*, based on Robert Penn Warren's story of a corrupt Governor of Louisiana. 'How dare he do this picture because people might think that Hughie Long was a little too like Stalin?

He told them to shove it where the sun don't shine. They wanted him to become a party hack because he was real good, he was smart, he was tough. He said "Adios".'

As she says: 'One of the reasons my father walked out of the party was that they wanted to meddle with his work and the one thing he would not allow is people to meddle in his work.' In an unused part of the interview for my BBC radio programme, she said: 'In no way did Communism ever catch on in this country. A generation was in despair, really.'

Robert Rossen remained a liberal after leaving the Communist party. 'He was gone. Then 1947 hit, they all rallied. My father wanted to tell the truth. They decided to stay as one. They thought it would get them off. They wanted to squash the subpoenas. They were not heroes.'

Carol Rossen recalls 'an almost institutional paranoia in Washington, but on the Communist side, they, too, were duplicitous and the people in Hollywood, certainly before the Soviet-Nazi Pact, were quite innocent and had committed themselves to group-think.'

After the HUAC appearance, Rossen returned to New York, but still couldn't get satisfactory work. The blacklist, which most people assume didn't affect the East Coast, certainly did in his case, according to Carol.

Others went back to Hollywood and gave names in camera. 'My father tried not to do that and waited too long. By the time in 1953 that he finally decided to give in to his particular demons – and had to for financial reasons and most essentially for work reasons – he was not a writer who could take an alias.' His passport had been taken away from him. 'All sorts of people had gotten passports, but he couldn't and couldn't work.'

The committee wanted to rub salt in his wounds and refused to allow Rossen the privilege of a secret hearing. The indignity of it all appeared the committee's priority from the moment he went to HUAC for this second time. Carol Rossen added: 'They were trying to save their souls. They didn't go there for constitutional reasons. A tidal wave of evil was coming at everyone. There was no answer that wasn't evil. I believe in evil. That word has meaning for me.'

When she uses that word, she automatically goes back to the second hearing. 'They made him crawl. They called him "Mr. Rosen" [his original name]; they did everything to humiliate him – and then asked him if he could get them house seats for the Broadway plays that were current at the time. We are talking of cynicism on the right and left . . . it has nothing to do with idealism.'

Rossen testified, got back to work abroad – 'but he was told he had to check in to various FBI people at various times and both right and left treated him with contempt. He had buckled to them, so therefore he was just a victim and on the left he buckled, so therefore he was an informer.

'Oh, God!' she says now. 'It was a time of shame, a time of confusion, a time of alienation, a time from the kids' point of view, I would later put it in the context of a sort of Holocaust victim where you know your parents' lives seem to be more important and more crisis-filled than your own – and therefore it must be paid attention to.'

The effect on her family was traumatic. 'We were moving, moving. That's what we did for a living. We were moving, moving.' It certainly had a serious effect on Rossen's marriage to his wife, Sue. 'There was a pall around the household all the time. And a lot of booze, I'll tell you that.' Not helped by the fact that, while awaiting the original subpoena, she knew there were 'Feds in the house across the street, filming everyone going in and coming out of my father's house.'

Rossen died as a result of complications brought on by skin lesions at the age of 58, with most of his work far behind him, although Carol says she is convinced his best work was made after blacklisting and after leaving Warner Bros. 'I think he was very keyed in to the idea of environment and the way it affected human beings.' There was one very late blooming as writer, director and producer – the 1961 Paul Newman film *The Hustler* in which he used all his skills. 'Some say,' maintains his daughter, 'that he died of shame. My father never got over the shame of giving names.'

Chapter Sixteen
Exile

I wouldn't be allowed to make The Best Years of Our Lives *in Hollywood today. That is directly the result of the activities of the Un-American Activities Committee. They are making decent people afraid to express their opinions. They are creating fear in Hollywood. Fear will result in self-censorship. Self-censorship will paralyse the screen. In the last analysis, you will suffer. You will be deprived of entertainment which stimulates you and you will be given a diet of pictures which conform to arbitrary standards of Americanism.*

William Wyler, *Hollywood Fights Back*, 1947

The blacklist changed everything for its victims – the Unfriendly victims, that is, despite what Dalton Trumbo maintained. The biggest change of all was knowing what to do, which essentially meant where to go. Work in the United States was impossible for named actors. Directors who didn't rat couldn't work in the country either and no studio was going to trust a Commie with the responsibility of producing a movie.

For the others there was one hope – escape. In some cases, escape entailed escaping from their names, employing others to submit scripts on their behalf for a fee. For others, escape was literally that: getting out of Los Angeles and, in many cases, out of America altogether. These were, after all, talented people with proven track records, too young and too energetic simply to go into retirement or wait for HUAC to pull out its tent pegs and move on

Some went to Mexico – a comparatively easy option for those who had had their documents taken away, since the Mexican authorities didn't demand passports. Chris Trumbo said there was no option but to go abroad. 'Moving back to Beverly Hills or Los Angeles would have been moving back into the lion's den.'

Others went to Europe, where they made films for companies they had previously never heard of, or, like Carl Foreman and Michael Wilson, wrote important movies that won Oscars – even though they didn't receive them themselves until much later and posthumously.

Ben and Norma Barzman went first to England and then to France, where they had a remarkably productive time, making new friends and great professional strides.

'My husband, Ben, hated exile,' Norma told me when I interviewed her for the BBC programme. To the extent that he inserted an emotive line into the 1961 film he wrote for Sophia Loren and Charlton Heston, *El Cid*, saying just how bad it was to be in exile. As she explained: 'He felt the United States had put him out. As a naturalised American [he was born in Canada] he felt the exile even worse because they kicked him out and wouldn't let him back in.'

Norma herself would have been more welcome back in the US. In fact, people said she should return, to name names, something she manifestly refused to do. So she made a film in Italy and Ben worked with Edward Dmytryk on what had originally been called *Christ in Concrete*.

'We went to work in Europe so we could work. I went to London to have a baby and worked desperately hard to find an apartment.' Meanwhile, Ben was working in New York – 'I didn't see him for a long, long time.' When in England together, they made new friends, like Sam Wanamaker, an outstanding actor whom she found extraordinarily attractive, both as a fellow blacklistee and as an actor.

From London they went to Paris, where the air was unsullied by fog. As Norma said: 'Ben said that Paris is the only city in the world for which you feel nostalgic even while you're in it.' Meeting and becoming close friends with people like Pablo Picasso, whom they admired both for his unique talent and his Communist politics, was another huge plus. 'He was,' she says in her book *The Red and the Blacklist*, 'us'. In an interview in the 1980s, Norma said: 'I feel we were very fortunate in that the blacklist and the McCarthy period was destructive for many careers, families, lives. If we hadn't have gone abroad, we'd have stayed provincial screenwriters on Sunset Plaza Drive and what it really meant was the world really opened up for us.'

On the other hand, Jules Dassin saw a much blacker picture. One should never imagine, he said, that anything which 'deprived every artistic aspect of citizenship' and of writing films in his own native language, could be anything but bad.

A close friend of the Barzman was a French Jewish intellectual called Vlodya – real name Vladimir Pozner – who had spent the years of the German occupation in America. From France, Ben and Norma went to Israel, where Norma experienced her first Passover seder at a kibbutz. She wrote a film in 1952 called *Young Man with Ideas*, which was based on her own experiences at Radcliffe college and her sister's at a Swiss finishing school. It had originally been called *Finishing School* and ended up as *Luxury Girls*, complete with lurid promotional posters which had nothing whatsoever to do with the story.

It took until 1999 for Norma to get an on-screen credit for that film – at the same time as Ben was allowed to have his name on *El Cid*.

Christ in Concrete or rather *Give Us This Day*, much, no doubt, to the secret delight of HUAC, who were presented with new evidence against the Barzmans' unfriendliness, was featured at the Prague Film Festival and won a prize – at the same time as a special award for Paul Jarrico's and John Berry's documentary, *The Hollywood Ten*. The result of the Prague award was that the State Department tried to find a way of bringing Norma back to America so that she could face the noise. She resisted.

Instead, the couple returned to Paris, where Ben teamed up writing with their friend and fellow Communist, Jules Dassin, resulting in a film in 1957 called *He Who Must Die*, which Dassin also directed. There was also a film shot at Elstree studios, outside London, *Time Without Pity* the same year, directed by another blacklist refugee, Joseph Losey. Owing to his exile, Barzman had phone conferences with Losey about the script, and the director even flew out to Paris on one occasion. Barzman's other film credits at this time included the Italian *Stranger on the Prowl* in 1952, *Blind Date* (1959) and *Oasis* (1955). Later came his most heralded works, the sweeping dramas *El Cid*, *The Fall of the Roman Empire* in 1964, *The Heroes of Telemark*, 1965 and *The Blue Max*, 1966, along with an uncredited adaptation of Costa-Gavras' 1969 classic *Z*.

The Barzmans stayed in exile for 16 years. They arrived back in Los Angeles in 1976. After their return to a vastly changed city and film industry, work was scarce. Although Ben was hired to work on several screenplays, none was ever made into a film, and he never again saw his work on the screen He died in 1989, at the age of 78. Norma settled down to writing, including the brilliant *The Red and the Blacklist*.

In her book, she recounts her affair with Bernard Vorhaus, who, once the catch-me-if-you-can shenanigans around the house(s) with the FBI were over, also went to France. Vorhaus' career had been damned by the projectionists' union which refused to show any film he had written. They went further and said they would ban all films made by United Artists. 'So I lost all my money.' He had a good contract to work in Italy, but couldn't get a permit. He couldn't remain long in France either, although he stayed there for a few weeks – enough to be with Norma Barzman. But he was married to an Englishwoman and a solicitor advised him to lie low in Britain for a time, where he went into business converting old houses.

'I returned to Italy on a tourist visa for one month and hoped I would be able to straighten out my position. In other words, to take up the contract that was begging to be fulfilled. He had only been in the country a few days when he was picked up by the police in the resort town of Positano. 'They wouldn't say why.' He was told to go to Naples, where he could present any problems to the American consul. 'I didn't want to talk to the American consul. I had been in the Air Force during the war and had [known some] secrets. But I wasn't interested in betraying any of it. It was the time that the Rosenbergs were on trial and the last thing *I* wanted was to be sent back to America.'

Vorhaus, who once said that he liked working on shoestring budgets because it forced him to use every means he had available to tell a story succinctly, had an entirely different military career and worked on the first American radar installations, the first swing-wing plane and the first vertical take-off aircraft. 'The Chief of Police in Naples was very annoyed. Thank God, with their usual inefficiency, he had not been sent my file. His assumption was that "I don't know why this son of a bitch is here". He thought I had insisted on seeing the consul, so the only thing to do was to get as mad as I could. He said, "Take this son of a bitch and send him over the border. He's not going to see the consul". That's why I was told to lay low.'

The Jarricos settled in France, too. Sylvia Jarrico now says: 'We associated with friendly people – as we did here [in America] and the French have a very superior school of education in the history of modern thought and in philosophy of government and so on. So they felt very strongly the issues of freedom of speech on which the black-listed people had made their commitment. They were very supportive, those who were friendly to us. I don't remember meeting any who were hostile.'

Even if there had been hostile neighbours, the Jarricos would have been comforted by the others who were in the same boat. 'There were so many who came through. Some stayed for a while, some went. The

Wilsons had a very nice country estate, so there were a lot of parties there. We knew all the Americans who were there. And we used to have an American-French Thanksgiving party. The French insisted that they made the best stuffing for a turkey and if you have to stuff a turkey, make it the best!'

Michael Wilson's family took time to get together in France. Michael went first but it took his wife six months to get a passport, a frequent problem for potential refugees. But then things got moving. Rosanna Wilson-Farrow told Barbra Paskin: 'It happened really fast because my mother was afraid that we had a small window of opportunity when our passports would be valid and then they might be revoked again later – which is actually what happened in France later on when our passports were revoked for a few years and we couldn't return to the States even if we had wanted to.' Her memories of that time are wonderful blends of family affection and childish wonder. 'I remember on the ship, one of my memories, being on deck outside, looking into the night and there were little lights in the distance, as we were approaching the French coast at Le Havre and I kept saying, "Is that Daddy with the lights?"'

Nothing was certain for the Wilsons, like so many others. 'I do remember being told we were only going there for a while. We were only going for six months, I think was what I heard. I'm not quite sure why they told us that . . . maybe they didn't want to scare us. But I do remember them telling us, first it was six months, then it was a year – which became eight years.'

After four years of attending a French school in Paris, the family moved to the country and Michael Wilson's daughters, Becca and Rosanna, went tó a British school. 'It was at that British school that I actually encountered my first experience of threat, this time from a kind of neo-Nazi teacher, which was very threatening to me. At that time, there was this Algerian independence movement and there were bombs going off in Paris. And one day, one of the teachers at our school, a Spanish teacher, came up to me in the hallway and said, "I know who your father is and you'd better watch out because we know what he is. We know he's a Communist, we know all about him, so you'd better watch out." Just like that.'

At school, she says she was always aware of carrying secrets. 'We had to protect, we had to be secretive. We couldn't just tell anybody or [even] our good friends who our parents were and why we were in France. We felt like outsiders and we were treated that way at high school.'

Wilson himself also found settling in France difficult, says his daughter. 'He was still frustrated over his career. Politically, he became increasingly cynical. He was more driven as a writer, as he felt he was getting older and I think the culmination of years of struggle in terms of his need for recognition as a writer – it was all taking its toll on him – and so I knew he also wanted to return to Hollywood soon. He was a melancholy person. He was an alcoholic as well – but the fact is he didn't get the acknowledgement he would have liked also. And that was important to him.'

What was hard was that nobody knew he had written *Lawrence of Arabia* or, with Carl Foreman, *Bridge on the River Kwai*. 'Let's face it, this was painful for him, because had there not been the blacklist, who knows what other projects he might have been offered? Even without these unknown projects he would have been regarded publicly, and critically acclaimed, as one of the great screenwriters of his time.'

It wasn't so easy on his wife either. Her daughter says: 'For my mother, there was a whole other thing going on, which was that she had to give up her career as an architect when we went to France and it was going on for too long. So after a few years, she began to get really antsy and wanted to get back and have her career back. And that created a lot of strife between my parents. I do remember fights. I do remember arguments, some having to do with that, others having to do with other things. I can't say it was a peaceful household at all times because there was so much frustration on the part of both of my parents.'

Settling in, she says, despite all the nice things, there were difficulties for the children of émigrés, too. But a sense, too, of companionship. 'A feeling you're part of something, part of an extended family of persecuted people, fine people who took a brave stand on the principles on which this country was founded.' There was also 'the feeling of being an outsider, and feeling like we had something to hide. I think that was the big thing.'

A number of the friends of the young French-dwelling refugees were children of military people working for SHAPE (Supreme Headquarters Allied Powers Europe). 'Ironically, some of the parents of these kids were actually involved in espionage work against the Soviet-Communist threat in Europe. I had a really good friend in school and her dad was in the English Secret Service and he had top secret clearance.'

There were more serious problems. Abraham Polonsky lived near the Wilsons and had a bomb thrown into his apartment.

Looking back now, Norman Corwin says that this exodus of film people 'was very injurious when you think of all the good men and women who fled the country.'

Artie Shaw chose to go to Spain. Recalling his sessions with HUAC, he told me: 'There was a scandal. That was why I left America and went to Europe for five years. America had become a cesspool at that time. I got down to Australia at first and the [American government] wouldn't give me a [new] passport. They would give me a limited passport. I said, "I'm not going to Australia with a red flag over my head." In the end, they gave me a passport. It cost $15,000 in legal fees.'

He recalled getting an invitation to meet a senior Australian judge, who had a copy of Shaw's book, *Troubled Cinderella*, on his desk. 'I was appalled by some of the things you have told me,' said the judge. 'You are guilty by association,' he told the clarinettist and band leader. 'I said it was true. I couldn't work on prime-time television again. Ever. My life has never been the same since. Not that I liked television, but it paid the rent. I could do TV shows and go back to my farm and buy a tractor. But I couldn't do that any more. After two weeks, I was told by my agent that I would never work in television again. I asked why and he said, "They've got a tower somewhere and there's a man working in it and he has a list and your name is on the list. If someone mentions your name, he looks down the list, sees your name on it and says, "No. He's not kosher".'

In 1954, Shaw needed that money badly. It was the year he played his clarinet, perhaps the most famous in the world, for the last time, although he fronted an orchestra and did appear on late-night TV which, he assumed nobody was watching. 'I went on Nixon's enemies' list. They said I owed $100,000 in taxes. I didn't. I couldn't cheat.'

Paul Jarrico's stay in New Mexico was an exile of sorts. There wasn't quite the hedonistic atmosphere of Beverly Hills there, but it enabled him and his fellow blacklistees to make *Salt of the Earth*, which hardly surprisingly, ran into all the problems of production and distribution and – not least when Rosaura Revueltas, its star, was deported over the border. 'They said that when she came into the country, she failed to get a stamp in her passport.' The film, written with Michael Wilson and Michael Biberman, directed by Herbert Biberman, couldn't get a conventional showing in America. The picture, which also featured Will Geer, playing a sheriff, was made in 1952. But in 1954, a theatre owner in New York said, according to Sylvia Jarrico (who also worked on the movie), 'that it would be a pleasure to have the world première there.

They didn't rent us the theatre in the normal way, they gave it to us.' But the Jarricos, too, ran up against the projectionists' union, who banned their members showing it. 'So it showed in very few theatres.' In some, it was shown in secret. Few were surprised about that. History now describes the movie as the only wholly blacklisted film made in the whole era. And the only one to win the prize at the Czechoslovakian film festival.

There was a call for a national, industry-wide boycott of anything to do with the filming and post-production.

Ed Asner was among those who tried to get *Salt of the Earth* shown in the United States, via the co-operative Playwrights. 'Biberman and company came to Playwrights, looking for a venue to have a screening of *Salt of the Earth* and the producers said OK. One of the actors, a veteran who's a little more leery, came and said, "If they show that here, it's going to indict us as well. Do you feel they should be taking that kind of position with your futures?" And the majority of us said, "Maybe not." So we voted against it and had to say sorry.'

Adrian Scott went to London with his wife Joan. He stayed there, without making another picture. Several projects fell through: a film that would have starred Warren Beatty, a picture directed by Vittorio De Sica, and one by Joe Losey. 'The tragedy,' Joan Scott told Barbra Paskin, 'was that he thought he had his chance there and everything fell apart.'

Adrian did get to work with other blacklist refugees who came to Britain, like Ring Lardner Jr, Waldo Salt and Robert Lees, and wrote the immensely popular *Robin Hood* TV series for the producer Hannah Weinstein who was offering a courageous refuge for many blacklisted writers. Howard Koch was the script editor. All of them worked under assumed names.

Things seemed to get better, says Scott's wife, when Jennings Lang, the veteran producer supervising new products at Universal, persuaded him to come back to Hollywood. At first it seemed wonderful to him. 'He was deliriously happy. I was not. I wept all the way back on the plane; he was ecstatic to be coming back home and working in Hollywood. It was redemption. I was miserable, but he didn't want to know. I hated change. But also I'd fallen in love with London.'

Neither of them fell in love with the new Hollywood.

'He got assigned to work under this little pipsqueak of a kid who was young enough to be his son, an awful young guy. He was not nice and it was such a putdown, so demeaning. And that's when he was 61 and got diagnosed with lung cancer. And I think he just gave up and died. The triumphant return was a disaster.' That was in 1973.

The Trumbos went to Mexico at the same time as Hugo and Jean Butler. Jean Butler said she and her husband chose the country over the border because 'they were refurbishing the Japanese camps [the ones to which Japanese-Americans had been sent after Pearl Harbor]. It seemed stupid to wait for it to happen. We decided [to go to Mexico] because 'we never had passports and knew we couldn't get one. So Mexico was the best thing.' Mexico was 'a country that was 'free, chaotic.' Jean: 'We felt very secure in Mexico.'

'There were a few expulsions which made us a little nervous. They were hiring men to kidnap people, lefties, and dumping them on the other side of the border.' But they didn't have anything to do with Hollywood. Butler made two documentaries in Mexico, one of which won an Academy award – although it took until 1997 to have it presented with the right name on the plinth. In 1941 Butler was nominated for an Oscar with Dore Schary then his co-writer for the 1940 *Edison, the Man*. In 1954 Butler's uncredited adaptation for *Robinson Crusoe* won an acting Oscar nomination for Dan O'Herlihy. But there's no record of his having won an Oscar at any time, though, in 1997, the Screen Writers' Guild posthumously restored Butler's credits to *Crusoe*.

The Butlers and Trumbos drove in tandem down to Mexico City. Nikki Trumbo said the change in the family's life from California to Mexico was like the switch from black and white to colour in *The Wizard of Oz*. 'It was exciting. I, of course, was sad about leaving my friends behind and probably I must have been sad about leaving the animals because I'm such an animal lover. But there was also a great sense of adventure. We were all headed off on this new adventure together.'

In Mexico, the Trumbo children went to the American School – where there was a strange mixture. 'It was a school for both Mexican children and American children and most of the Mexican families were upper class. The rich were pretty rich and the poor were awfully poor. And then the American kids were the children of ambassadors or political appointees or corporate executives.' And the offspring of people on the blacklist.

Mexico was also where Albert Maltz and his family went. It was very hard for his daughter, Katharine. Her daughter, Maltz's granddaughter, Gabriela Maltz Larkin, told Barbra Paskin: 'It was awful, awful. I think it scarred her for pretty much all her life. She adjusted seemingly well and picked up the language very fast – a girl growing up in Los Angeles and suddenly her parents are asked to leave the country and she's not quite understanding why and she goes to a foreign country. Mexico was very foreign at that time. She learns a whole new language and culture but I think it affected her terribly for a very long time. She didn't really fit in.'

Gordon Kahn also chose Mexico, a country forever linked in his mind with a heavy conscience. 'If now,' he said, 'in full flight from any principle I possess, I went and recanted everything and every decent thing I believe in, it wouldn't be enough.'

Bernard Gordon went to Madrid, with mixed fortunes. 'I didn't just decide to try Europe. I had an opportunity there and I had very little choice. I was very glad to have the opportunity. What happened was a friend of mine, Irving Lerner, had been hired to direct a film for Phil Yordan. Anyway, when he got through the picture, it didn't work.'

Gordon was asked to come up with some thoughts on improving the pictures. It worked and he went to Paris to write *The Day of the Triffids* in 1962, one of the most popular science-fiction movies of the 1960s. The writer credit went to Yordan, the producer. 'I was not exactly under the carpet, but . . . I didn't know how much of a front I was supposed to be presenting. Phil was no help because he expected me to be sensible enough to stay in my own place and not make problems for him. He was supposed to be writing the scripts because he had an Oscar which he never earned but he got it and he had about 60 scripts, most of which he didn't write.'

Gordon's daughter hated living in Spain. 'She lost all her friends here [in California] and she had to live in a strange place. She now looks back on it as a great experience but she sure didn't then. We talk frankly about it now and she hated it and she became very disjointed from the whole thing.'

He wasn't happy working in London. There was a brilliant cameraman, but 'we had British special effects people and so on and they just shit all over us. They wouldn't do anything to be helpful. They hated the idea of Americans working there. If you were American, the Brits hated you.'

Going to Europe was the only outlet for so many Hollywood people in difficult circumstances, and despite some professional problems between the Yanks and the Brits, the UK film industry benefited from the exile. As Michael Cole said: 'Yes, because of all those people like

Jules Dassin, all of them could go and they could write. Because in Italy, in France, in England, you could still write. And in the United States, you couldn't.'

Lester Cole went to England for that reason. 'The English had their problems with civil rights in my opinion, but it didn't extend to the incredible paranoia of these individuals.'

To Robert Rossen, going to Europe seemed the only salvation from his conscience as well as hope for his career. He went to Spain and made *Mambo* in 1954 and *Alexander the Great* two years later, Carol Eve Rossen told me: 'They stopped him at the border because they had an old list.' When a new list became available (one which took into account his defection), he was cleared for entry. 'I will tell you something,' she now says, 'I was grateful for the time we spent in Europe. We lived in Rome, in London, where I matriculated.'

If there were a matriculation certificate for the study of adapting to new lives, the blacklistees would pass with flying colours, even if some of those colours were not quite as red as before.

Chapter Seventeen
Back to the Front

The House Committee, we have found out, has been in existence for about nine years . . .

. . . spending tax payers' money, investigating what it calls subversive activities. The idea was that the committee would come up with legislation that would counter anything subversive. Well, in nine years, it has proposed exactly one piece of legislation – and that was rejected as unconstitutional, along with scathing denunciation by the United States Supreme Court.

John Huston, *Hollywood Fights Back*, 1947

It was as if a clever student was bribing a fellow pupil to cheat by copying his exam paper. The difference when the blacklist victims did just that was that they were making a plea for their professional lives and for the welfare of their families. At the same time, they were losing a great deal of money and a huge amount of their integrity.

It worked like this: a blacklisted writer would work on a screenplay or a TV script and then, when it was finished, pass it over to someone else. That someone else would then submit it to a producer under their own name for a fee.

Sometimes that someone else was also a writer, probably not as successful as the one to whom this procedure threw a lifeline. Occasionally, it was the writer's spouse who doubled for them. Frequently, the name used was that of a person who had never written a word for any kind of publication in his or her life. Sometimes, that person had never even used a typewriter before. They were the 'Fronts', like those in the Woody Allen movie.

Allen was too young to have been blacklisted himself, but he portrayed the 'Front' in the story with all the conviction of one who had suffered from the curse of McCarthy or HUAC. His character of the simple restaurant cashier-turned-acclaimed screenwriter grew ever more confident until he began to make his own demands on authors – not merely *suggesting* changes, but demanding them.

It was a familiarly true story that the blacklisted writer Walter Bernstein said he was drawing from life. He told us about the man who fronted a script that he wrote as an entry for an award. 'He wouldn't accept any money. But he liked to go to meetings, smoked a pipe and looked like a writer.'

The idea of using fronts wasn't a surprise to producers, says Bernstein – although not in the manner that eventually became almost the norm. Charles Russell, the producer who sacked him from the *Danger* project at CBS, suggested that Bernstein should simply use a different name. 'That went on for a while. Then the networks, like the studios, decided that the writers were a shifty bunch' and were probably doing exactly what they were accused of. They decided that writers had had to appear in person. That was when the 'live' 'Fronts' first showed themselves. 'It was difficult,' said Bernstein. 'Some people did it for the money. You would ask around, like looking for an apartment. Some who wanted to be writers did it for credits.' And some, just for altruistic reasons.

How could a writer with integrity accept a state of affairs which manifestly took away his pride? 'We had to come to terms with it,' Bernstein told Barbra Paskin. 'The basic question was one of survival. I was getting money. I was much better off than the actors and directors who could not use 'Fronts' because they had to show themselves. But it is no fun when you see other people getting credit for what you have done.'

Frequently, the biggest problem was in arranging the right front, one who could be trusted. 'Nobody showed up and said, "I want to be your front." We all helped each other, trying to find jobs. We helped each other trying to find 'Fronts'. I knew cases where people didn't have fronts of their own. They were using 'Fronts' that I had.'

It was one way to avoid the feelings of loneliness that being blacklisted inevitably brought. 'It was painful', Bernstein now recalls. 'It was isolating, because people you knew wouldn't return telephone calls, they'd cross the street when they saw you. At the same time, there was a great sense of camaraderie, we circled the wagons, as it were. We helped each other. The comradeship was something I'd look back on and I miss . . . aspects of generosity I didn't know was there. They would collect money, writers would help other writers to find jobs.'

At first, the 'Fronts' were paid a fairly modest stipend. In some cases, they got no money at all for their trouble – they were merely trying to help. But market forces proved too tempting for some, whose only fear was being found out. In the movie *The Front*, Woody Allen's crunch-time came when a producer demanded changes from him immediately. There are reports of one 'Front' going as far as saying to his writer: 'All *you* have to do is sit at your typewriter. *I* have to go to meetings.'

Then came the problem of distributing the material. Michael Wilson licked the difficulty by taking his work in an envelope to a nearby pharmacy. It was as if he were delivering details of pills and potions he needed to take – only, in this case, the word 'script' (shorthand for 'prescription' in the professional terminology) meant something entirely different. At the same time, the pharmacist would hand over another envelope – the fee for the job, minus the Front's commission, of course.

Jeff Lawson recalled for Barbra Paskin how his father, John Howard Lawson, wrote several of what he called 'black-market scripts'. One of them was the remarkable 1951 film about black life in South Africa, *Cry, The Beloved Country*. Lawson's name did not appear on the script until after he died.

Some 'Fronts' were already established writers, like Ian McLellan Hunter, who won an Oscar for William Wyler's famed film starring Gregory Peck and Audrey Hepburn, *Roman Holiday* in 1953. Hunter later admitted that the story was written by Dalton Trumbo. 'He asked me to "Front" for him,' he said. The Academy Award was for the story. 'Had it been for the screenplay, I could have convinced myself that I had done most of it.' But Trumbo got the fee that had originally been paid to Hunter.

Most of the writers had their favourite 'Front'. Lester Cole used his wife. Joan Scott fronted for her husband Adrian. 'I remember one script conference on a film that I was fronting for him. He was one of the first to do this "tough-guy" dialogue and I was fronting for this script. A lot of it sounds funny now, but he'd be driving me in to the studio [while] I had pneumonia, or was just getting over flu. I had a conference with the studio and he had to do the rewrites – and he's complaining!'

The complaints could do him no good. 'On the way to the studio, I'm looking at the rewrites and I said, "Adrian, there's a new scene on page thirty. You didn't tell me about that." He said, "I must have forgotten."' That wasn't good enough for a woman who had to face the masses, or so it seemed. 'Sometimes, I'd be in a conference and there'd be six or seven men in the story conference and more would come in. This was the era of girls in fluffy petticoats. They'd read the script and they wanted to meet the girl who wrote like a man. So there I was in this fluffy skirt and they came in under one pretext or another to meet me. It seems funny now, but it wasn't then.'

Writing under other people's names not only provided money for the authors, it also enabled their philosophies to get across to the public – without HUAC members or the FBI looking for Reds under their beds. As far as the fronts were concerned, for the most part neither group went looking for people they would never have thought had anything to be guilty of. Which is a further indictment of the committee and its system. HUAC was after names of people on whom they could hang alleged crimes. Those very same crimes, 'committed' by other people whom HUAC had no reason to suspect, didn't seem to be crimes at all.

The 'Fronts' even had 'Fronts' of their own. Many of them wrote under assumed names, men who were anonymous to everyone but *their* writers, not just at the time, but for ever afterwards. It wasn't enough for the real authors to use assumed names. As we have seen, the 'Fronts' had to exist – so that they could attend meetings, answer the telephone, argue with producers. Some had taken oaths never to reveal the titles of films on which they had worked. Abraham Polonsky once said: 'If we refused to credit any of them, they'll imagine we wrote the best.' Waldo Salt was one of those who worked with fronts, notably on *Robin Hood* episodes which were made in London.

His wife remembered: 'Everybody was doing the same thing. Everybody was living on *Robin Hood* or *The Twilight Zone*. He did some screenplays for some of the Eastern countries, like Poland. Some of those countries wanted documentaries written by good United States, American, screenwriters. We were so accustomed [to using 'Fronts'] . . . it was important to get that sort of work. Of course, it was humiliating. But that wasn't the main emotion. The main emotion was not having enough money to live on. I never thought of him as a hero. The rest of my life, I have. We were not living the life of a hero; we were living the life of a man struggling to live.'

Robin Hood stands out today as the finest hour of the 'Fronts'. It was perhaps the most popular black-and-white series of the 1950s in Britain and did well in America, too. What few Americans realised was that the fictional stories had as many left-wing sentiments in them as the statements the Hollywood Ten were unable to deliver when called to HUAC hearings.

The idea of robbing the rich to give to the poor and the legend of Robin Hood himself was so well known that it defied most suspicions. But the American producer Hannah Weinstein, herself a Communist who took refuge in Britain, saw the series as both a good business venture and a means of helping her fellow party members.

'Hannah worked with all these blacklisted writers on television productions,' said Joan Salt. 'She was hiring every blacklisted writer in town,' Salt wrote in 2002 in the SAG journal *Written By*. 'She was very gutsy.'

Ring Lardner's daughter Kate is a little more sceptical about Weinstein's role in setting up her company. 'Her intention was to use blacklisted writers – largely because they were talented, but also because they were cheap.' Lardner and the other writers left their families, and in particular their children, with no doubt that this had to be treated like a military secret. 'I was followed up to bed by my dad and told I could not mention this because he needed the work.'

The assumed names the 'Fronts' adopted remained mysterious for the best part of the next half century. Nobody at the time realised that the first episode of the series *The Coming of Robin* was written by Ring Lardner Jr. Any member of the public who read the credits – and, surprisingly to some producers, there *were* people who read the credits, even if most of them were in the business – would have no idea that this was Lardner's work. As far as they could see, the writer was Lawrence McClellan. The name was based on the same Ian McClellan Hunter, who had fronted for Dalton Trumbo. He also wrote about six of the episodes himself under his own name.

Weinstein's outfit, Sapphire Films, which became Official Films, turned into one of the most successful independent production companies in British TV history. At about the same time, Walter Bernstein and Abe Polonsky, along with Arnold Manoff, were writing one of the most elegant and intelligent American series ever, *You Are There*, introduced by Walter Cronkite, in which events such as the trial of Galileo or the Salem Witch Hunts were portrayed as though they were current events – which, with the activities of HUAC and McCarthyism in the news on a daily basis, they practically were. The team worked 'as a kind of commune,' Bernstein would later say.

Cronkite knew the series was being written by blacklisted writers with the help of 'Fronts', but never revealed the facts. As Walter Bernstein now says: 'I asked if he knew blacklisted writers had been responsible. He said he wondered why no writer was ever there. He [knew] after that. He didn't mind. He was against the blacklist, the reconstruction of historical events . . . it was a great "Front".'

Bernstein added: 'You were living in a kind of suspended animation.

We had to meet outside the studio, in somebody's house, in a bar, in a restaurant somewhere.'

Albert Maltz had his own favourite 'Fronts'. One was the writer Michael Blankfort. Another was himself – operating under the name John B Sherry. Sherry was his mother's maiden name. That is the name on the credits for most copies of *The Robe* which was made in 1953, the first movie shot in Cinemascope. Recent DVD versions have the real Maltz credit.

Plainly, a great deal of imagination was needed in finding the right 'Front' *for* the right Front. Bernard Gordon also started using a 'Front' by being one himself, which is about as complicated as it could get. It started when a producer named Charlie Schneer had seen Gordon's film with Rock Hudson. 'It was a good Western and he needed a good Western and did I have one in the trunk that I'd like to have him see? This was his way of saying, "Would you write something on spec?" which they're not supposed to do. And I happened to know about a play that had been written by friends of mine, Janet and Phil Stevenson. They had written for Broadway . . . So I called the Stevensons and I told them that somebody wants a Western. I don't have one, but if they want, I'll send him their play. "Do me a treatment of it and I'll say it's mine – and we'll split the money". Before I knew it, they liked the treatment and wanted me to go ahead with a script for them for Columbia Pictures.'

As he said: 'That's how I got into working with the blacklist and with a 'Front'. But they were blacklisted, too, so I couldn't use their name on the play.' The complications became . . . well, even more complicated. 'So the name I used . . . I had another friend who was blacklisted and he had a brother who wasn't. He was working in a camera shop in Beverly Hills.' Gordon told his blacklisted friend, 'Give me a 20- or 30-page treatment you've prepared.' He explained, 'I wasn't willing to do any work on this. Everybody agreed.'

Therefore he had someone to whom he would give 50 per cent of the writing fee for the treatment. 'The Stevensons would get a third because it was their story.' His friend's brother, however, was the one who had to pay the tax. 'It was just too complicated to work out.'

When Gordon himself put in scripts, his front was Ray Marcus, the owner of the plastics factory where he was working as a salesman. Eventually, like the whole business of the blacklist, the 'Front' ceased to be necessary. In a way, it died out because the process of taking away people's names as well as their livelihood no longer seemed reasonable to those who had cheered the defeat of Hollywood's Commies.

Chapter Eighteen
Blacking the Blacklist

We found out that the committee has been making friends and enemies during all these years. Here are some people who didn't like them. As far back as 1938, when the committee began, Franklin D Roosevelt saw what it was up to. He said, 'most fair-minded Americans hope that the committee will abandon the practice of merely providing a forum for those who seek headlines which they could not otherwise obtain.'

Danny Kaye, Hollywood Fights Back, 1947

It is generally accepted that it took 12 years for the blacklist to be taken out of producers' desk drawers, scrunched up and thrown into wastepaper baskets. Yet even if Otto Preminger had not ordered Dalton Trumbo's name to go on to the credits of *Exodus* and Kirk Douglas had not done the same with his *Spartacus*, it still could only have been a matter of time before the list was consigned to history.

With the arrival of the 1960s, the idea of blacklisting, to say nothing of a House Un-American Activities Committee, was becoming abhorrent. Political correctness had not yet arrived, but the election of John F Kennedy to the White House seemed to offer a new kind of hope which was incompatible with the HUAC's Red-baiting. Mogul power was already proving to be a lot less effective than flower power. Meanwhile, young men about to be sent to fight in Vietnam were taking draft cards out of their envelopes and burning them, as their sisters were making bonfires of their bras.

Of course, the world was changing and Hollywood was changing with it. Television was proving to be more important than any of the studios could have imagined. Faced with the rise of the small screen, Warner Bros had for a time even banned television sets from scenes in their films. All the studios, but with 20th Century Fox leading the pack, thought they only had to make screens wider and the sound louder to bring the customers back. But they were wrong. They were also wrong in thinking they could manage without some of the most talented people who had either gone abroad or flown to New York where they worked on the live stage or, say it quietly, for television.

Many former movie people who were forced to switch to TV gave their best work – work that was diametrically opposed to the HUAC tenet that they were merely dishing out propaganda. To this day Walter Bernstein is proud of the *You Are There* shows. 'We did Salem witch-hunts, the persecution of Galileo. We were very scrupulous in making sure we did both sides. We were very careful and did not want it to seem it was a biased production in any way, which is why many schools used it as a kind of textbook.'

It was not surprising that schools did, in fact, use the films as textbooks. What is perhaps more surprising is that there have been comparatively few fictional movies about the most cataclysmic events in the Hollywood story. There have been some – like the Barbra Streisand-Robert Redford 1973 film *The Way We Were* and *Guilty by Suspicion* in 1991 – but few were specifically set in the McCarthy era, unlike George Clooney's *Goodnight and Good Luck* in 2005, which addressed the subject head-on.

The real reason *The Front* succeeded was Woody Allen. He liked the project and it was made – but, like most Allen films, it didn't exactly make a fortune. The only problem with having Allen was that he diluted the all-blacklist cast. But that was a minor detail. Said Walter Bernstein: 'We selected as many blacklisted actors as we could. Apart from anything else, we were making a statement – saying "we are here, we haven't gone away". It was bittersweet. It was revenge in a way. "You did your best to drive us out, you didn't succeed. Here we are, working at our business, our craft, our art". It was a wonderful feeling seeing people like Zero and Hersh Bernardi. I suppose there were tears. All I remember is the first day of shooting. I had cut myself in so many places, shaving. There were a lot of people who didn't survive – and we thought of them.'

Mostel no longer needed the big challenges to show HUAC members who was the real survivor and, perhaps, the victor of the period. In the intervening years, he had earned an impressive reputation as an artist. His friends are of two minds about the sort of pictures he painted. Several of them say they see the anger he felt in his work. Others describe it simply as artistic licence.

He was, however, given a couple of great chances to get back to acting, which he grabbed with all the force that his huge hands could muster. He featured in a British-made movie *Great Catherine* made in 1968, a not marvellous picture about the times of Catherine the Great of Russia. 'It was on the set of that film that I met Mostel for the first time. Was he was angry? "I'll show you how angry I am," he said, grabbing the mike from my hand. "I am now eating your microphone," he said in the best imitation of *Deep Throat* I had ever seen. "Angry? When Fascists took over America and killed my close friends! When those Nazis tried to kill my career! Of course, I'm angry."'

Great Catherine was a mere blip in the remarkably recovering Mostel career. By then, he had starred in the original Broadway production of the stage musical *Fiddler on the Roof*. This led to a different kind of anger, when the film role went not to Mostel, the internationally renowned actor, but to the young Israeli actor Topol, who until he starred in the movie was virtually unknown outside his home country and beyond London, where he had introduced the role in the Her Majesty's Theatre production. Zero had as great a triumph in the original 1966 production of *A Funny Thing Happened on the Way to the Forum*, the skit on ancient Rome, which contained a litany of references to the blacklist. For one, it co-starred his friend Jack Gilford. For another, the choreography was by Jerome Robbins – whose appointment was full of ironies.

The suggestion of employing Robbins was made by the show's producer, who thought he knew from the beginning what the response was going to be. Gilford was adamant: under no circumstances could he employ the man who was responsible for blacklisting his wife Madeleine Leigh. Madeleine told Barbra Paskin that for her it was far less of a problem: 'Jack and Zero were very intimate friends. Jack called Zero into his dressing room. Zero said, "Does he know how we feel?" And then it became clear that he was going to give way – "So long as I don't have to have coffee with him." The crunch of the matter, as far as Mostel was concerned, was that "we on the left do not blacklist".'

When *Fiddler on the Roof* opened, Zero had used the great opportunity with which he was being presented to tell the world what he thought of Mr Robbins. At certain stages of the production, Mostel would go to the footlights to welcome Mrs Greenberg to the theatre or ask Mr Shapiro what he had done to his wife that night. He also used the moment to tell the audience his none too flattering thoughts about the personality of Jerome Robbins and what had happened between them. In rehearsal, he would begin the day by saying, 'Mr Robbins, say good morning to everybody.' He made Jerry [Robbins] behave like a gentleman.

Seeing Zero on stage was an experience to be treasured. But had it not been for HUAC he might never have had his biggest successes. For, as Madeleine Leigh put it, he didn't really enjoy stage acting. 'Zero had a very healthy profile. He had a studio and made enough money to buy the building. He would go to the studio every day, then go to the theatre. He really didn't like the theatre. He wanted to paint. Every night, he would go home, his wife would make him chicken in the pot, with some gefilte fish and pumpernickel bread.

'He went about his business. He would go home and with his pot of chicken, he would look through his art books. His wife didn't think they had a life because they couldn't go to dinner parties. How could you go to dinner parties when you have eight shows a week? He would only care about painting.'

Eric Sherman emphasises the extent to which economics played a part in that end-of-blacklist era. People had been shown their marching orders as much because they were expensive as because they were on the wrong side of the political spectrum. As he said: 'Now, instead of a thousand movies a year, there were going to have to be tens of thousands of products to fill the airwaves. The banks were looking at having to finance [these] products, the sudden need for product. Now you can't go and tell my dad and Bette Davis and Joan Crawford that they have to take a salary cut because we need more product from them. So all were removed from their jobs.'

Proof of this lay in the number of blacklisted writers who were rehired under either their pen names or of those of their 'Fronts' – as part of that same economics escapade. The producers at last recognised the 'Front' game being played out *in front* of their very noses. They knew it to the extent of rehiring the writers at a quarter of their previous salaries.

What has become known as the 'Robin Hood family' – led by Lardner Jr and Hunter – produced so much of what was good about American TV drama. Maurice Rapf was among its stable of contributors. The cameraman also worked for a company in New York called Transfilm, which made promotional films for companies like General Motors and the Bank of America. His daughter Joanna Rapf says: 'It always amuses me that these major corporations would hire these blacklisted writers to write their promotional films for them. They didn't put their names on them, but a lot of blacklisted writers did those films and he did some wonderful animated films.' As she said: 'My father travelled all over the world, making these movies for these big capitalist companies.'

Even the writers who had used fronts sometimes bared the enemy in their lairs. Waldo Salt, for instance, would go on the set of his films like the much later *Midnight Cowboy*. Paul Buhle would say that Salt was actually 'able to play a larger role in formulating the film as it was being made – something that before 1950 just couldn't happen.'

Before he was set free by Douglas and Preminger, Dalton Trumbo can be seen as the philosopher of the blacklistees. He once said: 'This blacklisting is going to collapse because it is rotten, immoral and illegal. I am one day going to be working openly in the motion picture industry. When that day comes, I swear to you that I will never sign a term contract with any major studio.'

He was so well established and respected that he never had to. Films like 1965's *The Sandpiper*, *The Fixer* in 1968 and *Hawaii* and in 1966 proved his point. For his children, the frustration in the early years was keeping the secrets of his achievements. 'There is NOTHING,' Nikki Trumbo said, 'that you want to do more than brag, but, of course, we couldn't.'

Certainly, the children of the blacklistees continued to suffer, as they wondered just what their parents could have achieved. While Ring Lardner Jr was an amazing, if unheralded success, thanks to Hannah Weinstein and *Robin Hood*, that was never going to be enough. His daughter still contemplates how different his life might have been. 'I know,' she told Barbra Paskin, 'he would have gone on to produce his own material. He even said he would have directed, even though he was never outgoing in a director's way. Mom was affected. She got to teach [and] work was taken away from her. He was a drinker, he was an alcoholic. I am sure he had bouts of depression. If he had been engaging with other people, who knows what it would have been like? He did a very honourable thing. He refused to co-operate with this committee and he would never have named names because he didn't want to get other people into trouble.'

Despite all, there had been a constant wave of optimism about the anti-blacklist fight. In February 1957, Paul Jarrico wrote to friends, asking for money for a new campaign which was going to centre later that year on the United States Supreme Court. In his letter, Jarrico mentioned the appeal to that court on behalf of Michael Wilson, against Loew's Incorporated, MGM's parent company: 'As you may have heard, fish are jumpin' on the anti-blacklist front,' he wrote. Loews was being confronted by '23 blacklisted folk including Gale Sondergaard, Howard Da Silva, Anne Revere . . . Abe Polonsky.' The people listed 'including me are suing the whole fucking industry and some of the members of the Un-American Committee for some $51,000.' He said that 'although there are several other legal hassles going on, like Wilson vs Allied Artists et al for taking his name off *Friendly Persuasion* and *Salt of the Earth* against the world for conspiracy to violate the anti-trust laws, the case of the 23 is the key to the works. If we win this one, the chances are enormous that it will be the end of the blacklist for everyone.'

If ever there was an example of optimism overriding trends and evidence, this was one. But optimism had to be paid for and Jarrico was writing to collect money from friends both at home and abroad – a total of $1,000 from those in Paris and the same from London and in Mexico, all centres for blacklist émigrés.

He was aiming for $3,000 from New York and $9,000 from California. Like most of the optimistic plans, these came to nought. There were others who were a lot more adventurous. As Jarrico reported: 'Trumbo is embarked on a personal campaign to end the blacklist, which means it's doomed. He has written to Eisenhower, Hemingway, Steinbeck, Faulkner, all the guilds and is also writing to Nixon, Dulles, Cardinal Spellman and others.'

That list of right-wing personalities illustrated in the letter shows just how optimistic – and doomed – Trumbo's plan was.

But Jarrico went on to say that things were getting brighter. 'Guy Endore is reliably reported to have sold his bestseller to a Hollywood independent. 20th Century Fox is releasing *Oh Men, Oh Women* without any credit for Eddie Chodorov in its advertising. But *Variety*, reviewing the film yesterday, gave Chodorov full credit. Mike Wilson was just nominated for an Academy Award for the *Friendly Persuasion* screenplay, with the Academy announcing that he's inelligible and a big fuss [is] ahead. And now they're trying to put Marilyn Monroe's mate in jail. Can you imagine her public sitting still for that? Yep, they've gone too far. Send us the thousand.'

The Academy presentation that year was the perfect example of the word that was increasingly associated with the blacklist: farce. The crunch came with Deborah Kerr at the podium to announce the winner of a now long-abandoned category: best motion-picture story. Kerr, star of recent box-office hits like *The King and I* and *From Here to Eternity*, opened the envelope, while an audience ranging from top stars to top electricians, sat waiting for the big moment. The winning film was *The Brave One*. The winning writer was Robert Rich. You could hear the stage whispers as the winner was revealed to a group of the most attractive and influential people in Hollywood, the people who knew everybody who was anybody. The problem was that none of them knew Robert Rich, none of them. It took Jesse Lasky Jr, who that evening was deputed to put out the fire that was slowly enveloping the audience, to rush to the microphone to pay tribute to his 'very good friend' who couldn't be there that evening because his wife was in a nearby maternity hospital, waiting to give birth.

The whispers continued, but the people out front seemed to accept what he said, even though they wanted to know more about the Oscar winner who had somehow escaped the attention of the selection group. As it turned out, the only birth in the Hollywood community that evening was of a loud series of guffaws from the mouth of Dalton Trumbo. A search was made of local maternity hospitals, all in vain. No one could find Mr Rich – because he didn't exist. Other than as the shy Mr Trumbo, that is. It was the most dramatic stab at the blacklist yet – and a whole lot more effective than the letter Trumbo was writing to Eisenhower, Cardinal Spellman et al.

It took time, however, before the truth was out. There was uproar at the Academy once they realised they had been hoodwinked. Yet it wasn't until just a few months before Trumbo's death that his name was finally engraved on the plate beneath the statuette. It was presented to him by Walter Mirisch.

In the meantime, all sorts of claims were made on Mr Rich's behalf. Could it really be Orson Welles? Frank King said he knew Rich as 'a brilliant young writer I met in Munich,' who was aged between 33 and 35. Eventually, someone had the courage to ask another writer if he was really Robert Rich. 'Hell no,' said Dalton Trumbo. 'I'm Dalton Trumbo,' and then came the real chutzpah. Trumbo entered the speculation stakes – and put forward his own candidate, Michael Wilson. It wasn't that he wanted to hide from his pen name. He was just enjoying putting people off the scent. Wilson couldn't get the *Friendly Persuasion* Oscar, Trumbo explained, and submitted *The Brave One* 'so that he had something to show for a year's work'.

It was a wonderful opportunity for a bit of sport from a man who declared that for a decade he had been 'among the professional dead men.' *Variety* commented that for the first time in its 29-year history, 'the winner is clouded in such doubt and mystery'. The blacklistees laughed a little more after that. But no one could say they were a happy bunch.

Nor could every one of the blacklisted people accept that they were all equal in their needs. Albert Maltz's granddaughter recalls: 'He didn't agree that they were equal victims, that they had suffered themselves. He didn't feel that they were in the same boat. He felt that if some of these people had stood up to HUAC, had said, "We're not going to name names, we're not going to do this", the blacklist would have gone away a lot sooner.'

And perhaps those who lost jobs would have found new ones sooner, too. Bernard Gordon could certainly be forgiven for thinking that. 'When I came back from Mexico,' he said 'I was really nowhere in terms of work. I'd had that first trip to Europe. My poor wife was living with her mother and my child in the little house up in the Hollywood Hills and everyone was wondering what the hell Bernie was doing running around the world. I came back and the question was where are we going to live? What can we afford to live in? How do we make a life here? And they are now listening on the radio, everyone in Hollywood was listening to the radio and my wife was scared to death that my name would come up. Rightly so.'

Actually, he had built up quite an impressive CV. He wrote *The Lawless Breed*, then *Crime Wave* starring Sterling Hayden – the man who couldn't remember Gordon's name – and *Hellcats of the Navy* in 1957, a film that had an amazing resurgence in the early 1980s. It was the only film Ronald Reagan and his wife Nancy ever made together. There was also one big blockbuster, the 1963 wide-screen epic *Fifty-Five Days in Peking*, starring Charlton Heston, David Niven and Ava Gardner about the Boxer Revolution against foreign influences in the Chinese Imperial court. For the first time since the blacklisting, his name appeared as a writer in the credits, as the Writers Guild had finally decided it was time to try to sort out which film credits belonged to whom – and that the names appeared in the right place on the credits list.

Gordon's political credentials improved, too. Nikita Khrushchev made his famous speech renouncing the dogmatism and repressiveness of the Stalin era, and Gordon, along with hundreds of thousands of others, left the Communist Party of the United States. 'We were all horrified that we had supported this monster, he told us.' It has to be said that not everyone in the Communist Party of the United States was equally horrified about this 'monster'. But it is true that almost none of the blacklistees was prepared to accept their treatment lying down. Most of the victims tried to find ways of using the talents which, for a brief period before the arrival of the pink slips, had earned them fabulous salaries. Not all of them found 'Fronts'. Not all of them carried on writing screenplays. A great many of them taught. And not just teaching actors as Jeff Corey had done or school mathematics like Sam Jaffe. John Howard Lawson lectured to an encouragingly large audience and wrote books. His *The Hidden Heritage* was going to be the first volume of a history of the United States. As it was, he lectured on the blacklist, too.

But being welcomed back into the film community officially did not mean that everyone welcomed everybody. Chris Trumbo told Barbra Paskin: 'The blacklist was resilient. The people in Hollywood who had been [my father's] political enemies didn't change overnight. Ward Bond, John Wayne, other people like that . . . The blacklist was a good thing to them. Others didn't care. Nobody brought out a marching band and said, "Welcome back." The blacklist didn't break. Not everybody was suddenly rehired. All had to persuade a producer, but now had the example of "If Trumbo could do it, *you* could do it".'

It took until 1985 for the Academy to recognise the fact that Oscars withheld from blacklistees should go to their true winners. The Awards that should have gone to Carl Foreman and Michael Wilson for *Bridge on the River Kwai* were finally presented in their names – but to their widows. Both writers were already dead. 'It was a thrill, but a bitter-sweet experience, for sure,' Wilson's daughter, Rosanna, recalled.

Wilson's story had been particularly poignant. It was at the fiftieth wedding anniversary party of his dear friends Helen and Al Levitt (who had also been blacklisted). 'At the end of his speech [to them], he said these words: "All that remains in the end is the gold of our friendship," and then he walked over to his seat and he slumped over and he died.'

It was a time when almost anything connecting HUAC with Hollywood would have enormous resonance. But some events were more significant than others. On 2 November 2000 the death of Ring Lardner Jr was announced. The world was told that he was the last of the Hollywood Ten.

All the time, one name associated with the blacklist comes up constantly – that of the man who was probably Hollywood Eleven – or should that be Twelve? The fact that such a thing matters is an indication of the value and sadness of what happened to Larry Parks. He made one more significant film, 1962's *Freud*, in which, fully bearded, he gave a great deal of pleasure to his wife Betty Garrett. Not that he didn't have other successes in life, like being a great father to his two sons. He and Betty did a double act with which they toured America and appeared at the London Palladium and other remnants of old-fashioned variety. That was after taking dancing lessons which Larry regarded as seriously as he had the prospect of opening his mouth, moving his tongue and then hearing Al Jolson's voice coming out. 'He became such a good dancer,' Betty remembered.

Even more successful was the entirely different profession that he took on. Parks went into the property business, building apartment blocks. 'He did it so well,' Betty remembers. Did it well, from working on the original drawings to getting his hands (and his feet) wet and dirty on building sites. Later, he managed the blocks, liaised with tenants and real estate agents. He was the proverbial duck dipping into the pool and swimming away happily. But it wasn't all he could wish. Betty asked him if he wouldn't have preferred to be an actor. 'Well, of course, I would,' he replied.

Marsha Hunt played opposite Parks in the play *Tunnel of Love* in Detroit. 'Larry and I did it together and in all the time we played, which was only a few weeks, neither of us ever mentioned the blacklist. I found him so haunting that that was the last thing I was going to bring up. And he didn't either.'

The other Larry, Larry Adler, made a totally new life for himself in England, never as financially secure as he had been in his native homeland, but as the years passed, he found success as a columnist and author of his autobiography: 'I told a TV hostess that I was writing my autobiography. "Great," she said. "Who of?"' Adler was constantly in demand on radio and television, as the last survivor of the golden age of Broadway and Tin Pan Alley, the only one who could give personal testimony to the work of Gershwin. (Recordings were issued of Adler playing 'Rhapsody In Blue' 'accompanied' by a piano roll made by the composer himself.) He gave concerts virtually right until his death in 2001 and played his mouth organ (never call it a 'harmonica') on cruise ships.

For years, Adler didn't go back to the States to play. 'The only thing I regretted,' he said, 'and that is a real regret, is that my manager managed to get me, at the height of the blacklisting, an engagement in New Orleans at an hotel called the Monte Leone, and I flew from London to New Orleans. Then the American Legion stepped in and said, "If Adler opens, we picket". And the manager, a Mr Montelikoni said, "I've got to live with these guys." Well, I *wouldn't* live with these guys.

'One of Washington's top law firms, Thurman Arnold and Fortis, wanted to know if I would sue the American Legion, but I already had a libel case in which a woman called me pro-Communist. The case lasted for four weeks and ended in a hung jury – with no decision and I couldn't afford another trial. But if I had sued the Legion, I could have broken the blacklist single handed. But I could not submit my family to the publicity of another court case. I think this was the one cowardly act of my life – that I didn't sue the Legion. I could have done a good thing for all the other performers.'

Some blacklistees did a great deal for their profession simply by carrying on from overseas. Carl Foreman's work on *Bridge on the River Kwai* connected him (eventually when the fact could be told) with history, via one of the most significant movies about the Second World War. He was able to say just what he wanted to HUAC – by the judicious choice of 'Col Bogey' as both the theme music for the picture and for the march of the prisoners. The traditional lyrics were obscured in the on-screen singing. But almost everyone seeing the film realised that the number was a verbal two fingers to the tormentors. It wouldn't take too much of a stretch of the imagination to believe that Foreman was directing his digits towards HUAC.

The actor Sam Wanamaker came to Britain to act in films and on the stage. What no one could predict was that his memorial would be a stage that he built himself – a whole theatre in fact. Building the Globe Theatre, to the original sixteenth-century plans and producing the plays of Shakespeare, was inspired. Had there been no HUAC investigations, London would have lost what has become a new landmark.

Larry Parks was not the only HUAC victim to go into entirely different work. Some of the choices of blacklisted victims were surprising. The idea of Lionel Stander – with his extreme left-wing background – going into the world of stockbroking is astounding, even though he wasn't exactly a brilliant success. A friend suggested to Jay Gorney that he go into the same business. His wife remembered: 'Jay went off. He came home in tears. He said, "How can I sell stocks to my friends? I wrote 'Brother, Can You Spare A Dime?' about the decline of Wall Street and how people lost their money on Wall Street – I can't sell stocks."'

Another friend asked him to collect rents for him. He couldn't do that, either.

Bernie Gordon had two fallback positions once he knew that he couldn't work as a screenwriter. He was a salesman for a plastics firm, but when he tired of that he became a private detective. He wasn't a great success at either – selling plastics didn't pay the rent. He told me: 'My wife went to work as a secretary and we managed to get by. Then I was fired. I was really a very poor salesman.' Gordon quite enjoyed the private eye work. 'The cases were almost all where we felt it was honest work. We weren't dealing with marital problems between husbands and wives, which we didn't want to have anything to do with. We were representing people who were injured in accidents and who did not have the common sense or the awareness to get themselves a lawyer to defend them. So a lawyer who would hire an investigator did a favour and we were doing him a favour. We were actually doing investigations which helped them to collect from the goddamned insurance companies who had everything going for them. So it was not a regressive thing to do. We had to rationalise our actions.'

Plainly, the evils of the time and its memories were (and remain) a long time a-dying. In July 2001, Robert Rehnu, the Academy's President, declared: 'The rift the blacklist created in Hollywood hasn't healed, even though more than 50 years has passed. Maybe it can never be healed, but any era with that long-lasting impact needs to be carefully studied.'

Carol Eve Rossen is not sure that the rift *has* healed. 'The blacklist created a greater diversity of consequences as any event might have. There were those who really did commit suicide, who couldn't handle it; others who became bankers and business people. Ring Lardner was able to get a passport and work in England. My father was not one of the above, his passion, the God point in his life, was his work. He couldn't work without that.'

And neither could he live with what had happened in his life. 'He died at the age of 58. Some say he died of his shame, the mythology of the Left. My father never got over the shame of giving names.'

The children suffered along with their parents. Carol once met some very old friends in a New York store. They ignored her.

Could it all happen again? The answer from many of the people to whom we have spoken was, not just yes, but that it *is* happening – although not necessarily in the HUAC form. But sometimes it has happened in almost that same way. Ed Asner says that, without doubt, he was blacklisted from getting work because, in the producer's words, 'I think he'd be a political liability.' 'You have the liberal director and producer-director, he's got his very special baby and he wants it to get done; he knows that he'll get a lot of static and perhaps cancellation if he uses you, so his subconscious takes over. So he says, "No, he's too fat, he's too thin, he's too bald, he's too old." A big casting person I'd done favours for, very successful tops in town, told my agent, "I think he's over exposed." So no jobs.'

Asner is convinced that his highly popular TV series in which he played a newspaperman, *Lou Grant*, was cancelled because of his politics.

So what did it mean to be on the blacklist and survive? The writer Larry Gelbart put it like this: 'It has become a badge of honour. We are entitled never to have answered that question.'

That question, the $64,000 question, is probably not going to be asked again. But there are other demands being made. In these, Gelbart echoes Ed Asner's experience. 'There are people in this town who will tell you they have been deprived of work because they are too conservative. There is now a form of censorship. There is no inclination on the part of any major company to tackle on an entertainment level, subjects like war, political matters. They are afraid of the power and the naked use of power that the Bush administration has inspired over the past six years.'

Ever since Martin Dies first banged his gavel, people have been thinking of what might have been. The nonagenarian Norman Corwin reflected to me: 'I was grey-listed. I did not suffer from it as many others did, but still there were friends who would rather not be seen with me, rather not dine with me. There were work opportunities that were lost. However, I survived, continued to work. My sympathies were always with the victims of this hysteria.'

Victims who suffered in all sorts of ways. Hugo Butler had, according to his widow, 'a rich, wonderful time' in Mexico, but he died of a massive heart attack at the age of 53. 'The tension killed him,' she told Barbra Paskin.

The time has really come to assess who were those principal victims. Paul Buhle puts an interesting perspective on the picture. He points out that even celebrity blacklistees like Abraham Polonsky were not the main sufferers from the HUAC disease. 'Those who survived the best were the ones for whom going [into] the movies was only the third or fourth thing they did. Polonsky had written for radio, he'd been an OSS figure in World War Two, he'd been an educator before that. So it didn't kill him that all this had been taken away from him. But there were many people who came in very young, and lost everything.' To this, Buhle added a coda: 'Those are the people I didn't interview – because it had killed them.'

Rosanna Wilson-Farrow said: 'My feelings about the blacklist are by nature very conflicted and ambivalent. This was a painful and ugly period in our history, but conversely it also forced us to witness something of beauty: the integrity, courage and loyalty of many fine people. When my father and others faced and defied HUAC, they were so brave in the face of such intimidation, fear, humiliation and punishment. They chose to defend themselves as well as our democracy by standing up to a government committee they felt was defiling our Constitution by its very existence.'

Strangely, historians of the period point to one thing: the lack of bitterness. 'I think,' says Paul Buhle, 'that is partly because they've made a correct assessment – when all this horrible stuff is finished, in the USA, if it's ever finished, those who are benign and generous will say the entire oppressive apparatus was run by less than 10 per cent of the population and supported by 10 per cent of the population.'

If there were such people as patron saints in the mainly secular Hollywood writing community, then the names Kirk Douglas and Otto Preminger come to the top of the nominations list. Both were actors and both were producers and, it was in the second category that they ended the blacklist in 1959 – when they handed Dalton Trumbo that most precious of gifts – credits on screen.

As Kirk Douglas told Barbra Paskin: 'I have been working in Hollywood for 60 years, made 85 pictures, but the thing I am most proud of is breaking the blacklist. That was a terrible thing. I am ashamed to say I started off like everyone else. We were making the movie *Spartacus*. I employed Dalton Trumbo under the name of Sam Jackson. I was so ashamed of the hypocrisy of putting writers in a hold. One day my producer and my director discussed that and I said "You can't put Sam Jackson's name on screen." I thought about that and next morning I decided we're going to put Dalton Trumbo's name on the screen as the writer. I never made a public announcement because a few months before that, Frank Sinatra announced that Maltz would be the writer and it never happened. I said I didn't want to tempt fate. I told Dalton Trumbo I'd use his name. For the first time in 10 years [actually, 12 years], I wouldn't [let him] use a pseudonym.'

Because there were no announcements the news took time to leak out. 'Universal was perplexed. But my agent was Lew Wasserman of MCA and they were in the process of buying the studio.'

It wasn't an easy decision to make. 'Lew Wasserman had doubts if I should do that. It would hurt my career. But he was sympathetic. It was the worst kept secret in town.'

And, of course, there is one thing that can be guaranteed about badly kept secrets: somebody, somewhere, will always find out and copy it. In this case, that somebody was Otto Preminger. 'He was very upset I was going to use Trumbo,' says Douglas. 'He was going to hire him for the film, *Exodus*. A few weeks after that, he announced he was going to use Trumbo's name.' For the Hollywood community, it was the big topic of conversation in the Polo Lounge of the Beverly Hills Hotel. Producers gathering for brunch at Nate 'n' Al's deli on Beverly Boulevard talked of nothing else. For them, it was a moment of history. For the blacklist, it was a death sentence.

Lary Gelbart seemed to sum it all up. 'It was a bad dream – but one we are dreaming again.'

Select Bibliography for Further Reading

Barzman, Norma, *The Red and the Blacklist*, Nation Books, New York, 2004

Bentley, Eric, *Are You Now or Have You Ever Been?*, Grove Press, Cambridge, 1981

Thirty Years of Treason, Thunder's Mouth Press, New York, 2002

Bernstein, Walter, *Inside Out*, Da Capo Press, Cambridge MA, 2000

Bessie, Alvah, *Inquisition in Eden*,

Bessie, Dan, *Rare Birds: An American Family*, University Press of Kentucky, Lexington, 2000

Bosworth, Patricia, *Anything Your Little Heart Desires*, Pocket Books, New York, 1998

Buhle, Paul & Wagner, Dave, *Blacklisted*, Palgrave Macmilan, New York, 2003

Ceplair, Larry & Englund, Stephen, *The Inquisition in Hollywood*, University of Illinois Press, 2003

Cole, Lester, *Hollywood Red*, Ramparts Press, Palo Alto, 1981

Dmytryk, Edward, *Odd Man Out*, Southern Illinois University Press, Carbondale, 2003

Fariello, Griffin, *Red Scare: Memories of the American Inquisition*, Avon, New York, 1996

Fast, Howard, *Being Red*, Dell Publishing, New York, 1991

Friedrich, Otto, *City of Nests*,

Garrett, Betty, *Betty Garrett & Other Songs*, Madison Books, Lanham, 2000

Goldstein, Patrick, *Birth of the Blacklist*,

Goodman, Walter, *The Committee: the Extraordinary Career of the House Un-American Activities*, Farrar Straus & Giroux, New York, 1968

Select Bibliography for Further Reading

Gordon, Bernard, *Hollywood Exile*, University of Texas Press, Austin, 2000

Gorney, Sondra, *Brother, Can you Spare a Dime?*, Scarecrow Press, Lanham, 2005

Hellman, Lillian, *Scoundrel Time*, Little, Brown, London, 2000

Kahn, Gordon, *Hollywood on Trial*, Arno Press, New York, 1976

Kazan, Elia, *Elia Kazan: A Life*, Alfred Knopf, New York, 1988

Killian, Crawford, *Growing Up Blacklisted*,

Lardner, Kate, *Shut Up He Explained*, Ballantine Books, New York, 2004

Lardner, Ring Jr, *I'd Hate Myself in the Morning*, Thunder's Mouth, New York, 2001

Lorence, James J, *The Suppression of Salt of the Earth*, University of New Mexico Press, Albuquerque, 2001

Miller, Arthur, *Timebends*, Methuen, London, 2005

McGilligan, Patrick & Buhle, Paul, *Tender Comrades*, Saint Martin's Press, New York, 1999

Mostel, Kate & Giford, Madelene Lee, *170 Years of Showbusiness*, Random House, London, 1978

Navasky, Victor, *Naming Names*, Penguin, New York, 1991

Radosh, Ronald & Radosh, Allis, *Red Star Over Hollywood*, Encounter Books, New York, 2004

Rouverol, Jean, *Refugees From Hollywood*, University of New Mexico Press, Albuquerque, 2001

Schary, Dore, *Heydey*,

Schrecker, Ellen, *The Age of McCarthyism*, Palgrave Macmillan, New York, 2002

Schulberg, Budd, *Moving Pictures*, Ivan R Dee, Publisher, Chicago, 2003

Sherman, Vincent, *Studio Affairs: My life as a Film Director*, University Press of Kentucky, Lexington, 1996

Vaughn, Robert, *Only Victims*, Limelight Editions, Pompton Plains, 1996

Articles from *Cinema Journal*:
'A Different Childhood' by Nicola Trumbo
'Behind the Curtains: The Blacklist Years' by Geraldine Van Dusen
'Commie, Kiddie-Porn Days Gone By' by Daniel Gorney
'Shock Waves' by Michael Butler
'The Blacklist Through New Eyes' by Bill Jarrico

'The Senate Small Business Committee Pizza Parlor' by Tim Hunter
'What Was It Like To Have A Blacklisted Father' by David Eliscu
Wives of the Hollywood Ten, For Justice and Peace, Committee for the
  Hollywood Ten, Los Angeles, 1950

Pamphlet:
Red Channels: The Report of Communist Influence in Radio and
  Television, Counterattack, 1950

Blacklisted! NPR radio series by Tony Kahn
Stage play Trumbo: *Red, White & Blacklisted* by Trumbo, Christopher.

Select Filmography

The Hollywood Ten
In 1950, while the Ten were waiting for their appeals to be completed and sentences handed down, they made a documentary called *The Hollywood Ten* in which each made a speech denouncing McCarthyism and protesting the blacklist. They all sat around a table and spoke. John Berry directed the 15-minute documentary. When his role in it became known, he, too, was blacklisted and left America for France.

Salt of the Earth
This was a film made in 1953 about the historic zinc miners' strike in New Mexico in 1951. Three of the blacklistees – Mike Wilson, Herbert Biberman and Paul Jarrico – came together and formed a production company in order to continue making films under their own name. Looking to film a social issue, they were deeply affected by the infamous strike for better working conditions – an event every bit as historically important as the Salinas' lettuce strike of the 1930s, and chose the subject for their first film. It has become a valued film over the years because of its tremendous social significance in showing the role that the Mexican-American women played in changing the outcome of the strike, as when the men were legally forced to return to work or be fired, the women took over the picketing line.

The film was shot in New Mexico where the original strike took place. Donald Jackson, a congressman on the HUA committee, was convinced that Communist influence was involved and that the film was part of an attempt to undermine the US war effort in Korea. He urged the film industry to ban the movie from cinemas – and the government to harass its production and distribution. Such a national outcry to boycott anything to do with the film caused great hardship just to get the film shot. He sent a telegram to Howard Hughes, asking, 'Is there any action that industry and labor in motion picture field can take to stop completion and release of picture and prevent showing of film here and abroad?' which evoked an extraordinary list of specific suggestions from Hughes. During the filming itself there were several nasty incidents, a small plane kept buzzing overhead and numerous attempts were made to disrupt the shooting. Post-production services were hard to effect: Pathé Labs, who had been paid in advance for the processing, responded to the boycott by returning the money and refusing to handle the footage. It was a miracle that the film was completed. It had to be edited in secret and was stored for safekeeping in an anonymous wooden shack in LA.

There have been many stories, books and documentaries made about the making of *Salt of the Earth*. It has become an important contribution to the history of film and recognised as such by film bodies such as the American Film Institute and the Library of Congress, and been selected for preservation in the National Film Registry. The film and leading actress Rosaura Revueltas have won awards around the world, including the coveted Grand Prix in 1955 from the Académie du Cinema de Paris. In 2000 the film was adapted into an opera named *Esperanza,* a source of great pride to the filmmakers. No wonder then, as Rosanna Wilson-Farrow told me, that her father who had written it 'wept tears of joy' when eventually they saw it together in a cinema on the Champs-Elysées. In 1999 the film was digitally restored and the DVD reissue includes a copy of the short documentary, *The Hollywood Ten.*

Appendix:
Prison sentences vs actual time served by the Hollywood Ten

Ring Lardner Jr served 9½ months
Lester Cole served 10 months
Alvah Bessie served 10 months
John Howard Lawson 10 months
Samuel Ornitz served 9 months
Adrian Scott served 9 months
Dalton Trumbo served 11 months
Albert Maltz served 10 months
Herbert J Biberman served 5 months
Edward Dmytryk served 4½ months

Index

Index

Index